The *Marshall* Decision and Native Rights

MCGILL-QUEEN'S NATIVE AND NORTHERN SERIES
BRUCE G. TRIGGER, editor

1 When the Whalers Were Up North
   Inuit Memories from the Eastern Arctic
   Dorothy Harley Eber

2 The Challenge of Arctic Shipping
   Science, Environmental Assessment, and Human Values
   David L. VanderZwaag and Cynthia Lamson, Editors

3 Lost Harvests
   Prairie Indian Reserve Farmers and Government Policy
   Sarah Carter

4 Native Liberty, Crown Sovereignty
   The Existing Aboriginal Right of Self-Government in Canada
   Bruce Clark

5 Unravelling the Franklin Mystery
   Inuit Testimony
   David C. Woodman

6 Otter Skins, Boston Ships, and China Goods
   The Maritime Fur Trade of the Northwest Coast, 1785–1741
   James R. Gibson

7 From Wooden Ploughs to Welfare
   The Story of the Western Reserves
   Helen Buckley

8 In Business for Ourselves
   Northern Entrepreneurs
   Wanda A. Wuttunee

9 For an Amerindian Autohistory
   An Essay on the Foundations of a Social Ethic
   Georges E. Sioui

10 Strangers Among Us
   David Woodman

11 When the North Was Red
   Aboriginal Education in Soviet Siberia
   Dennis A. Bartels and Alice L. Bartels

12 From Taking Chiefs to a
Native Corporate Elite
The Birth of Class and
Nationalism among
Canadians
Marybelle Mitchell

13 Cold Comfort
My Love Affair with
the Arctic
Graham W. Rowley

14 The True Spirit and
Original Intent of Treaty 7
*Treaty 7 Elders and Tribal
Council with Walter
Hildebrandt, Dorothy First
Rider, and Sarah Carter*

15 This Distant and
Unsurveyed Country
A Women's Winter at
Baffin Island, 1857–1858
W. Gillies Ross

16 Images of Justice
Dorothy Harley Eber

17 Capturing Women
The Manipulation of
Cultural Imagery in
Canada's Prairie West
Sarah A. Carter

18 Social and Environmental
Impacts of the James Bay
Hydroelectric Project
Edited by James F. Hornig

19 Saqiyuq
Stories from the Lives
of Three Inuit Women
*Nancy Wachowich in
collaboration with
Apphia Agalakti Awa,
Rhoda Kaukjak Katsak,
and Sandra Pikujak Katsak*

20 Justice in Paradise
Bruce Clark

21 Aboriginal Rights and
Self-Government
The Canadian and
Mexican Experience
in North American
Perspective
*Edited by Curtis Cook
and Juan D. Lindau*

22 Harvest of Souls
The Jesuit Missions and
Colonialism in North
America, 1632–1650
Carole Blackburn

23 Bounty and Benevolence
A Documentary History
of Saskatchewan Treaties
*Arthur J. Ray, Jim Miller,
and Frank Tough*

24 The People of Denendeh
Ethnohistory of the
Indians of Canada's
Northwest Territories
June Helm

25 The *Marshall* Decision
and Native Rights
Kenneth Coates

26 The Flying Tiger
Women Shamans and
Storytellers of the Amur
Kira Van Deusen

The *Marshall* Decision and Native Rights

KEN S. COATES

McGill-Queen's University Press
Montreal & Kingston · London · Ithaca

© McGill-Queen's University Press 2000
ISBN 0-7735-2104-6 (cloth)
ISBN 0-7735-2108-9 (paper)

Legal deposit fourth quarter 2000
Bibliothèque nationale du Québec

Printed in Canada on acid-free paper

McGill-Queen's University Press acknowledges the financial support of the Government of Canada through the Book Publishing Industry Development Program (BPIDP) for its activities. It also acknowledges the support of the Canada Council for the Arts for its publishing program.

Maps were prepared by Starshell Maps.

Canadian Cataloguing in Publication Data

Coates, Kenneth, 1956–
The Marshall decision and native rights
Includes bibliographical references and index.
ISBN 0-7735-2104-6 (bound). –
ISBN 0-7735-2108-9 (pbk.)
1. Micmac Indians – Government relations.
2. Micmac Indians – Legal status, laws, etc.
3. Natural ressources – Government policy –
Maritimes Provinces.
I. Title.
KE7709.C63 2000   323.1'1973   C00-901227-3

Typeset in Palatino 10/12
by Caractéra inc., Quebec City

Contents

Preface ix

Acknowledgments xxi

1 Of Eels, Judges, and Lobsters: The *Marshall* Challenge and the Supreme Court Decision 3

2 Paying the Price for History: Mi'kmaq, Maliseet, and Colonists from Treaties to Irrelevance 21

3 Mi'kmaq and Maliseet Frustrations: Social Crises and Government Responses 51

4 Prelude to *Marshall*: Aboriginal and Treaty Rights in Canada 72

5 Thomas Peter Paul and the Mi'kmaq Logging Dispute 94

6 The *Marshall* Crisis and East Coast Confrontations 127

7 Postlude to *Marshall*: Joshua Bernard, Lobster Licences, and the Refinement of Mi'kmaq Rights 169

8 What Does It Mean? The *Marshall* Decision, East Coast Fisheries, and Aboriginal Rights 186

APPENDICES

A Maritime First Nations Communities: Population 209

B Lobster Quotas and Mi'kmaq Fishing Rights 212

C *Rex v. Syliboy*, Nova Scotia County Court, 10 September 1928 www.mcgill.ca/mqup/marshall

D *Regina v. Donald Marshall Jr.*, Nova Scotia Court of Appeal, 26 March 1997 www.mcgill.ca/mqup/marshall

E *Regina v. Peter Paul*, New Brunswick Court of Queen's Bench, 28 October 1997 www.mcgill.ca/mqup/marshall

F *Regina* v. *Peter Paul*, New Brunswick Court of Appeal, 22 April 1998   www.mcgill.ca/mqup/marshall

G *Regina* v. *Marshall Jr.*, Supreme Court of Canada, 17 September 1999   www.mcgill.ca/mqup/marshall

H *Regina* v. *Marshall Jr.*, Supreme Court of Canada Motion for Rehearing and Stay, 17 November 1999   www.mcgill.ca/mqup/marshall

I Treaty of 1760   220

Notes   223

Index   237

Preface

The events of the fall of 1999 caught Canadians unaware. No one – Mi'kmaq, Department of Fisheries and Oceans personnel, officials from the Department of Indian Affairs, academic experts, or the public at large – anticipated either the specifics of the Supreme Court decision on the case of Donald Marshall Jr or the controversy that followed.[1] It is easy with hindsight to criticize people in positions of authority for failing to plan for the fallout from the Supreme Court ruling. Even though the decision was unexpected, it was not outside the pattern of recent judgments on Aboriginal matters.

The scenes of conflict between First Nations and non-Aboriginal fishers which followed disturbed observers across the country. Canada had, for the most part, managed the difficult and often tense relationship between indigenous and transplanted societies over the past twenty years without violence and public anger. Major conflicts like the Oka standoff in Quebec and the Gufstanson Lake controversy in British Columbia stood out as exceptions to a general rule. The widespread anger and frustration sparked by the *Marshall* decision seemed to drag on and on, from community to community, engulfing a region generally known for the absence of conflict on First Nations issues.

Making sense of the *Marshall* decision, both as a legal decision and as a symptom of the broader tension between indigenous and other Canadians in the Maritimes, is an important endeavour. Almost a year after the initial judgment, the issue remains as timely and urgent as it did in September 1999. Tensions run high, particularly at Burnt Church, the centre of the confrontation. More broadly, Maritimers are gradually understanding that the *Marshall* decision has potent implications for the region as a whole. First Nations people, despite their concerted efforts in the past, rarely figured prominently in Maritime politics. Similarly, compared with provinces like British Columbia and Alberta, Aboriginal issues in the Maritime provinces seldom generated much public debate. The Supreme Court judgment touched off a storm of protest, Aboriginal and non-Aboriginal, and transformed the discussion about the nature and extent of First Nations rights in the region. Bitter protests by non-Aboriginal fishers were matched by equally angry assertions of authority, even sovereignty, by First Nations groups. Many Maritimers assumed – erroneously – that the long-term absence of western-type conflict signalled First Nations' satisfaction with the status quo. A lot has been learned on all sides over the past year. To a degree that most Maritimers do not yet appreciate, the *Marshall* decision (along with the broader agenda of Aboriginal legal rights) promises to change forever the face of natural resource use, economic and political relations, and indigenous-newcomer contact in the region.

What follows is, by design and execution, an overview. It endeavours to explain, in general terms, why there is a debate over Aboriginal rights in the Maritimes; why eighteenth-century treaties are important in the first years of the twenty-first century; why Mi'kmaq and Maliseet people have so many hopes and aspirations imbedded in legal and political processes; how Maritimers reacted to judicial involvement in regional life; and how federal, First Nations, and provincial politicians responded to the intense pressures of the 1999-2000 dispute over Aboriginal rights. The broader goal is to alert Maritimers and other Canadians to the historical, contemporary, and future significance of the *Marshall* decision and to offer some insights into how this fundamentally important debate might transform the region in the years to come. First Nations rights will not disappear, regardless of what opponents and critics of recent decisions hope and believe, and demands will increase over time, not decrease. Aboriginal groups feel – with justification and relief – empowered by a legal process that finally accepted arguments they have been making for generations. I hope that this book, by explaining the historical context, summarizing the events of the past year, and contemplating the future, will help Maritimers and Canadians understand this fundamentally important Supreme Court ruling and encourage them to reflect on the need for more positive, supportive approaches to the situation of First Nations people in the region and across the country.

The *Marshall* decision will no doubt be the focus for many other books and studies in the years to come. First Nations researchers will, by drawing on the unique and powerful insights of elders, situate this decision within the rich oral traditions of Mi'kmaq and Maliseet communities and provide a level of understanding that is not possible through the documentary record. Historians will re-examine and debate both the documentary evidence surrounding the eighteenth-century treaties and the use of historical evidence in Canadian courtrooms. Legal scholars will consider the immediate and long-term implications of the judgments on *Marshall* and offer far more nuanced analyses of the legal aspects of the case and their implication. Political scientists will, with more time, distance, and documents, consider the manner in which federal politicians and civil servants, together with their provincial counterparts, responded to the controversies surrounding First Nations rights in the region. And so the list goes on, for this issue has ramifications that cross cultures, academic disciplines, and professional interests. Resource managers will follow the increased Aboriginal use of Maritime resources with great interest and, one hopes, take seriously Mi'kmaq and Maliseet understandings of ecosystems and environmental knowledge. Economists will be confronted with a variety of issues relating to the changing dynamics of the regional fishing industry and, potentially, other sectors as well. Students of intercultural relations will find much of interest in the volatile and fluid relationships between indigenous and non-indigenous peoples.

Pulling this book together so quickly has been a formidable challenge. I have had access to a substantial array of published historical, legal, anthropological, and sociological studies on regional and national indigenous affairs. The legal process has produced a variety of substantial reports, decisions, and documents, as have the government departments charged with responsibility for this matter. Further, a small but growing body of published oral history material draws on the rich cultural traditions of Mi'kmaq and Maliseet people and speaks to the continuity of cultural and historical understanding that underpins community response to the *Marshall* case. I followed the events, issues, and debates very closely in the regional and national media, although, inevitably, press attention heightens during periods of conflict and dissipates when standoffs end. I have benefited from the informal discussions I have had on this subject with dozens of Maritimers and from the assessments of early drafts of this manuscript – some supportive and others quite critical – by anonymous reviewers. The latter, in particular, alerted me to a variety of issues and perspectives that I had not covered adequately in my initial work.

A book that relies heavily on newspaper reports runs into a particular problem in the Maritimes. Although scholars in general have been uneasy about the relationship between news reporting and corporate ownership, the issue is particularly strong in this part of Canada. The Irving group of companies, in addition to formidable holdings in logging, pulp and paper, transportation, and other industries, publishes all the major newspapers in New Brunswick, controls many radio stations, and exerts tremendous power throughout the

Maritimes. Observers are sceptical about the independence of Irving newspapers and about the media generally. While it is easy to understand the concern, it is also easy to exaggerate the extent of the problem and the degree of corporate influence. The Saint John *Times Globe* provided me with unrestricted access to its electronic files, making it easy to search back issues of all the major New Brunswick newspapers and stories filed with the Canadian Press. In reviewing the hundreds of articles, editorials, and letters to the editor published on matters relating to Aboriginal rights in the Maritimes, several themes stand out: the media reacted/overreacted to conflict and crisis and provided relatively little background information (contextual material was generally limited to the history of the court cases involved and, occasionally, the eighteenth-century treaties); the editorials generally ran in favour of the First Nations' positions or of responding positively to their aspirations and needs, although perhaps not to the extent that the more assertive advocates of Aboriginal rights might have wished; letters to the editor included numerous submissions by First Nations people, covering a range of arguments on the issues at hand; the news stories themselves regularly included First Nations voices and opinions; and the papers published a wide variety of opinion pieces on the subject.

If there is a fundamental bias in the debate surrounding the *Marshall* case, it is the predominance of non-Aboriginal perspectives. Other than the letters to the editor (a few of which are cited in this book) and quotations from First Nations people in news stories, First Nations perspectives and insight are generally not well canvassed. This imbalance remains a fundamental problem in Canada with news reporting, analysis, and even jurisprudence, all of which offer a preponderance of non-indigenous voices and little systematic First Nations coverage. As a consequence, there is consistent emphasis on how things like the *Marshall* decision create a "problem" for the Maritimes, and less understanding of how this decision provides hope to a people who have faced generations of discrimination. News reports on this conflict highlighted the threat to east coast fishing communities, and rarely commented on two hundred years of economic marginalization for the Mi'kmaq and Maliseet. Numerous reports represented the "threat" posed to the east coast lobster fishery by expanded First Nations harvesting, but recent arguments by fishers that the harvest could be enlarged substantially were rarely reported, and little attention was given to the very small cumulative size of the total planned First Nations fishery. (According to several estimates, the planned Aboriginal harvest represented a meagre 1 per cent of the total east coast lobster fishery, an amount hardly likely to destroy the resource.) Great concern was expressed about the ability of First Nations people to "manage" their affairs, and much less about the roots of the social, economic, and political difficulties facing indigenous communities. For generations, newcomers have debated, analyzed, and sought to solve the "Indian problem" in Canada without addressing seriously the basic responsibility of newcomers for the difficulties facing indigenous peoples. The rhetoric and ideas that circulated around the *Marshall* decision continued very much in this same vein.

While the view of *Marshall* and other issues within the First Nations communities varies widely, it is important to acknowledge that Mi'kmaq and Maliseet people often, and legitimately, see historical and contemporary situations in fundamentally different ways from other Maritimers. One of the truisms of the study of history is that the "winners" generally get to tell the story of what happened, muting the different stories that emerge from the memories of those who have been shouldered aside. I am not a First Nations person and, although I have devoted my adult life to an effort to understand indigenous-newcomer relations, I know that I do not necessarily see events, processes, and realities in the same way as First Nations observers. The very fact that, as an academic steeped in the Western intellectual tradition, I place greater weight on objective scientific evidence than on the accounts preserved in Aboriginal oral tradition, for example, reveals a fundamental set of assumptions that might well be described as bias. Similarly, I cannot begin to argue that I share the same sense of grievance, hurt, isolation, and frustration that is felt by those who have been on the receiving end of several generations of discrimination and dispossession. Further, in asserting that I am a Canadian (no other place makes any sense, given my family history), I must recognize that my claim to territory sits atop Aboriginal ownership of the land that is centuries old. In what follows, I will endeavour to reflect First Nations perspectives on the issues at hand and, wherever possible, to use the words and arguments of the First Nations people. But, as a relative newcomer to the Maritimes and as a non-Aboriginal person, I know that my understanding is partial and still under development.

Canadians are a polite people, and we tend to approach even contentious issues such as indigenous land and treaty rights through negotiation and the search for mutual understanding. On occasion, and I believe this is one, the gentleness of voices obscures the fundamental anger, even fury, that rests beneath the surface. These frustrations run in both directions, including non-Aboriginal people who are angry about Aboriginal and treaty rights, and First Nations people who believe that the newcomers simply do not realize the extent of their inherent and treaty rights. The non-Aboriginal protest is relatively well known. The *National Post* has provided critics of contemporary policy with a country-wide platform; an early May 2000 editorial on the need for a policy of assimilation for First Nations people revealed both the depth of resistance to current laws and the continuity between nineteenth-century and contemporary ideas. Thomas Flanagan, a political scientist from Alberta who comments regularly on Aboriginal issues, and magazines like *Alberta Report* routinely demand a rethinking of First Nations rights and, at their most extreme, insist on the elimination of special status for First Nations people. The reverse is also true. Articulate and active Aboriginal spokespeople, particularly such individuals as Ovide Mercredi, Phil Fontaine, and Matthew Coon Come, the past and current grand chiefs of the Assembly of First Nations, have offered strongly worded critiques of Canadian history and national policy. They have presented clear demands for the recognition of the inherent right to self-government, greater respect for treaty and Aboriginal rights, the need for apologies for past government actions, and increased funding to address the social and economic challenges facing First Nations people.

But even as the debate rebounds across the country, one is left with the sense that the arguments rarely penetrate to the heart of the matter. Canadians generally understand the reality of historical injustices, but see them as problems of the eighteenth and nineteenth centuries, not issues to be addressed in the twenty-first century. Canadians acknowledge the extent of Aboriginal poverty and respond anxiously to stories of suicide, alcohol and drug abuse, or overrepresentation in the Canadian prison system. But the population generally does not recognize culpability and responsibility for dealing with these issues. The problems are reasons for sadness, it seems, not for action. For First Nations people, even those supportive of conciliatory gestures and cooperative approaches to legal and political issues, the willingness of non-Aboriginals to ignore historical responsibilities and contemporary conditions is a painful reminder of how much people can hear without really listening. Other Aboriginal leaders and speakers, unconvinced that the gradualist approach will bear fruit, are more blunt in their assessment of the situation. They believe that contemporary policies are little different from historic regulations and that entrenched patterns of racism remain dominant across the country.

Non–First Nations readers should try to imagine the story of Canada, the Maritimes, and Aboriginal policy as an indigenous person might see it. Aboriginal people know that their ancestors had a rich and vibrant culture, one rooted in thousands of years of partnership with the land. They realize that, at several levels, the arrival of the Europeans was an unmitigated disaster, bringing new diseases that devastated the population and altered the economic and resource base of their society. The newcomers brought religious ideas that were imposed on the First Nations, and they began, slowly at first and later with great speed, to occupy traditional territories. French and British leaders alike spoke in grand terms of permanent alliances and lasting friendships, and First Nations chiefs agreed to peace treaties that ended conflicts and promised a future of partnership and mutual prosperity. First Nations in the Maritimes reject the notion that these treaties constituted a formal land transfer and argue that the land and resources remain theirs. To the extent that the treaties were formal agreements and contained promises of protection and economic freedom, Mi'kmaq and Maliseet observe, the treaties were virtually ignored. The partnership between cultures implicitly promised in the treaties was replaced by an ideology of individuality and competitive use of resources, a situation that ignored First Nations' collectivist systems and less material orientation. The new order was also based on human domination over the environment, a complete reversal of Aboriginal approaches to land and resource use.

To many First Nations peoples, the nuances and twists of history are obscured by the broader and more painful realities. Contact with Europeans meant being pushed from their lands, stripped of independence, dominated by foreign governments, relegated to tiny and marginal reserves, cut off from resources and the means of making a living, assailed by an aggressive clergy, and, later, subjected to an intrusive education system capped by the now infamous residential schools. In the eighteenth century, Mi'kmaq and Maliseet moved freely throughout their traditional territories; by the 1950s they had only a few plots of land to call their own, and even there they lived under the watchful and intrusive eye of the federal Department of Indian Affairs. Every decade of oppression is, they assert with good cause, reflected in the poverty and despair of contemporary Aboriginal communities. Non-indigenous peoples worrying about the potential threat to resources from Aboriginal harvesting conveniently leave out of their public comments any criticism of non-indigenous resource exploitation which has, over two centuries, damaged ecosystems and, as with the cod fishery, put key stocks at risk. First Nations live with the consequences of a brutal, dehumanizing history in a way that non-Aboriginal people simply do not.

The Aboriginal interpretation of the past makes it clear that First Nations demonstrated resilience and creativity. They did not cave in to the dictates of the "superior" Europeans, but sought to adapt and respond to the newcomers and to the changing realities in their homelands. Efforts to accommodate, however, were repeatedly blocked by a combination of ignorance, misunderstanding, and self-interest on the part of the settler society. In this understanding of history, to focus unduly on the details is to evade responsibility for the broad pattern of racial domination, dispossession, and disempowerment. In this depiction of the past – one commonly held by First Nations people but rarely presented to non-Aboriginals – the courts have become a last resort, a final chance for Aboriginal communities to receive a measure of justice. The Supreme Court decision on the *Marshall* case is but a tiny bit of retribution, a small step towards recognition and far from the achievement of the final goal.

Rather than being the end of a process of asserting treaty and Aboriginal rights, *Marshall* represents but a small stride along a lengthy path. Success, defined in First Nations terms, awaits further attainments: full recognition of the authority of the treaties; acceptance of Aboriginal resource and other rights; acknowledgment of the inherent right to self-government for First Nations communities; formal apologies for past injustices; financial and other compensation for lost lands and resources; public recognition of the importance and value of Aboriginal culture, languages, and world views; and the establishment of a genuine partnership between indigenous and non-indigenous peoples. For non-Native peoples still reeling from the sweeping impact, as yet not fully realized, of the *Marshall* decision, discovering the depth of First Nations frustration and disappointment and the scope of their aspirations can be troubling indeed.

It is crucial to acknowledge the huge gulf dividing First Nations and non-Aboriginal concepts of the past. While people of European ancestry no longer speak uncritically of the "progress" of Western civilization and recognize the inequalities and injustices that emerged along the way, they still talk of the "opening" of frontier regions, praise the early settlers, and remember fondly the political and economic efforts of politicians, business people, and community leaders. Contemporary prosperity, such as it is, rests on their actions, efforts, and determination. The history of the newcomers, however, is offset by a bleaker image – of peoples whose lands were "stolen" through various political manoeuvres, whose culture was systematically attacked and undermined, and whose ability to manage their own affairs was confiscated by colonial powers. These are more than different renderings of the same image: rather, they are overlapping pictures of the Maritime past that often exist without reference to each other. Preparing a sustainable portrait of regional history will ultimately rest on the ability to speak and write across the chasm, and to seek an understanding of the past that draws these contradictory but interconnected images together.

Readers should also take a moment to reposition the camera lens and consider the *Marshall* decision from the perspective of non-Aboriginal fishers and communities. These settlements have faced their own set of challenges. Fishing has rarely been a lucrative enterprise, buffeted constantly by uncertainties in the ocean stocks and the international marketplace. Canada's mismanagement of the cod fishery devastated entire communities and forced many fishers into poverty or unemployment. For these people the lobster fishery – the initial battleground arising from the *Marshall* decision – was a financial salvation, providing a reasonable income and promising some hope for future prosperity. The coastal communities of the Maritimes were not seedbeds of racism. First Nations reserves often sit alongside fishing settlements, and relations between the two groups have generally been reasonably placid. Compared with other parts of Canada, social contacts have been friendly and there has been a fair amount of commercial interaction.

For the non-Aboriginal fishers, the *Marshall* decision was frightening. One seemingly stable element in the regional economy – the lobster fishery – was under attack. The prospect of expanding Aboriginal rights seemed very real. First Nations neighbours, rarely a source of conflict, spoke in grandiose terms of their authority and control over natural resources. The First Nations rhetoric of dispossession and anger surprised many local residents, who discovered an undercurrent of hostility they had either ignored or misunderstood. The federal government offered little leadership or reassurance. Suddenly, the stability of the Maritime economy seemed threatened yet again. Certainties of the past were in doubt. Fishers and their communities wondered why historical grievances were being settled on their backs and from their incomes, for they represented one of the poorest regions of the country. In their unease and disappointment, the fishers erupted in anger and frustration, adding fuel to the controversy and providing First Nations with a unique insight into the thoughts and opinions of their neighbours.

This book does not try to present a single perspective on the *Marshall* controversy or to argue for a particular side of the debate. Some non-Native observers will say of this work, as they have of my public comments, that I am biased in favour of First Nations people and their legal rights. Some First Nations commentators will criticize me, as they have in the past, for not pushing the agenda far and fast enough, and for not supporting their more general claims for public recognition of their rights and resource needs. On an issue as complicated and emotional as the *Marshall* decision, it is virtually impossible to satisfy everyone – and that should not be the goal of this or any other study.

What follows represents a personal understanding of the historical and cultural context of the *Marshall* decision, a narrative reconstruction and analysis of the two major cases (*Thomas Peter Paul*[2] and *Donald Marshall Jr*) that have framed the contemporary debate, and a contemplation of what lies ahead and what might be done to address the fundamental and underlying problems. I claim no absolute insights into the legal, cultural, and political web in which contemporary First Nations claims exist. I declare a passionate concern about this issue and about the fundamental need for non-Aboriginal Canadians to acknowledge and respect the legal rights, aspirations, and requirements of indigenous peoples in the Maritimes and in Canada. I share with some, but not all, observers a concern about the reliance on the court system to mediate a basic cultural relationship, and I worry that regular recourse to the courts will not address the country's need for a systemic transformation of First Nations affairs in Canada. I share with many non-Aboriginal commentators and virtually all First Nations people an abhorrence of the poverty and injustice that surrounds indigenous communities in this country. And I am deeply concerned about the ability of contemporary policies and programs to address the fundamental flaws and failings of the indigenous-newcomer relationship in Canada. I believe that we must respond to the needs and visions of the First Nations, but despair of the growing opposition in non-Aboriginal circles to the enhancement and extension of First Nations rights. These are troubling times, and there are no simple solutions to the morass created by over three centuries of conflict and the tangled web of legal rights and political solutions.

The *Marshall* decision did not cause the deep divisions that have subsequently been revealed between First Nations and other Maritimers. It is, instead, a symptom of a long-term, fundamental inequality between indigenous and non-indigenous peoples in the Maritimes. The challenge before us is several-fold. First, we must seek to understand the origins of the conflicts, tensions, and relationships that resulted in the legal contest settled finally by the Supreme Court of Canada. Second, we must remember the events surrounding the *Paul* and *Marshall* cases so we do not forget the sharp reaction, hostile comments, conciliatory gestures, and political interventions the accompanied these court decisions. Third, we must reflect on what the decisions and the reaction to the judgments tell us about the Canadian court system, the place of First Nations people in Canadian society, and the entrenched barriers to full Aboriginal participation in Canadian life. Finally, it is imperative that all Canadians, First Nations and non-Aboriginal alike, respond to situations like the *Marshall* conflict by generating new ideas – and a heightened level of commitment – about how to restructure the relationship between First Nations and other Canadians. I trust this book will be considered as a small contribution to this vital endeavour, one that is integral to our success as a nation committed to justice, fairness, and human decency.

Let me conclude with a simple, but important, observation. The *Marshall* decision, and the other court cases that are part of the Mi'kmaq and Maliseet effort to assert their Aboriginal and treaty rights, generated a harsh public response across the Maritimes. Less well known is the fact that First Nations, along with provincial and federal officials, have worked extremely hard to secure both interim and long-term settlements on the outstanding and controversial issues. While it may seem somewhat optimistic in the context of the hostilities of 1999–2000, there appears to be a Maritime pattern of reconciliation at work that holds great promise for the future. Provincial governments, in particular, are determined to find workable solutions, and New Brunswick merits special mention in this regard. Similarly, and behind the often heated public rhetoric that attends such controversies, First Nations leaders are working with their communities and governments to identify solutions and to use the court decisions as the foundation for a new relationship. There is reason for hope in the Maritimes, and the real possibility that the region will develop a model of Aboriginal/non-Aboriginal relations that could well be emulated by the rest of the country. Out of conflict and controversy can arise hope and solutions.

Acknowledgments

McGill-Queen's University Press is a well-known haven for Canadian authors and Canadian scholarship. That this book has seen the light of day is due almost entirely to Aurèle Parisien, an acquisitions editor for MQUP. He approached me with the idea for this book in January 2000 – and then insisted that the manuscript be ready by April. All along the way, even as the deadline was extended into August, he prodded, cajoled, and encouraged. He sent copies of news clippings, CBC audio files, and a steady barrage of other information and ideas. He was as committed to the project as I was, and took an active interest in every aspect of the book. I thoroughly enjoyed our many discussions and debates about the issues surrounding the *Marshall* decision. If this book has any merit, it is due in large measure to Aurèle's zeal, friendship, and persistence. Joan McGilvray, coordinating editor at the press, did a superb job of pulling the manuscript together under unusually tight deadlines. Rosemary Shipton edited several versions of the manuscript; the final product is immeasurably better for her careful attention and sharp editorial eye. Susanne MacAdam and the production team have turned the book out in record time to ensure that it contributes to the ongoing debate.

This work has benefited from the professional assessments of a number of scholars. Don Desserud, a political scientist at the University of New Brunswick at Saint John, offered comments on an early draft, as did Greg Poelzer, a good friend and political scientist at the University of Northern British Columbia. A former student and friend, Al Grove, made his extensive knowledge of Aboriginal law available to me; his comments were helpful and our numerous discussions on indigenous issues have been inspirational. Because of a collective desire to get this book into production while the issues of the *Marshall* decision remained in the public's mind, McGill-Queen's University Press called on several professional and academic reviewers under trying conditions. Although these anonymous reviewers were given a "work in progress" to assess, they tackled the assignment with good grace and great insight. I hope they will see in the final product the extent to which I heeded their excellent advice. These reviewers and advisers bear no responsibility for the errors that remain in the manuscript. They deserve a great deal of credit for whatever merits it may have.

I offer a special word of thanks to Bill Morrison of the History Program at the University of Northern British Columbia. Bill and I have worked on numerous projects over the years. Despite a distressingly short deadline and at the beginning of a heavy term of teaching, Bill agreed to give the manuscript a careful proofreading. His sharp eye, sheer love of the English language, and vast erudition saved me from many errors.

This book came together in my final year as dean of the Faculty of Arts at the University of New Brunswick at Saint John. I benefited greatly from the encouragement and support of Dr Rick Miner, vice-president (Saint John), and John McLaughlin, vice-president (academic) for the university. The UNB library system saved me on numerous occasions, and I give special thanks to the staff at the UNB-Fredericton Law School for their assistance in tracking down court materials. The staff in my office, Tamara Beatteay and Tanya Pitt, created a delightful working environment and kept distractions to a minimum during key writing periods. Many thanks, as well, to Scott Brittain, my research assistant, who took an active interest in the project.

This project received a great boost from Rob Linke, editorial page editor at the Saint John *Times-Globe*. Rob and Editor Carolyn Ryan provided me with access to their electronic news archives, making it possible for me to examine a substantial portion of the press coverage of the issues at hand. Their "no strings attached" support is greatly appreciated. Further afield, staff in the communication branches of the Department of Fisheries and Oceans and the Department of Indian Affairs and Northern Development were prompt and gracious in responding to my research requests.

This project would not have been possible without the contribution of Ms Sarah Devarenne. Sarah runs the dean's office at UNBSJ – and she ran my life exceptionally well during the past eighteen months. On the Marshall project, she was exemplary. Sarah tackled research assignments, corrected rough drafts, and kept me on schedule. It was a joy working with her.

My final words of thanks are for my family. Bradley, Mark, and Laura Coates know a great deal more about what I do than they did when they were younger. I hope that this understanding justifies or explains some of the many hours I have taken from them to devote to my research and writing. One of the great delights of parenthood is watching children develop into young adults and seeing them take an active interest in the world around them. Carin Holroyd, my wife and best friend, truly believes that ideas matter and that works of scholarship can influence our broader world. It is her enthusiasm and support that keeps me motivated. Her endless optimism keeps me trying. With great pleasure and much love, I dedicated this book to her.

KEN COATES
Saint John, New Brunswick,
and Saskatoon, Saskatchewan

The *Marshall* Decision and Native Rights

"This appeal should be allowed because nothing less would uphold the honour and integrity of the Crown in its dealings with the Mi'kmaq people to secure their peace and friendship, as best the content of those treaty promises can now be ascertained."

Supreme Court of Canada,
17 September 1999

CHAPTER ONE

Of Eels, Judges, and Lobsters: The Marshall Challenge and the Supreme Court Decision

Donald Marshall Jr. was back. A Mi'kmaq from Membertou Band, Cape Breton Island, and son of a grand chief of the Mi'kmaq people, Donald John Marshall Jr was pushed into the national spotlight in the 1980s. Only a teenager, he was accused of the murder of a young man in Sydney, Nova Scotia. Protesting his innocence, Marshall found himself dragged quickly through the court and the prison system. He spent eleven years in prison, convicted of second-degree murder, before he was finally exonerated. When the Nova Scotia royal commission set up to investigate Marshall's wrongful conviction reported in 1989, it exposed a judicial system rife with hostility and discrimination towards First Nations and African Canadians. Marshall became synonymous with the short-comings of Canadian law, and his experiences symbolized the deeply imbedded racism that lay so close to the surface in eastern Canada. Marshall's adjustment to life outside the prison walls was not always smooth, but, for a time, he assumed a low profile, endeavouring to bring some semblance of order back to a life largely destroyed by police and judicial incompetence.

It was hard not to be surprised, then, when Donald Marshall Jr re-emerged at the head of one of the most significant Aboriginal rights court challenges in the history of the Maritime provinces. Contrary to some expectations, Marshall is a quiet man, not given to radical pronouncements and political activism. He typically leaves the spotlight for others and seems to crave privacy. The events of the late 1990s thrust him back both front and centre. As with most Aboriginal rights cases, Marshall's second major foray into the legal system started in a fairly innocuous way. In August 1993 Marshall was fishing for eels in Pomquet Harbour and his catch was seized by officers from the Department of Fisheries and Oceans. Convinced that he had a right to fish, he contacted the chief of his reserve, who told him to keep fishing. The department stopped him again, and Marshall went back onto the water. Officials grabbed his

210 kilogram catch – worth close to $790 – and charged him with fishing without a licence, selling eels without a licence, and fishing during a closed season.

Donald Marshall Jr fought back – and this time he was not alone in his struggle. He had the backing of more than a dozen Mi'kmaq chiefs and the official support of the Union of Nova Scotia Indians and the Confederacy of Mainland Mi'kmaq. He was supported, as well, by his lead attorney, Bruce Wildsmith, a Dalhousie University law professor and senior legal counsel for the Union of Nova Scotia Indians, who advanced the *Marshall* case as one of a series of legal challenges brought forward on behalf of Nova Scotia Mi'kmaq. Many of Wildmsith's cases focused on resource issues – these were, in the late 1990s, the focal point for Aboriginal legal activity. Unlike some lawyers working in the field, Wildsmith was not given to broad and sweeping legal claims of the type favoured in British Columbia cases. Instead, he built careful, historically based arguments that focused on the contemporary relevance of the eighteenth-century treaties between the Mi'kmaq and the British, arguing that these agreements were still in force, had long been ignored, and provided the Mi'kmaq with significant rights and privileges under the law.

Marshall, Mi'kmaq leaders believed, was the right person to lead the legal fight for Aboriginal fishing rights. As his girlfriend, Jane McMillan, noted: "He's a name. He's somebody who's going to get support from the public, the sympathy that's needed in a case like this." The trial was just that – a formidable challenge. The case was heard in the same courtroom where he had been tried and found guilty of murder over a decade earlier. "I got sick a couple of times," Marshall observed. "I thought I'd never be in this court again." Being singled out as the symbol for First Nations' aspirations placed a sizable burden on Marshall's shoulders. He was, according to a journalist who visited him during the court proceedings in 1995, "a hard, lean 41 years – a crude blue MOM scratched on a hand isn't the only hint that prison gets under the skin. His name has more baggage than Samsonite. He has carried it all his life. It is the name of the father, Donald Marshall, the late, revered leader, a Micmac statesman who met the Queen and the Pope. It is the name of the son, a name synonymous with injustice."[1]

To the First Nations in the Maritimes, the charges were an affront to their Aboriginal right to harvest food and, most significantly, a breach of the Mi'kmaq treaty right to sell their catch. Through a series of court challenges in the 1970s and 1980s, First Nations across Canada had secured state recognition of their "Aboriginal right" to harvest resources for subsistence purposes. While these fishing, hunting, and gathering rights were important – country food remains a substantial part of community diet in many parts of Canada – the authority was limited. First Nations could not legally sell their harvests for commercial benefit, and government officials went to considerable pains to limit fishing and hunting to legitimate subsistence activities. The treaty argument, based on treaties signed with Britain in 1760 and 1761, held that these eighteenth-century agreements guaranteed Mi'kmaq the right to fish for commercial purposes and to benefit substantially from their resource activities.

Marshall lost the first round of his legal contest. Judge John Embree ruled in June 1996 that the treaties were valid, but that the eighteenth-century instruments of commercial rights – truck houses and Indian trading agents – no longer existed, thereby eliminating the Mi'kmaq right to sell their catch. Reaction was swift and hostile. The defence lawyers declared their determination to bring the case before the Court of Appeal and, if necessary, the Supreme Court. Marshall himself stated: "We have been fighting to get this whole thing out for a long time and this is the first stage. I'm not the one convicted here. All Micmacs are convicted."[2] Highlighting the fact that his arrest was a test case, Marshall reported that he had no intention of returning to the eel fishery: "I wouldn't give that job to my worst enemy. It's hard work and it's dirty." Mi'kmaq chiefs reacted with bitterness. Chief Lawrence Paul of the Millbrook reserve near Truro demanded that the case be heard by a foreign judge, arguing that it was impossible to get a fair hearing from someone who was a "descendant of the enemy."[3] Paul was one of the first to threaten publicly that First Nations would ignore the law if the decision was not overturned.

Court processes moved slowly, and the case did not appear before the Nova Scotia Court of Appeal until early February 1997. Wildsmith again presented his argument, which, to oversimplify a complex historical and legal account, suggested that the trading opportunities promised in the original treaties (truck houses and licensed Indian traders) represented an assurance that commercial resource harvests could continue. The fact that this right had been largely ignored for two hundred years did not make it any less valid: "These treaties are as relevant today as they were then. They just have to be understood in a modern context."[4] The Court of Appeal disagreed and rejected the attempt to overturn Marshall's conviction. Rather, it accepted the argument that the truck houses promised in the treaties were an administrative expedient and did not represent an open-ended guarantee that the Mi'kmaq would have special and protected access to resources in perpetuity.

Having lost for a second time in Nova Scotia courts, Donald Marshall Jr and his lawyers prepared themselves for an appeal to the Supreme Court of Canada. From the beginning they and their Aboriginal supporters had known that his case would end up before the Supreme Court. The only way of ensuring that the eighteenth-century treaties were honoured in the present time was to have the Supreme Court rule on their relevance. With a combined sense of anticipation and nervousness, the Mi'kmaq launched an appeal of the Nova Scotia Court of Appeal ruling to the Supreme Court. The hearing – a pivotal one – was granted in October 1997, and arguments commenced in November 1998. The case attracted further interventions: from the government of New Brunswick, alarmed about the dangers of an expansive interpretation; from the Union of New Brunswick Indians, in favour of Marshall's case; and from various industry associations, worried about the impact of extending Aboriginal treaty rights to the fishery. Four hours of arguments before the Supreme Court were completed in early November and, as expected, the judges reserved their decision. A resolution of the *Marshall* case would await their judgment, which was not expected for at least eight months. In making Marshall's case, Wildsmith aimed for the "middle ground," arguing that the Natives' right to fish and to sell their catch was a clear treaty right. Under such an arrangement, the lawyer said, the government could regulate the fishery, but only after justifying the regulations.[5]

In the winner-take-all world of the courtroom, a great deal was at stake. The First Nations of the Maritimes had contributed a lot of money and effort to the case. Vast amounts of evidence had been gathered from the historical and legal experts who routinely appear at Aboriginal rights cases, along with oral testimony and thousands of pages of historical documents. Supreme Court justices do not listen to new testimony, however, and their challenge was to review the legal and constitutional status of the *Marshall* case to determine whether the Mi'kmaq people had an existing treaty right to harvest eels for commercial purposes. Everyone knew that this decision was not solely about eels. If the Mi'kmaq had a right to harvest one species for sale, that right could logically extend to other fishery resources. Potentially, it could extend to timber, minerals, and other natural resources as well.

The Supreme Court, by dint of the Constitution Act, 1982, particularly the Canadian Charter of Rights and Freedoms, and the Court's own activist bent in recent years, held formidable power in its hands. If it ruled in favour of Marshall, First Nations would secure a long-denied commercial right in the Maritimes. Almost inevitably, groups across Canada would attempt to have this right extended to their area. The opposite was also true. The Supreme Court could deny the appeal and provide a clarification and limitation of Mi'kmaq and Maliseet treaty rights with Britain. Although there were various shades of grey between the possible extremes, the Court was expected to go in one direction or the other. Sentiment in the field among Aboriginal rights specialists and lawyers appeared to lean against Marshall and the Mi'kmaq, though in recent Court decisions there had been a relatively steady extension of rights to Aboriginal people.

When the Supreme Court of Canada rendered its decision on 17 September 1999, the judgment went further than even the Mi'kmaq had expected. Donald Marshall Jr was, by a vote of five to two, acquitted of the charges. Justices Lamer, L'Heureux-Dubé, Cory, Iacobucci, and Binnie supported Marshall; Judges Gonthier and McLachlin dissented. The Court spelled out, in considerable detail, the significance of its ruling. The eighteenth-century treaties between the British and the First Nations covered the commercial use of resources. The right to use the resources – in this case, eels – was not unlimited. First Nations could earn a "moderate income" (not defined) and were obliged to operate within the framework of federal government rules. The decision made it clear that the Supreme Court judges believed that the right to fish extended beyond eels to other ocean resources and to hunting. The Court also held that maintaining the integrity of the treaty was of paramount importance in ensuring that Canada honoured its legal obligations to First Nations.

THE RESPONSE TO THE *MARSHALL* DECISION

The Mi'kmaq were ecstatic: Marshall was vindicated, and they were, too. Chief Terrance Paul of Membertou hailed the decision: "We no longer want Micmac people to go hungry. As of today, there is no more hunger and no dependence."[6] Surrounded by Mi'kmaq leaders and his legal team, Marshall observed that "at times I almost gave up, but in the back of my mind I wasn't giving up." He was pleased with his accomplishment: "I give myself a pat on the shoulder that I'm a Mi'kmaq and I'm proud to be a Mi'kmaq ... When I went to the Supreme Court for the fishing, I wasn't there for myself. I was there for my people. I had to represent my people, and it was really more touching than anything else when you represent your people and not yourself."[7]

Mi'kmaq claims about long-ignored treaty rights and government responsibility had been proven true. The decision came during the start of the lucrative fall lobster season, and the First Nations believed they now possessed the right to a share of the bounty. The 1760 treaty survived, and it extended to commercial fishing rights. The Mi'kmaq and Maliseet people of the Maritimes had reasons to believe there would be a place for them in the eastern economy after all. Some First Nations, in the Maritimes and across the country, interpreted the ruling very broadly and claimed that it extended commercial access to resources to all Aboriginal people. More radical individuals argued, without success, that communities should assert their right to the commercial use of other resources in the Maritimes. Excitement reigned. The Court had ruled, and the First Nations had gained the place in the regional order they always felt they deserved.

The regional reaction to the *Marshall* decision was conditioned by the fallout from the 1997 court case involving Thomas Peter Paul (see chapter 5). Paul had been arrested for harvesting trees for commercial purposes and, much to the surprise of legal and political observers, the provincial court in New Brunswick agreed with his argument that he had a treaty right to cut and sell logs. Mi'kmaq and Maliseet people immediately headed into the woods to exercise their newly regained right, causing anxiety throughout the forest industry and euphoria among First Nations. The provincial government struggled to find a solution, seeking a compromise between licence holders and First Nations, and eventually it offered Mi'kmaq and Maliseet communities a share of the New Brunswick harvest. Paul's victory was overturned on appeal, but not before providing the Maritimes with a rude awakening. Before the *Marshall* decision, the non-Aboriginal people of the Maritimes had had a taste of the potential power of legal judgments on First Nations harvesting rights.

Andrea Bear Nicholas, chair of Native Studies at New Brunswick's St Thomas University and an outspoken critic of federal Aboriginal policies, offered a celebratory commentary on the significance of the Supreme Court decision:

K'cikwohahtiba (You did a great deed for the people) to Donald Marshall Jr, to his legal team, to the organizations that supported the case, to all the researchers who contributed, and especially to those Wolastokwiy and Mi'kmaq hunters, fishers and harvesters who faced guns and punishment for more than two centuries to maintain our original teachings, responsibilities and practices.

What the Marshall decision has done is to recognize a truth that has existed all along – that we, the Wolastrokwiyik and Mi'kmaq, have neither sold our lands nor surrendered our access to sources of life in the land. It has also recognized that the colonial prohibitions against trading or selling the products of the land were unduly oppressive. That it has taken more than two centuries for these truths to be recognized is a measure of the fact that courts of the immigrant society were truly never impartial.

The new concern being voiced by elders and traditionals is which set of values will be practised now that Junior Marshall and our whole way of life has been vindicated, now that the oppression is lifting and our access to the courses of life may soon be assured? There is now no need to buy into Western values and practices as the only way for some to survive. The final step in liberating our own values and ways is now in our hands.[8]

The sense of accomplishment and opportunity in the First Nations communities was profound.

The federal government was caught unaware by the Supreme Court judgment and its implications. Fisheries Minister Herb Dhaliwal was not available for comment, and an official response to the ruling was delayed several times. The Department of Fisheries and Oceans, having suffered a severe loss in credibility over its handling of the cod fisheries and the imposition of a lengthy moratorium on commercial use of the resource, now found itself in the middle of a potential standoff between Aboriginal and non-Aboriginal fishers. Officials asked for calm and for time to sort out the ruling, as First Nations prepared to exercise their newly defined right and as non-Aboriginal fishers complained bitterly about having to surrender a sizable portion of their industry.

The non-Aboriginal response in the Maritimes mirrored the reaction to the *Thomas Peter Paul* decisions in New Brunswick. Fishers railed against the Supreme Court and wondered aloud why their rights to the resources were dispensed with so readily. They demanded federal government action, and found themselves waiting for a formal response. They flinched as Aboriginal leaders spoke of the enthusiasm on the reserve for returning to the commercial fishery, and worried openly about the impact of First Nations' competition on both their incomes and the lobster stocks. Anti-Aboriginal sentiment bubbled to the surface, and hastily organized meetings provided the fishers with opportunities to vent their frustrations. Conservation groups called for federal action and asked First Nations to proceed with caution. David Coon, policy director for the New Brunswick Conservation Council, warned: "The ball is in the government's court right now and they have got to respond fairly quickly. With no rules, there will be deteriorating relations within the communities, between the aboriginal people and the other folks."[9] Provincial governments, for the most part, stood aside, relieved that the challenge rested with the federal authorities and that they were not obliged to repeat the tense negotiations that followed the *Paul* case.

Professor William Wicken of York University, one of the historians who provided expert testimony on the Mi'kmaq treaties, responded to the criticism of the Supreme Court decision by reminding people of the troubled history of Mi'kmaq-newcomer relations. As he wrote, "If many Mi'kmaq took to their boats after the Supreme Court's decision, it was because for the first time they were provided with a legal right to become equal partners in the Canadian economy. The Supreme Court's decision will free many families from welfare ... It is not possible to return to them all of what was once theirs. We cannot give them back the children who died. But what can be done is to treat them fairly so their children may thrive in the future. The Supreme Court's decision is a bold but necessary step in that direction."[10] While many Maritimers shared the general sentiments, those closest to the industry worried about the potential for economic hardship.

The *Marshall* judgment sparked an enormous national debate – one of those rare occasions when the rest of the country paid more than passing attention to the Maritimes. Aboriginal leaders and their supporters hailed the decision as a major victory for all First Nations and applauded the Supreme Court's willingness to extend Aboriginal harvesting rights into the commercial realm. Just as strongly, and with more than a hint of bitterness, non-Aboriginal resource users across the country protested the potential intrusion by First Nations into their industry and worried about the seemingly unending extension of Aboriginal rights through the courts. Academics and lawyers weighed in on the issue, interpreting the ruling for the press and commenting on the implications of the *Marshall* decision for the country. Debate continued for weeks after the Supreme Court handed down its judgment, rising and declining in temper alongside other developments in the east coast fishery. One theme ran through this regional and national discussion – the decision had fundamentally changed the Maritimes – but no one was sure what it really meant.

EXPLAINING THE JUDGMENT

Supreme Court judgments are complicated, and making sense of the seventy-page *Marshall* ruling will take a great deal of time and effort by legal and academic specialists. The judgment contains a number of provisions which must be understood to appreciate the impact of the ruling and which can be summarized in eleven key points. (The text of the *Marshall* decision can be found in appendix H.)

- In a key statement, Justice Binnie wrote, "I accept as inherent in these treaties that the British recognized and accepted the existing Mi'kmaq way of life."

- The court ruled that Donald Marshall Jr had a treaty right to catch and to sell fish. That right was not unlimited, but was subject to controls. In words of assurance to the non-Aboriginal sector, Binnie wrote: "The ultimate fear is that the appellant, who in this case fished for eels from a small boat using a fyke net, could lever the treaty right into a factory trawler in Pomquet Harbour gathering the available harvest in preference to all non-aboriginal commercial or recreational fishermen. (This is indeed the position advanced by the intervenor Union of New Brunswick Indians.) This fear (or hope) is based on a misunderstanding of the narrow ambit and extent of the treaty right."
- The Court agreed that Mi'kmaq people could earn a moderate living from the proceeds of their harvest. This point is critical. The Supreme Court did not grant First Nations ownership or control of resources, nor did it permit them to dominate the sector to the exclusion of all others. Instead, the Mi'kmaq could legitimately expect to be able to earn a reasonable income, not to enjoy windfall gains. For the Court, the crux of the decision rested with the idea that "the treaty rights are limited to securing necessaries (which I construe in the modern context, as equivalent to a moderate livelihood), and do not extend to the open-ended accumulation of wealth." Commercial use of resources that exceeded these limits would be subject to government action. A moderate livelihood was defined as "such basics as food, clothing and housing, supplemented by a few amenities, but not the accumulation of wealth. It addresses day-to-day needs. This was the common intention in 1760. It is fair that it be given this interpretation today."
- The Court declared that the federal government, as the steward of ocean resources, could "within its proper limits" regulate the coastal fishery, including Aboriginal fishing activity. Regional fishers and governments worried in their interventions before the Supreme Court that an unregulated right would give First Nations effective control over the fishery. The Supreme Court acknowledged this concern and asserted that the treaty authority was a "regulated right," subject to government control.
- In addition, the Court held that any regulations limiting Aboriginal fishing rights had to be fully justified, explained, and reasonable. These limits had to respect the federal government's fiduciary, or trust, relationship with First Nations. Infringement of fishing rights would, in normal circumstances, involve compensation.
- The Supreme Court interpreted the historical context of the treaty process to mean that the Mi'kmaq treaty makers had connected trade with peace. On the one hand the First Nations had asserted in 1760 that, to enjoy peaceful relations with the newcomers, they

had to be able to care for themselves; on the other hand the British worried about the Mi'kmaq becoming a drain on the public purse in the colony or in Britain. Treaty protections for Aboriginal harvesting rights, then, were based on the realization that the Mi'Kmaq needed to provide an adequate living for themselves.
- The Court declared that the treaty right to fish commercially – and to negotiate on matters concerning that right – is a "collective right" held by each band, reflecting the fact that the treaties were negotiated by bands, not individuals.
- The Supreme Court decision included an extended commentary on the importance of using external evidence in determining the content of and intent behind the agreement. In other words, the historical context in which an agreement was made is an integral part of the consideration of the terms and conditions of the treaty.
- The Supreme Court ruling once again highlighted the importance of looking for evidence beyond the specific and detailed wording of a treaty, or other legal agreement, in determining what was meant or intended in the accord. As the majority decision stated, "that extrinsic evidence of the historical and cultural context of a treaty may be received even absent any ambiguity on the face of the treaty." First Nations have long argued that the written text of a treaty often did not include all the promises and understandings that formed the agreement. The Supreme Court agreed that oral or separate promises, sometimes documented in the written record and other times recorded in First Nations oral tradition, can figure into judgments about treaties.
- The dissenting opinion (Justices Gontier and McLachlin) argued that the treaties did not grant a "general right to trade." Instead, the treaties represented an exchange – with the Mi'kmaq surrendering their "trading autonomy" in exchange for trading outlets, which proved to be only a temporary expedient designed to ensure peace. The Mi'kmaq were left with the same general non-treaty right to hunt, fish, and trade possessed by all British subjects in the region. Not surprisingly, non-Aboriginal fishers preferred the minority opinion to that of the majority.

THE MI'KMAQ RESPONSE

Aboriginal people along the east coast were emboldened in the wake of the Supreme Court judgment.[11] The *Marshall* victory had vindicated their long-standing argument that their treaty rights extended into the commercial realm. Within days, fishers from the Lennox

Island First Nation on Prince Edward Island and Burnt Church in New Brunswick headed out to the lobster grounds, defying federal regulations. The activism of Burnt Church, in particular, was understandable, given the long-standing hostility between First Nations and non-Aboriginal fishers in that region. Politicians and local industry people asked First Nations, in the words of Prince Edward Island member of parliament Wayne Easter, to "cool it," but they had no intention of holding back. First Nations had waited long enough for the ruling.[12] The fishers from Burnt Church set out more than 1,000 traps in direct violation of the legal lobster season (1 May to 30 June), infuriating non-Aboriginal fishers who had to watch and wait for a government response. In other areas, where the lobster fishery was open, First Nations headed for their boats. Robert Levi, chief of Big Cove, exalted, "Today is a good day to be an Indian."[13] On Lennox Island, the First Nations set quota limits (per fisher and per household) and announced to the band that the fishery would be carefully regulated.

Even in the excitement of the first days after the Supreme Court decision, words of disquiet could be heard among Mi'kmaq and Maliseet people. For Mi'kmaq lawyer Bernd Christmas, the *Marshall* victory was only a tiny step forward: "We've never surrendered our land or our resources and that's the question that has to be answered. In our view, the treaty is just an off-shoot of that notion of aboriginal title. And aboriginal title covers all aspects – whether it's hunting, fishing, mining, land, or return of our land."[14] He also argued that any attempts to impose tight limits on Mi'kmaq fishers would be rejected: "If some fisherman gets 300,000 pounds of snowcrab, then we expect to get that quota for every single Micmac."[15]

Why, Native people asked themselves, were they being restricted to a "moderate" income, particularly when so many non-Aboriginal people had become wealthy from the exploitation of the region's natural resources? The Court did not rule – in large part because it was not asked to – about the long-standing question of Aboriginal land entitlement arising out of the 1760–61 treaties. To those people looking for a more substantial reordering of First Nations–newcomer relations and power in the Maritimes, the *Marshall* decision was but a tiny step along a long and difficult path. After all, the Supreme Court was, at its most basic level, simply acknowledging that a right claimed by Mi'kmaq people for over two hundred years did exist – exactly as countless First Nations people had argued over the years. Moreover, those portions of the decision which referred to the conservation and regulatory regimes of the federal government seemed designed to limit the influence of First Nations governments and to bind First Nations fishers to government agencies and conservation schemes. First Nations in the Maritimes, and the rest of Canada, have been asserting their "inherent right" to self-government, and have been demanding more sweeping powers than those granted by the federal government under its self-government agreements. First Nations, in particular, assert the right and the need to establish conservation and resource use regulations, arguing that traditional knowledge and Aboriginal management systems are more sustainable than those used by provincial and national governments. The *Marshall* decision indicated directly the pre-eminence of federal and provincial regulation systems, and implicitly drew borders around the anticipated authority of First Nations governments.

In this context, it is possible to see that, while the decision represented a move in the correct direction, it was hardly a revolutionary acknowledgment of the legitimacy of First Nations' aspirations in the Maritimes. That some First Nations, even amidst the celebrations of their colleagues and communities and the anguished protests of many non-Aboriginal people, questioned the legitimacy and scope of the Supreme Court ruling illustrates something of the gulf that remains between indigenous and newcomer political communities in the Maritimes. Non-Aboriginal people reacted vigorously to this relatively minor extension of First Nations rights, while, to many Aboriginal communities, the *Marshall* decision granted only a small portion of the power and resource rights they claimed. It is in this gap in understanding that the greatest potential for future disputes lies, for most non-Aboriginal residents simply do not appreciate the scope and nature of First Nations' aspirations.

Non-Aboriginal observers worried openly about the rapid decision to start lobster fishing and hoped for a quick clarification. Fishers and conservationists alike questioned the capacity of the east coast fishery to absorb additional harvesters. The Maritime Fishermen's Union, for example, wondered if the extra harvests taken by the First Nations would come at their cost. The New Brunswick Salmon Council and the New Brunswick Wildlife Federation called for new laws and quick government action to head off conflict and the destruction of resources. Chief Lawrence Paul, co-chair of the Atlantic Policy Congress of First Nations, offered a sharp rebuke to non-Aboriginals who had long ignored Aboriginal requests for access to the fishery: "Due to the Supreme Court decision, the rules of the game have changed and they'll have to share, whether they like it or not. I think the bottom line on the whole thing is not conservation, it's not about saving fish stocks – the bottom line is greed. The Mi'kmaq and Maliseet people believe in sharing. But to the non-Indian, sharing is a very bitter word in their mouths."[16] By the end of September, tensions had risen, battlelines had been drawn, and anger was building.

CHALLENGING THE COURT

While most of the debate raged on the wharves, in restaurants, and in university classrooms and other meeting places, some activists took a more formal route. At the political level, the federal government appears to have toyed with the idea of asking the Supreme Court to set aside its ruling until the implications could be explored and remedies sought. This request, if made, would have been palpably inappropriate and would have generated enormous anger among Aboriginal people. Conservative politicians, led by Elsie Wayne, MP for Saint John, New Brunswick, argued that the ruling was too disruptive and should be revisited – a suggestion that earned contemptuous responses alike from First Nations and legal experts. Clearly, political leaders wanted to buy time and get some assistance from the Supreme Court in resolving the problems created by the judgment. Fishermen's organizations in the Maritimes took a more direct approach, petitioning the Supreme Court to withdraw its ruling and reconsider the judgment. Their formal appeals were unsuccessful, and the fishers were disappointed. It is instructive, however, that the organizations attempted to work within legal structures, rather than resort to direct action – as more than a few of their members suggested.

Perhaps the most interesting challenge to the *Marshall* ruling came from a New Brunswick history professor. Dr Stephen Patterson, a University of New Brunswick – Fredericton historian who had testified for the Crown during the trial, was quoted by Justice Ian Binnie in the reasons for judgment for those voting in favour of Marshall. But Patterson felt he had been seriously misquoted, and his disquiet with the use of his testimony soon became front-page news. As he told the *Times & Transcript*: "I guess one is not supposed to say that the Supreme Court made errors, but it seems to me that strictly on the basis of historical fact, the justices in the majority decision may not have a view of the facts that would be adopted by an historian."[17] Patterson argued that the treaty, seen in context, endeavoured to provide the British with control over the area, and the First Nations with stable trading opportunities: "What I said was that the treaty gave the Micmac permission to bring the goods they had for sale to a truckhouse. What the judge did with that at the trial level was to say they had a right to trade at truckhouses and when the truckhouses ceased to exist any right that was implicit in the treaty disappeared with the truckhouses. But Binnie doesn't see that."[18] Binnie used Patterson's words to argue that the treaties conveyed a permanent right to fish commercially. Patterson agreed with the use of historical interpretation by Justice Beverley McLachlin (now the Chief Justice), who voted with the minority against Marshall. The contretemps illustrated the profound difficulty involved with using historical material in court processes. Other academic historians, led by Professor Wicken and Dr John Reid of St Mary's University, testified on behalf of the Mi'kmaq.

Justice Binnie heard the complaints. In an unusual step, he deleted one section in the ruling and added a revised portion: "While he [Patterson] generally supported the Crown's narrow approach to the interpretation of the Treaty, which I have rejected on points of law, he did make a number of important concessions to the defence in a relatively lengthy and reflective statement which should be set out in full." Patterson held his comments, for he was then testifying before a New Brunswick court on yet another Mi'Kmaq case (*Joshua Bernard*), though he did offer a brief observation: "I think that Mr. Justice Binnie anticipates that historians may react to the provocative comment that he has made in the Marshall decision and his refinement of paragraph 37 suggests that he may even anticipate some reaction from me."[19]

Not surprisingly, the debate about the *Marshall* judgment included a vigorous and at times heated exchange about judicial activism. Through the 1990s, the Supreme Court was accused by its critics of assuming greater authority and becoming increasingly active in setting the nation's political and social agenda. Wide-ranging rules on divorce, Aboriginal issues, the rights of same-sex partners, and many other topics had turned the Court into a focus for public attention and debate. Many Canadians welcomed the interventions, which compelled politicians to address issues that would otherwise be ignored or delayed. But some protested that the appointed Supreme Court judges, selected by the prime minister with no formal review of their qualifications, opinions, or perspectives, had gained an authority that rivalled, if not surpassed, that of Parliament. In particular, critics of Aboriginal rights argued forcefully that the Supreme Court had systematically expanded the authority of First Nations and had granted them sufficient powers not only to constitute a new order of government but to threaten the viability of long-standing economic sectors. At the same time, some critics have argued that the recent series of favourable Supreme Court decisions are not the unalloyed victories for First Nations that many people have assumed. Even the often quoted *Delgamuukw* decision mandates a substantial and difficult burden of proof for First Nations attempting to capitalize on the ruling. Historically, the Supreme Court of Canada has rarely strayed far from the economic and political status quo. Expecting an instrument of the federal government to provide a wide-ranging and comprehensive critique of the place of First Nations within Canadian society is, some argue, based on false hopes. While criticisms, like the laudatory statements, went too far, both arguments found support across the country.

The *Marshall* decision seemed to provide excellent proof of the far-reaching authority of the Supreme Court. In one quick move, the Court reinvigorated an eighteenth-century treaty, empowered Maritime First Nations, rewrote the rules for the east coast fishery, potentially undermined the non-Aboriginal economy, raised expectations and fears to previously untouched levels, and stirred enormous controversy. For those who looked to the Court for guidance, the judges had responded with a breathtaking decision. For those who believed that the Court was stepping far beyond the appropriate bounds, *Marshall* provided ample evidence that the politicians had to seize control of the agenda from the judiciary.

Legal appeals followed quickly. In November 1999 the Supreme Court heard a request from the West Nova Fishermen's Coalition that a stay of judgment be issued, pending a rehearing. The coalition specifically requested a further trial on the matter of the application of fisheries regulations to the Aboriginal fishery. It argued that rendering a judgment on Aboriginal commercial fishing rights based on the Mi'kmaq traditional eel fishery (a fishery that is not endangered, not commercial, and not subject to extensive competition) was inappropriate. The Court rejected the request, noting: "This Court has jurisdiction to entertain an intervener's application for a rehearing but will only do so in exceptional circumstances. Not only are there no such circumstances here but the intervener's application also violated the basis on which an intervener is permitted to participate in the appeal in the first place, namely acceptance of the record as defined by the Crown and the defence." The Court further stated that answers to the coalition's questions could be found in the original judgment: "The Coalition's application is based on a misconception of the scope of the Court's majority judgment of September 17, 1999 and the appellant should not have his acquittal kept in jeopardy while issues much broader than the specifics of his prosecution are litigated."[20]

CLARIFYING THE *MARSHALL* DECISION

The Supreme Court of Canada did not accept any of the appeals to set aside or to reopen the *Marshall* decision. But the judges could see what was going on across the Maritimes. They no doubt shared the concerns of many Canadians that the conflict and controversy along the coast could erupt into violence and civil unrest. It was also clear, as debate raged about the decision, that their ruling was being interpreted in widely different ways by proponents and opponents of Aboriginal rights. It must have galled the judges to see their words, concepts, and explanations twisted, turned, and presented in so many different ways. Perhaps, as well, they were concerned that the lack of precision in their ruling gave too much latitude for debate, controversy, and potential conflict.

In an almost unprecedented step, the Supreme Court of Canada issued a clarification of the *Marshall* ruling in November 1999, while simultaneously rejecting the West Nova request for an appeal. The decision to revisit the judgment, without hearing additional arguments or considering new evidence, seemed designed to dampen public anger and quell the discontent swirling around the Court's earlier action. The clarification shocked observers, who were used to the Court standing by its initial decisions, then narrowing or more sharply defining the judgment only when presented with additional cases. As the Court's statement noted, the decision "did not rule that the appellant had established a treaty right to 'gather' anything and everything physically capable of being gathered. The issues were much narrower and the ruling much narrower." The justices specifically indicated that they had not heard evidence and arguments relating to such issues as logging, mining, and off-shore natural gas. The door was not barred on these issues, but a clear burden of proof was established: "Equally, it will be open to an accused in future cases to try to show that the treaty right was intended in 1760 by both sides to include access to resources other than fish, wildlife and traditionally gathered things such as fruits and berries." The statement continued: "It is of course open to native communities to assert broader treaty rights in that regard, but if so, the basis of such a claim will have to be established in proceedings where the issue is squarely raised on proper historical evidence." Any contemporary treaty right, in other words, would have to be within the spirit of the original accord and the historical practices at the time of the treaty. The Court also clarified that governments had the authority to impose regulations over Aboriginal treaty rights. As John McEvoy, a law professor at the University of New Brunswick at Fredericton, summarized the Court's statement: "Well, we were concerned only with eels – you're going to have to prove you had a treaty right [to lobster]." Henry Bear of the Union of New Brunswick Indians disagreed with McEvoy and argued that the definition of "fishing" was sufficiently broad to incorporate both lobsters and eels.[21]

Having raised Aboriginal expectations exponentially in the initial *Marshall* ruling, the Supreme Court's clarification seemed to represent an attempt to bring the First Nations back to earth. The Mi'kmaq response was, predictably, one of anger. Chief Lawrence Paul commented: "The Supreme Court has given in to mob rule and vigilantism to let them get their way. The Supreme Court has hurt its credibility today. It has backtracked. I am not happy." Supporters found some positive signs. Lawyer Bruce Wildsmith was pleased that the clarification made it clear that the ruling applied to fisheries resources in general, and not just to eels.[22]

The clarification contained several key elements. First, it indicated that the *Marshall* decision related specifically to eels and that it was not obvious, as many First Nations claimed, that the judgment opened up all natural resource sectors to Aboriginal people. The extension of the treaty right to other resources, particularly forestry, would have to await separate court challenges. Second, and perhaps more important, the Court made it clear that the First Nations' right to fish had less priority than the conservation efforts of the federal government and did not automatically displace non-Aboriginal users of fishing resources. In the initial flush of victory, First Nations had asserted that their right was pre-eminent, overriding all other uses of the resource and operating under the protection of the highest court in the land. As well, the statement emphasized that the judgment applied to local groups, not to individuals, and should be managed in that fashion. The judges, in issuing the clarification, declared clearly that the Aboriginal right did not supersede conservation regulations and was not a first call on the resources. The Court, as it had done in the past, encouraged participants to consider negotiated settlements as an alternative to constant judicial review, something the government of New Brunswick, in particular, seemed keen to adopt.

The clarification was widely hailed as an important qualification, especially by politicians and opponents of Aboriginal resource rights. But it was a most unusual step, suggesting that the struggle within the Supreme Court over *Marshall* had continued and that the Court was determined to place some parameters around the assumptions about the inevitability of Aboriginal rights. The statement also puzzled and dismayed Aboriginal people: they felt that the Court had granted them a huge victory, then snatched it away before they could savour the success. For those who viewed the Supreme Court as a instrument of the federal government and a protector of economic interests (and who were likely surprised by the initial ruling), the clarification confirmed their initial expectations. Brian Fleming of the Halifax *Daily News* was less charitable: "Confidence in the court is now somewhere below the bellies of Mr. Marshall's eels," and "at best, this appalling attempt at damage control was an open admission of the court's failure in crafting its September judgement properly. At worst, Canada's highest court has, willy-nilly, created a new final final appeals procedure."[22]

The *Marshall* decision of September 1999, even with this clarification, was a momentous event. It changed, likely forever, the status and authority of First Nations in the Maritimes, and it generated a political and social response that further reshaped the regional order. As a legal text, situated within the growing body of Canadian jurisprudence on Aboriginal rights, the *Marshall* ruling speaks to the contemporary authority of pre–Second World War treaties, the growing power of First Nations groups, the need to share the diminishing natural resources of the country with the original inhabitants, and the determination of vulnerable non-Aboriginal resource communities to survive in the face of conflicting pressures. Perhaps more than anything, it indicates the difficulties, even the discomfort, that the courts experience in attempting to resolve long-standing differences between Aboriginal and non-Aboriginal people. As a court ruling, the *Marshall* decision will be widely cited in Canada and abroad, as indigenous groups endeavour to extend and define their legal rights, and as they continue to use the courts (in the absence of an alternative) to secure a more equitable place within Canadian society.

Making sense of the Supreme Court ruling in the case of Donald Marshall Jr requires a very broad and comprehensive perspective. It cannot be seen in isolation, apart from other court judgments, nor can it be understood outside the historical and contemporary reality of the First Nations in the Maritime provinces. The *Marshall* decision will reverberate throughout the region and across the country for generations. It has the potential to restructure, in positive and constructive ways, the relationship between First Nations and other Maritimers. It also contains explosive potential, and it could easily cause violent outbursts to set ethnic relations in Canada on a radically different path. It is potentially volatile, disruptive, helpful, and encouraging. Although it is far too early to tell whether the Maritimes will follow the path of reconciliation or confrontation, it is clear that the rules have changed, new realities hold, and the future is uncertain. To understand what the *Marshall* decision might ultimately mean, it is important to step back and then look forward, to place the Supreme Court decision in its appropriate context.

CHAPTER TWO

Paying the Price for History: Mi'kmaq, Maliseet, and Colonists from Treaties to Irrelevance

The debate over Mi'kmaq harvesting rights is founded on conflicting views of the past, although the fallout is completely modern. At the root of the court cases and public confrontation is a simple matter of responsibility for the past. For many non-Native Maritimers and Canadians, the details of a two-hundred-year-old treaty should be of little relevance in resolving sensitive issues surrounding fishing and logging rights. For the vast majority of Mi'kmaq and other First Nations people, the root of contemporary social, economic, and cultural ills lies in the past, in generations of oppression and broken promises. What appears, on the surface, to be a struggle over legal wording and judicial pronouncements is, at its most basic level, a battle over historical responsibility.

Understanding the current debate requires at least a basic appreciation of the evolution of Mi'kmaq-newcomer relations over the past four centuries. This relationship is, after all, one of the oldest of its type in Canada, complete with the twists, turns, and upheavals associated with the clash of European and indigenous societies around the world. Mi'kmaq people remember and discuss this history far more than non-Mi'kmaq people do. In the stories of the treaties, government policies, residential schools, racial discrimination, dispossession of land, and marginalization the Mi'kmaq find the means to understand their current condition. Other Maritimers pay relatively little attention to this historical legacy, for they find the record to be unpleasant, or overwhelmed by what they consider more compelling stories of European discovery, colonial politics, national building, military conflicts, and economic development and decay. Conflicting histories, then, have divided Mi'kmaq from other Maritimers, leaving the communities not only with vastly different understandings of the past but with a divided sense of collective responsibility for it.[1]

THE ORIGINS OF THE MI'KMAQ AND MALISEET PEOPLE

The Mi'kmaq – "the people who lived farthest east," or, more poetically, "the people of the dawn" – have a clear account of their origins. From the hands of the creator, Kisulk, came the Sun (Niskam), the Earth (Sitqamuk), and a teacher who gradually emerged in human form (Kluskap). Kluskap became known as the Teacher-Creator and is credited with bringing understanding and knowledge to the humans who emerged in this new world. Mi'kmaq society found its spiritual roots in this creation account, which also described how the people grew up alongside the animal kingdom. They were, from the outset, part of the natural and spirit world, neither separate from it nor superior to it. Mi'kmaq oral culture was rich, and the individuals who had responsibility for passing history and knowledge between generations were accorded honour. The first Europeans to venture into the Maritimes tended to see only heathens and barbarians, entirely missing the complexity, diversity, and intensity of the Mi'kmaq world view.[2]

Western science offers a different explanation for the emergence of the Mi'kmaq and Maliseet peoples. In this non-Aboriginal history of the Maritimes, the story begins with the initial habitation of the Maritime district, likely some 12,000 to 15,000 years ago. Canadians of European ancestry often have difficulty comprehending this time frame. Given that only 2,000 years have passed since the time of Christ, 1,000 years since the Vikings made their tentative approaches to North America, and slightly more than 500 years since Christopher Columbus voyaged to the hemisphere, the Aboriginal occupation of this region is stunning. Several thousand years before the Middle Eastern civilization of Sumeria and Babylon, long before complex societies had emerged in what became Europe, and at around the time that the first agricultural villages were appearing in various corners of the earth, the First Peoples inhabited the Maritimes.

The peopling of North America, what has been called "The Great Journey," is one the most remarkable episodes in human history. The occupation of the continent occurred without literary chroniclers, and the story has been slowly pieced together from archeological discoveries and research. According to this scenario, the earliest arrivals made their way from Siberia to Alaska and then moved south. Over time, these peoples settled the Americas, as their decendants established diverse cultures from the Pacific to the Atlantic coasts. These hunter/gatherer societies adapted quickly to the new ecosystems they encountered and developed strong attachments to their territories. In the process, they established the historical and cultural foundation for the indigenous people who, many centuries later, met the first Europeans to venture into their lands and waters.

Many First Nations people reject the "scientific" interpretations of the Aboriginal occupancy of North America. They point to the fact that archeological evidence of early habitation is sketchy and incomplete and that there are substantial differences of opinion within the academic community about the timing, direction, and nature of the initial occupation of the continent. As Vine Deloria, a leading Native American historian and scholar, recently observed: "How could I not have been skeptical of apparent truths so easily voiced by archaeologists when it seems plainly evident that many of their cherished doctrines are simply speculations that have become doctrines only because senior professors prefer to believe them...[A]rchaeology has always been dominated by those who waved science in front of us like an inexhaustible credit card, and we have deferred to them – believing that they represent the discipline in an objective and unbiased manner."[3] The academic, cultural, and legal battle over the remains of "Kennewick Man," a 9,000 – year-old skeleton found on the banks of the Columbia River, illustrates the potency of this debate. First Nations people often use the phrase "time immemorial" to describe the length of their occupancy of traditional territories and refer to oral history that asserts that the people emerged on these lands. The debate over the origins of the indigenous peoples of North America is far from resolved.

The first societies to emerge in the Maritimes were not static and unchanging. Shifting weather patterns – the initial migration came on the heels of the last ice age – brought changes in animal life, fish, and plants. Newly developed technologies, ranging from improved cutting tools to the bow and arrow and better boats, made harvesting easier and allowed for further alterations to work and living patterns. Contact with other groups, both peaceful exchanges and bitter conflicts, demanded social and cultural responses. Research on these early peoples provides a few insights into their lifestyle, revealing the balance between coastal and inland harvesting and the gradual emergence of new tools and clothing styles.[4]

The emergence of what scholars now connect to Mi'kmaq traditions can be traced, anthropologically, to approximately 2,500 years ago. Research sites reveal an increasingly complex society – certainly as well developed as many in Europe of this age – with strong pottery skills, a predominantly shellfish diet, improved tools, and extensive lodgings. We get but glimpses of indigenous cultural views from the physical evidence, but even for these early periods there are signs that the people have strong spiritual understandings and elaborate ceremonial activities. Adaptations continued, as the Mi'kmaq and Maliseet cultures began to develop in the form close to that the first Europeans encountered. Elaborate fish weirs demonstrated extensive knowledge of tidal pools and fish movements. Large shell middens, particularly around the Bay of Fundy, document the extensive use of shellfish by the first peoples. The inhabitants clearly understood their surroundings and made substantial use of the natural resources available to them.

The key to First Nations life was the movement among seasonal sites. Virginia Miller, an ethnohistorian, described the seasonal shifts as follows:

In the spring, the Micmac settled in villages along the coast. Here they remained until fall, living in nuclear family units in conical birchbark wigwams erected and painted with colourful designs by the women; extended families might live together in large, rectangular, cabin-shaped birchbark structures. Summer village sites were chosen for their proximity to fresh water and to marine food sources such as shellfish beds. Often a village was situated at the mouth of a river to permit easy travel by birchbark canoe to other coastal locations or to inland locations to hunt or dig ground nuts. Good campsites were returned to year after year.

The Micmac diet during this time consisted principally of products from the sea, with less reliance on land animals and plants. Food was never a problem from spring through fall. Oysters and clams were collected easily. With fish traps built across river and stream mouths, the Micmac took ample quantities of smelt, alewives, sturgeon, and salmon, as these fish returned to fresh water to spawn. Large fish and lobsters were attracted at night with torches and were taken using bone-tipped harpoons. Coastal ocean fish such as cod, plaice, skate and striped bass could be caught with bone hooks and lines or taken by weirs constructed in bays, although ocean fish apparently did not play a significant part in the diet …

In late summer, camps were moved inland, away from the impending harsh coastal winter storms. The men went ahead by canoe to choose and clear a winter campsite adjacent to a river or stream, while the women had the responsibility for transporting the household goods using backpacks and tumplines before once again setting up camp, this time covering their wigwams with birchbark, mats and skins to fortify them against the approaching winter cold. When the fall eel runs began, great numbers were taken either in traps or with leisters. Eels, still today a favourite food among the Micmac, were roasted or boiled and eaten fresh; quantities were also smoked for the winter.[5]

Long before the Europeans arrived, the Mi'kmaq and Maliseet people had established a firm presence across the Maritimes. The Mi'kmaq were the larger of the groups, their territories extending across what is now Nova Scotia, Prince Edward Island, eastern New Brunswick, Gaspé, and the Magdelan Islands (and, perhaps, Newfoundland). The Maliseet lived further inland, largely along the Saint John River valley, and sustained themselves by hunting, fishing, and agriculture.[6] It is difficult to judge the pre-contact population of the region, largely because the first ravages of introduced illnesses arrived before the initial European expeditions. First Nations in North America had no contact with the diseases of Europe. When the newcomers arrived, they unwittingly imported many illnesses that were new to the Mi'lmaq and Maliseet. These "virgin soil epidemics" hit with devastating ferocity, killing hundreds, if not thousands, of First Nations people in a matter of weeks. The indigenous population had no immunity to the diseases, so even a relatively gentle childhood illness like chicken-pox could cause enormous losses among the Aboriginal population. Early estimates suggest that the regional indigenous population was around 15,000 to 20,000 at the time of first extended contact in the early seventeenth century. This population had fallen to around 4,000 by the early nineteenth century. Getting a sense of the pre-contact numbers is important: for generations, settlers used the small size of the disease-depleted Aboriginal population to justify the confiscation and use of indigenous lands. The growing realization that pre-European contact populations were actually quite sizable has forced many commentators and governments to reassess their basic assumptions about First Nations land use, occupancy patterns, and land rights.

For many years, non-Aboriginal observers described the First Nations in disparaging terms – as savages, barbarians, heathens, and uncivilized people. Others, even in the early years of contact, viewed the First Nations more favourably, though with sadness. The "noble savage" now described an indigenous population that had once roamed across the land, free from the evils of a corrupted European age. But these people, said to be ravaged by the "inevitable" forces of progress and development, had been left behind in the race towards industrialization. This nostalgic and sorrowful image reflected growing dismay with the social and economic conditions of the marginalized First Nations, but did little to improve their standing within North American society. Nor did these assessments of First Nations history offer much in the way of criticism of non-Aboriginal actions, attacks, attitudes, and policies towards Mi'kmaq and Maliseet people. The fault for social despair was, implicitly, left at the feet of the First

Nations themselves. Gradually through the twentieth century, scholars developed a more realistic portrayal of indigenous cultures. *The Conflict of European and Eastern Algonkian Cultures, 1504–1700*, by New Brunswicker Alfred G. Bailey, was one of the first scholarly studies to provide a more sympathetic and nuanced perspective of indigenous history, but the book did not enjoy its well-deserved popularity until the 1960s, three decades after it first appeared. Bailey's work, in turn, has been critiqued and improved upon by more recent scholarship, including L.F.S. Upton's *Micmacs and Colonists* and recent work by William Wicken and Mi'kmaq historian Daniel Paul.[7] Gradually, Canadians and others came to appreciate more fully the complexity and diversity of Aboriginal cultures. Scholars moved beyond their documentary collections to use First Nations oral testimony and other records to develop a more comprehensive portrait of indigenous Mi'kmaq and Maliseet societies.

It is difficult for citizens of the twenty-first century to appreciate life in the early sixteenth century. Life expectancy was short, food supplies were often unreliable, harsh winters could result in considerable hardship, extended military conflicts caused deaths – and that was in Europe. Britain, France, and Spain constructed monumental buildings and made significant advances in science, navigation, and commerce, but they had not created equitable or stable societies, and life retained its harsh and uncertain edge. Indigenous societies in Meso-America (Mexico and Central and South America) had developed massive cities, elaborate religious systems, and remarkable agriculture complexes. Much further north, in the less temperate zones of Atlantic Canada, the physical structures of Mi'kmaq and Maliseet life were less dramatic. These peoples did not build cities or extensive economic projects, but they had developed societies that were stable, well suited to their natural surroundings, and sustainable.

The Mi'kmaq saw themselves as a single unit, loosely organized around the Grand Council of the Mi'kmaq (Sante Mawiomi). The council drew together the captains (*kep'tinaq*) who, in turn, appointed a Grand Chief (*jisaqamow*) and a Grand Captain (*jikeptin*). The Grand Chief when the French first settled in the region was a distinguished leader who attracted attention and respect from all who met him. The Mi'kmaq came from seven main districts – Sipekne'katik (Shubenacadie), Kespukwitk (southern Nova Scotia), Wunama'kik (Cape Breton Island), Siknikt (eastern New Brunswick and western Nova Scotia), Epelwik (Prince Edward Island), Eskikewa'kik (east coast of Nova Scotia), and Kespek (northern New Brunswick and Gaspe) – with local chiefs representing small regions within these districts. They had an active seasonal cycle of meetings, feasts, and celebrations, which brought them together in regional or larger groupings. Spiritual guidance could be found, somewhat informally, from the natural world and from human leaders. Shamans possessed spiritual authority and could call on their connection to the spiritual world to address all manner of personal and social ills. Wars were relatively few and focused primarily on the much-reviled Iroquois to the west. The Mi'kmaq and Maliseet were generally allied with each other, though squabbles and conflicts broke out on occasion. Experience in war and diplomacy provided two crucial routes to leadership within Mi'kmaq society.

The first Europeans were impressed with the Mi'kmaq, whose way of life straddled the wealth of the sea, rivers, and forests. The Mi'maq moved from coast to inland sites with the seasons and the availability of food, and generally found abundant resources within their traditional territories. They were "neither settled nor migratory. The environment of their birth has always been suited best to seasonal use so that, compatible with the rhythms of the earth, communities relied on a hunting ground, a fishing river or waters, and a planting home, and they travelled to other resources throughout the year. They lived within the beauty and cycles of their lands."[8] They developed tools and technologies appropriate to the region, including sophisticated fish weirs, movable bark shelters, and well-crafted birchbark canoes and toboggans for winter travel. Clothing made from the resources of the land provided excellent protection against the Maritime elements. The Mi'kmaq were particularly adept at harvesting fish and other sea life, providing themselves with a steady and dependable supply of food. The Maliseet followed a similar pattern, though their lifestyle was based more on the resources of the Saint John River than on those of the ocean.

Mi'kmaq and Maliseet life enjoyed the benefit of sustainability. Aspects changed slowly, but the passage of the centuries saw relatively slight shifts in social organization, harvesting, and spiritual beliefs. Although the people drew heavily from the resources of ocean, river, and forest, they lived lightly on the land. Each generation passed on to the next the rich bounty of their territories, protected from potential interlopers and capable of supporting a sizeable population. They relied, as well, on a rich oral culture as the basis for their society. Their stories and histories contained wisdom and insight, and were the primary conduit for the sharing of values and knowledge. Place names alone provided endless insight into the complexity of Mi'kmaq and Maliseet history and culture, for many of the names encapsulated stories of great importance to the broader society.

In more recent times, some non-Aboriginal people have romanticized indigenous pre-contact life. This new interpretation creates an interesting dichotmony between those who view the Mi'kmaq in "pure" Rousseauian terms – a bucolic conflict-free life, developed in harmony with nature – and those who see their experience in Hobbesian perspective: life was "nasty, bruttish and short." Such comparisons are more odious than helpful, for observers typically forget to look at life for most Europeans at a similar juncture. At the same time, overglorifying the past is just as misleading. Starvation was not unheard of among the Mi'kmaq and Maliseet, particularly during the deep cold of the winter, and life could be very hard. It was, however, a life that suited the First Nations well, one that represented thousands of years of adaptation and learning to the unique ecosystems of the Maritime region. Miller offers a striking description of the status of Mi'kmaq life at the point of European contact:

Adaptation that the Micmac people had evolved over hundreds of years allowed them to flourish and prosper in the climatically harsh but food-rich environment of eastern Maritime Canada. The complementary division of labour among male and female adults facilitated everyday life; the alliances and kinship networks brought about by marriages between bands and bilateral kin reckoning helped to bind the people together locally, while the Grand Chief, the Grand Council, and the system of political districts facilitated unified action of the Micmac people on political matters. The seasonal round permitted optimal use of the resources. With frequent feasts and dances for a variety of occasions, regional and Grand Council meetings providing an opportunity for visiting friends and relatives, and other social activities and pastimes, even war raids, life must have been full and eventful. From the early accounts of the culture, one gets the impression that the Micmac had made an eminently satisfactory adjustment to life.[9]

ENCOUNTERING NEWCOMERS

The Mi'kmaq and Maliseet likely knew about the unusual men and their enormous vessels long before they sailed into North Atlantic waters. News passed swiftly between indigenous groups, and the arrival of newcomers to the south and north probably circulated among Mi'kmaq and Maliseet communities. Similarly, diseases and European trade goods generally reached First Nations well before the initial face-to-face encounter with the outsiders. Because of their location on the east coast of North America, the Mi'kmaq made contact with Europeans some time before the early sixteenth century, for, when Jacques Cartier sailed into the region in 1534, they were used to trading furs. It would be a full three centuries before First Nations at the opposite end of the continent, in the upper Yukon River basin, had their first direct meeting with the newcomers. The Mi'kmaq provide one of the first glimpses of the encounter between First Nations and Europeans in northern North America, since the Maliseet were less well known to Europeans. Unlike the Beothuk of Newfoundland, who had little contact with the newcomers, yet perished as a result of settlement, the Mi'kmaq played a significant role in early contact.

Much contemporary commentary about early Maritime history uses the language of dispossession and colonization to explain what happened to the Mi'kmaq and Maliseet. In the initial decades of contact, relationships were based on mutual respect and shared need, but the First Nations soon found themselves locked in colonial struggles between Britain and France as they were evicted from land that had been theirs since "time immemorial." Early settlements relied heavily on the willingness of Mi'kmaq and Maliseet harvesters to sell produce to the forts and settlements. The French had many manufactured goods that the Mi'kmaq desired: metal tools, axes, and pots made immediate improvements to life among the First Nations. A vigorous exchange quickly developed, with the French anxious to buy beaver pelts in particular, and the Mi'kmaq willing to sample the manufactured goods, clothing, food, tobacco, and alcohol that the newcomers had to offer.

Involvement with the French brought benefits – and immediate consequences. Before they realized the full scope of the French-British rivalry, the Mi'kmaq and Maliseet discovered they had already chosen sides. The relationship was, at least in the early years, sufficiently balanced for the First Nations not to see any compelling reason to pull away from their trading partner. Still, the arrival of the French brought unprecedented assaults on the Mi'kmaq and Maliseet world view. At one extreme, the discovery of these strangers from across the ocean called into question Aboriginal assumptions about the order, size, and nature of the world. The technological advantage of the French in some areas gave them an aura of superiority, even invincibility, that was disconcerting. Diseases ravaged entire populations, and the often powerful shamans could rarely cope with the onset of foreign illnesses. The French also brought missionaries with them, determined to share the wisdom of the Catholic Church with the inhabitants of North America. When a priest cured Membertou from a severe attack of dysentery, the chief urged his people to join the Catholic faith. The priests, who also provided many of the best-written accounts of Aboriginal life in this period, were a determined lot. They typically lived and travelled with the people, learned their languages, and sought ways to ingratiate themselves into the society. With the knowledge gained, they offered the Mi'kmaq access to "the Word," using the scriptures, hymns, and Catholic ritual to draw the First Nations into the church's fold. They enjoyed considerable success, some argue, because the missionaries' arrival coincided with the onset of several vicious epidemics, diseases the priests did not catch. While some saw the Aboriginal acceptance of Christianity as representing a sign of cultural and spiritual desperation – traditional teachings and powers could not cope with the ravages of disease, for example – other scholars have argued that the Mi'kmaq spiritual world, with its belief in a life force that infused all things, could accommodate the single God of the Christian faith. The Catholic Church, initially acting in close concert with French authorities, also did a great deal to support the Mi'kmaq people during times of great difficulty. The missionaries' presence among the First Nations, and their tangible support during both good and difficult times, convinced many Aboriginal people to remain loyal to the Catholic faith long after the French had left the region. Perhaps this contact best explains the continuing power of the Christian church among Mi'kmaq and Maliseet people.

The advent of the fur trade brought opportunity and new trade goods, but it also created a new economy, one based on the supply of surplus products – in this case, pelts. The seemingly unlimited French demand for the pelts drove Mi'kmaq and Maliseet hunters into the forests, for they quickly came to desire many of the trade goods available from the Europeans. The commercialization of resources was not a case of the cleverer European exploiting the guileless Aboriginal, though the story has long played this way. Substantial changes followed the advent of trade. Responding to the fur-trading companies' desire for pelts, the Mi'kmaq spent more time hunting, at the expense of harvesting. They became more reliant on European foodstuffs and manufactured tools. Alcohol became a standard trade good, causing considerable hardship and difficulty for Mi'kmaq men and women, who had never before encountered such intoxicating drinks. Some traditional practices and tool-making skills fell into disuse. Mi'kmaq and Maliseet people understood the terms of trade and eagerly sought the new trade goods, which carried both practical and symbolic value in their communities. The conflicts occasionally escalated into major battles, resulting in a sizable expansion of Mi'kmaq territory towards the Gaspé. In rapid order, the fur trade introduced new economic assumptions that justified a substantial expansion from the earlier Aboriginal-to-Aboriginal trade in the region and altered First Nations relationships with the natural world.

In responding to the demands of the fur trade, the Mi'kmaq and Maliseet made errors, as all human societies have done, and overused certain resources.

Wars and military alliances figured prominently in the history of the Mi'kmaq and Maliseet. From the early days of European settlement in the Maritimes, the region became a focal point for the struggle between the British and the French for control over eastern North America. The British were firmly established in the Atlantic colonies to the south and, by the mid-seventeenth century, the French had entrenched themselves along the St Lawrence River. For reasons both strategic and symbolic, therefore, the area known as Acadia became a critical battleground. The French presence was initially quite small, restricted to a small outpost at Port Royal. As early as 1613, British forces attempted to evict the French from their posts. This temporarily successful endeavour had the important effect of convincing the Mi'kmaq that the French were their allies and, obviously, that the British were the enemy.

The French and English struggle for Acadia would continue for another 150 years, with the ebb and flow of the battle determined by the unstable state of relations between France and Britain, the aspirations of New France and British colonies in New England, and the activities of the Mi'kmaq and Maliseet people. Beginning in the 1630s, the French tried to establish a permanent colony. The French settlers, who lived along the Bay of Fundy and whose land use did not clash with that of the First Nations, co-existed well with the Aboriginal peoples. There was considerable trade and intermarriage, and a shared interest in the Catholic faith. They also had a mutual suspicion of the British, who remained an ever-present threat to their survival. (but who also traded with the Acadians). The battle for Acadia became, at times, a diplomatic chess match. The British captured the area in 1654 and returned it to French control in 1667. King Philip's War, a bitter and violent struggle between the New England colonists and the First Nations, spilled over into the Abenaki region and fuelled Aboriginal distaste for the British.

The Mi'kmaq and Maliseet found themselves in the middle of the growing conflict between the British and the French. The French encouraged the expansion of the Abenaki Confederacy and supplied their allies with arms and supplies. First Nations raiders routinely attacked New England settlements, escalating the struggle and adding to the bitter hostilities; Mohawk warriors joined the British armies in their attacks on French positions. Mi'kmaq support for the French proved critical throughout a series of attacks on Acadian outposts, and the seemingly constant struggles solidified relations between the two groups. The Mi'kmaq and Maliseet were dismayed, therefore, when Port Royal fell in 1710 and the French ceded control of Acadia – now called Nova Scotia – to the British in the Treaty of Utrecht of 1713. Their understanding of political realities was such that the Mi'kmaq soon make friendly overtures to the British at Port Royal. The French were not easily dissuaded, however, for they feared that Acadia would be used as a base to attack their larger settlements in New France. They quickly built a sizable fort at Lousibourg on Cape Breton Island, calling on the Acadians and the First Nations to continue to rally to their defence.

The French attempted to keep the Mi'kmaq on side from their new bases on Prince Edward Island (Ile St-Jean) and Cape Breton Island (Ile Royale). Meanwhile, the Mi'kmaq and Maliseet broadened their reach and joined in the Wabanaki (or Abenaki) Confederacy with the Algonkian tribes to the south and west, particularly the Penobscot of Maine. Encouraged by the French, they aligned themselves against both the British and the Iroquois. The British bitterly resented the French manipulation of the indigenous groups and unleashed their wrath on the Mi'kmaq. Organized campaigns designed to destroy the Mi'kmaq – the term "genocide" has been used by some writers to describe both the ferocity and the intent of the British campaign – fell short of the British goal, but severely weakened the indigenous resistance. The British effort was intense, sparked by a desire for revenge for earlier Mi'kmaq attacks on British outposts. Few historian would go so far as Virginia Miller in describing British actions:

British attempts at genocide took various forms: they served poisoned food to the Natives at a feast in 1712; they traded contaminated cloth to some Micmac in 1745, setting off an epidemic that caused the deaths of several hundred; they sent groups of English soldiers to roam Nova Scotia and destroy Micmac camps, murdering the Natives without regard to sex or age. The English even imported companies of Mohawks and New England Algonquians, traditional enemies of the Micmac, to track down and kill them. All these tactics cost of the lives of an uncalculated number of Micmac.[10]

The French maintained the support of the Mi'kmaq and Maliseet, in part because the British permitted their former and future enemies to continue trade with their First Nations allies. Occasional British tributes paled in comparison to French generosity, and Mi'kmaq allegiance to the French remained strong. Prodded by the French, the Mi'kmaq and Maliseet continued to harass would-be British settlers in Acadia and to resist British entreaties for peace accords. Conflicts further south sparked Dummer's War, which ended in a peace settlement with the Abenaki (including the Mi'kmaq and Maliseet) in 1760. Mi'kmaq leaders ratified the treaty the following year. An uneasy truce settled over the region, with its large Acadian population, still-agitated First Nations supporting the French, and a British population largely limited to a few military posts.

The battle was joined again in the 1740s, this time arising out of a European conflict over control of the Austrian throne. The Maritimes was once more engulfed in conflict, with the First Nations attacking British garrisons and with the French attempting to dislodge the British. The British capture of Louisbourg in 1745 temporarily ended the French threat, but did not convince the Mi'kmaq and Maliseet to throw down their arms. The French regained control of Louisbourg under the peace accord and decided to move aggressively into the region once more. The British responded by establishing a major base at Halifax in 1749 and by negotiating a peace agreement with the Abenaki and Maliseet that same year. Governor Cornwallis launched a widespread offensive against the Mi'kmaq, offering bounties for scalps and prisoners. After further skirmishes demonstrated their resolve, the British signed a peace settlement with the Mi'kmaq in 1752.

Only a few years later, Nova Scotia/Acadia was once more engulfed in conflict. In 1755 Governor Lawrence, believing he could not count on their loyalty, ordered the Acadians deported from the region. The French-Indian War, 1755–63, was the final act in the French-British struggle for the continent. The French prodded the Mi'kmaq into action, an easy task given their anger at the British for removing their Acadian friends and relations. The British gradually beat back the last French and Mi'kmaq challenge, capturing the major French posts in 1757 (Fort Beauséjour) and 1758 (Louisbourg). Even when it was clear that the French had been defeated in the region, some Mi'kmaq continued the struggle. Only in 1760–61 did they finally agree to a peace treaty. And only then was the long, difficult, and costly battle for Acadia/Nova Scotia finally over.

During the long period of French and English hostility, the Mi'kmaq had repeatedly demonstrated both their preference for the French and their willingness to reach negotiated settlements with the British. Treaties had been signed with the British in 1725–26, 1749 (primarily a treaty with the Maliseet), 1752, and 1760–61. As Wicken explains in his analysis of Mi'kmaq relations with England,

All the treaties were signed at English settlements and all contain articles regarding how relations between the English Crown and Mi'kmaq peoples would be governed. Many of these articles are similar. This is because the

1725 treaty served as the model for all subsequent treaties so that in later reaffirming their friendship and peace with the English Crown in 1749 and 1761, Indian delegates were actually re-establishing the laws which would govern their relations, laws which had been temporarily suspended as a result of war.

The common elements of these treaties can be quickly summarized. First, the signators recognized the English Crown's "jurisdiction and Dominion Over the Territories of the Said Province of Nova Scotia or Acadia" and agreed not to molest any English subjects who had already established settlements or would lawfully do so in the future. The treaties stated that in any wrongs committed against either Mi'kmaq peoples or in any misunderstanding with English subjects, redress would be made "according to His Majesty's laws." ... In return, the English, according to the 1726 ratification, agreed not to molest either the Mi'kmaq "hunting, fishing and shooting and planting on their planting grounds."[11]

The treaties were not casual affairs and they illustrate the determination of both the British and the Mi'kmaq to find a means of coexisting and of managing their political and economic relations in a sustainable and mutually acceptable way. They were far from perfect documents, for they failed to stand up when hostilities broke out between the British and the French. It is not clear whether the English and the Mi'kmaq possessed the language skills needed to communicate their intentions or their terms clearly, and subsequent actions and conflicts suggest that a great deal of misunderstanding surrounded the agreements. Wicken argues that the Mi'kmaq enjoyed too much independence simply to surrender control of traditional territories to the British; he suggests that the idea of allocating their lands to a foreign king would have be meaningless to the Mi'kmaq.[12]

The French-Indian War had also alienated British colonists from the mother country and provided the first sparks in what would become the American Revolution. As that struggle for independence unfolded, the war-weary Maritimes, populated by new settlers who had migrated north from New England and who did not, in general, share the southern hostility to Britian, stayed out of the fray. As the revolution wound to a tortuous conclusion, thousands of Loyalists, some by choice and some by circumstance, fled the American colonies. While some headed back to England, many thousands came to the St John River valley, where they found fertile land in the Maliseet homelands, and to Nova Scotia, where they quickly pushed the remaining Mi'kmaq into the margins. The wars were over and, by the early 1760s, peace treaties had been signed with most First

Nations in the Maritimes. But the end of hostilities had not provided security for the Mi'kmaq and Maliseet. In some ways, an ever greater challenge lay ahead.

Wicken offers a useful summary of the general pattern of Mi'kmaq-newcomer encounter:

> Previous researchers have tended to emphasize first the changes occurring among the Mi'kmaq as a result of contact and second, the alliance made with the French Crown. While those studies have viewed culture as a fluid mixture bending to the technologically advanced and militarily superior European societies, this thesis has emphasized that as long as the Mi'kmaq retained occupancy over their fishing and hunting grounds, their culture remained intact and thus also their collective sense of separateness from French and English society.[13]

Wicken stressed the centrality of the Mi'kmaq to Maritime history in the 1500–1760 period and the fundamental importance to the Mi'kmaq people of free access to resources and the land. The role the Mi'kmaq and Maliseet played in the early history of the region faded dramatically, however, in the years after the defeat of the French and the arrival of the Loyalist settlers.

At least during the fur trade era and the period of French-British conflict, the Mi'kmaq and Maliseet figured prominently in Maritime affairs. By the late eighteenth century, conditions had changed dramatically. The flood of immigrants associated with the establishment of Halifax – in particular, the Loyalists fleeing from the American Revolution in the southern colonies – swamped First Nations communities and destroyed traditional ways of life. The newcomers quickly established towns and farms, extended logging operations into the interior, and blanketed much of the region. The eastern fur trade proved to be no rival to the richer fields of the far west, and the flow of trade goods and pelts slowed to a trickle. First Nations people discovered they had little place in the new order: they might be used occasionally as labourers, but were actively discouraged from participating in the emerging agricultural and industrial economy. As their communities continued to experience the depredations of European illnesses, their population declined significantly. The newcomers concluded that the First Nations would experience a lingering but certain death. The Mi'kmaq and Maliseet had fallen into virtual irrelevance, all but ignored by governments and settlers, patronized by missionaries who offered salvation in return for loyalty, and marginalized in a region hell-bent on catching up to the economic prosperity of the new United States of America.

The non-Aboriginal settlers moved into the traditional Mi'kmaq and Maliseet harvesting territories, converted them into commercial farms, and logged trees in their hunting lands. By the middle of the nineteenth century the Mi'kmaq were virtually wards of the British Crown, granted little sympathy or attention. Although they were allocated only small reserves, their best land was occasionally carved off to meet the needs of non-Aboriginal people. The Mi'kmaq and Maliseet played no significant role in the economy – there was ample local and immigrant labour to operate the logging camps, sawmills, and shipyards – and city dwellers made it clear that First Nations were not welcome in their midst. Clergy and schoolteachers offered their version of hope, in the form of education through day and boarding schools, and spiritual redemption in the regular church services offered on all the reserves. Perhaps the most prominent image of the Mi'kmaq and Maliseet was of basket makers selling their wares near the reserves or in towns. The fine weaving indicated that key indigenous traditions flourished even in hardship.

It is difficult to judge the severity of the crisis, for government officials dealt largely with those in distress, and most Maritimers rarely encountered Mi'kmaq or Maliseet people in their daily lives. The First Nations continued to get most of their livelihood from the land, except in those areas where farms, towns, or commercial fisheries had pushed them aside. Hunting and gathering remained commonplace among the indigenous people, and only a few harboured ambitions of joining the non-Natives in the new society. Disease continued to exact a terrible toll, and the spreading scourge of tuberculosis – an illness, overwhelmingly, of poverty and destitution – worked its insidious way through the settlements. These endemic illnesses, which sapped the strength of the afflicted and made them look, to suspicious outsiders, like lazy ne'er-do-wells and further entrenched the impression that the Mi'kmaq and Maliseet could never fit into the evolving Maritime order. This was, after all, the most prosperous region in British North America, with major cities developing at Halifax and Saint John, a booming ship-building industry and world-famous sailing fleet, and rich farming districts across Nova Scotia, Prince Edward Island, and New Brunswick.

The Mi'kmaq were painfully aware of the degree to which they were falling behind the immigrant society. A Mi'kmaq petition of 1849 to John Harvey, lieutenant governor of Nova Scotia, spelled out the First Nations' sense of desperation:

Before the white people came, we had plenty of wild roots, plenty of fish, and plenty of cord. The skins of the Moose and Cariboo were warm to our bodies, we had plenty of good land, we worshiped "Kesoult" the Great Spirit, we were free and we were happy.

Good and Honorable Governor, be not offended at what we say, for we wish to please you. But your people had not land enough, they came and killed many of our tribe and took from us our country. You have taken from us our lands and trees and have destroyed our game. The Moose yards of our fathers, where are they. Whiteman kill the moose and leave the meat in the woods. You have put ships and steamboats upon the waters and they scare away the fish. You have made dams across the rivers so that the Salmon cannot go up, and your laws will not permit us to spear them.

In our old times our wigwams stood in the pleasant places along the sides of the rivers. These places are now taken from us, and we are told to go away. Upon our camping grounds you have built towns, and the graves of our fathers are broken by the plow and harrow. Even the ash and maple are growing scarce. We are told to cut no trees upon the farmer's ground, and the land you have give us is taken away every year ...

All your people say they wish to do us good, and they sometimes give, but give a beggar a dinner and he is a beggar still. We do not like to beg. As our game and fish are nearly gone and we cannot sell our articles, we have resolved to make farms, yet we cannot make farms without help. What more can we say? We will ask our Mother the Queen to help us. We beg your Excellency to help us in our distress, and help us that we may at last be able to help ourselves.[14]

The similarities in the Mi'kmaq and Maliseet appeals that surfaced in the years leading up to the *Marshall* decision are striking.

There is great irony in the presentation that the Maritime colonies chose to make at the Great London Exhibition of 1851. As the world's largest exhibition to that date, it offered an unprecedented opportunity to demonstrate the accomplishments of the colonies to Great Britain and Europe. What did the Maritime colonies put on display? Other than a few examples of agricultural produce, they presented a lovely set of Mi'kmaq handicrafts. Following the lead of New Zealand and other settler colonies, the Maritimes turned to one of the few things that set them apart from other areas – their Aboriginal population.[15] But this public display of First Nations artifacts did not reflect the standing of their makers in the region. As one historian recently wrote: "During the 1850s the whites considered most Micmacs as outcasts from civil society. They might be effective as hunters, guides, or producers of modest native crafts, but they had little chance to fit into the European customs of Maritime society and its market-oriented economy."[16]

The marginalization of the Mi'kmaq and Maliseet obscured an already forgotten reality in the Maritimes: Britain had signed treaties with the First Nations, seemingly guaranteeing them a significant place in the regional order. During the period of French-English rivalry before the 1750s, the Mi'kmaq were treated as valued allies and engaged in a variety of nation-to-nation negotiations with European powers. According to Mi'kmaq tradition, their leader Membertou established an alliance with the Catholic Church in the early 1600s. When the French were pushed out of much of the region, the British rushed in to stabilize relationships. Treaties were negotiated with indigenous groups along the coast and, in 1725, were extended to the Wabanaki Confederacy, a First Nations alliance that included the Mi'kmaq, Maliseet, and Pasamaquoddy people. This agreement has long been known as Dummer's Treaty. The Penobscot took the lead in negotiating the initial accord, but later British meetings with the Mi'kmaq resulted in their acceptance of the treaty in 1726 and 1728. As the British population and pressure on Maritime resources increased, the Mi'kmaq requested further negotiations. Jean Baptiste Cope, a key Mi'kmaq chief, signed a new agreement in 1752. This treaty, which included the promise to meet annually to discuss issues, highlighted the promise that the Mi'kmaq would enjoy considerable trading rights and that the British would open a "truck house," or trading store, to support Mi'kmaq economic activity.

The collapse of the French position in Acadia proved devastating for the Mi'kmaq and forced them to reassess their relationship with the British. The French had been generous with their presents and tributes, and longstanding and close relations with the Acadian population had solidified Mi'kmaq loyalty. During the seemingly endless French-English wars of the eighteenth century, the Mi'kmaq had been loyal and active allies; the British, in turn, viewed them as potential enemies and attempted to remove them as a military threat. Overtures to the Mi'kmaq brought temporary peace, but did not resolve the larger issues. The British decision to expel the Acadians in 1755 proved devastating, however, for it robbed the Mi'kmaq of their close allies and relations. Mi'kmaq and Maliseet warriors responded with fury at the removal of the Acadians, but their military position became increasingly tenuous. When the French lost Fort Beauséjour in 1757 and Louisbourg in 1758, the battle for the control of Acadia shifted decisively away from the French and their First Nations allies. When Quebec fell in 1759 and Montreal the following year, British dominance of North America had been settled. Without access to French supplies and support, the Mi'kmaq and Maliseet resistance collapsed.

The end of hostilities required ratification, and it came in the form of several new treaties. The first came in 1760, when the Maliseet and Passamaquoddy came to Halifax to sign a formal peace accord. Led by Mitchell Neptune of the Passamaquoddy and Ballomy Globe of the Maliseet, the First Nations agreed to a restatement of the earlier 1726 and 1749 treaties. In return, the British government agreed that they would maintain "truckhouses," where they would sell trade goods to the First Nations at set prices, and offered presents to mark the end of hostilities. As the treaty with the Le Have band, signed on 10 March 1760, states: "[W]e will not traffic, barter, or exchange, any commodities in any manner, but with such persons, or managers of such truck houses as shall be appointed, or established, by His Majesty's Governor at Lunenburgh, or elsewhere in Nova Scotia or Acadia."[17] The British signed ten similar treaties with the Mi'kmaq in 1760–61. The colonial authorities planned a ceremonial signing of a single, combined treaty, but the event never occured. The Mi'kmaq signed another treaty the following year, in 1761, agreeing to the same basic conditions as in the 1760 accords and ending their long-standing struggle with the British. In offering the treaty, Lieutenant-Governor Jonathan Belcher said: "Brothers ... I assure myself that you submit ... with hearts of Duty and Gratitude, as to your merciful Conqueror," and he continued: "Your Patriarch will still feed and nourish you ... The Laws will be like a great Hedge about your Rights and properties." He assured the Mi'kmaq that they were "in full possession of English protection and Liberty." The Mi'kmaq leaders, according to some historians, indicated that they had "intended" to surrender without condition and that the British willingness to help them through a winter of hardship in 1760–61 had convinced them of the British seriousness. They promised to hold to the treaty "as long as the Sun and Moon shall endure."[16] Other analysts, incidentally, dispute the idea that the Mi'kmaq accepted such a "surrender."

The treaties of 1760 and 1761 addressed a vexatious issue for the British. The Mi'kmaq and Maliseet people, although decidedly less of a threat without their French allies, had nonetheless presented a formidable challenge to the British presence in Nova Scotia. The treaties resolved the long-standing animosity and provided the First Nations with a measure of security and support under a new regime. The British were concerned, as well, about subsequent encroachments on Aboriginal lands. Two years later, the British government would issue the famous Royal Proclamation of 1763, which asserted British sovereignty over undeveloped indigenous lands, but sought to limit non-Aboriginal incursions onto these territories without a treaty first being signed. When Belcher sought advice, likely from the Catholic missionary Pierre Maillard, about lands requiring protection for the Mi'kmaq, he was told of the need to reserve the area "for a Common right to the Sea Coast from Cape Fronsac onwards for

Fishing without disturbance."[19] Belcher, in May 1762, formally set aside, by proclamation, a coastal area from Musquodoboit to Chaleur Bay. No widespread land settlement arose out of the treaty process, through a reserve system evolved slowly over time and generally resulted in First Nations people being relegated to unfavourable plots of land. Not surprisingly, many Mi'kmaq and Maliseet argue that there have never been land settlements in the Maritimes and that indigenous land entitlements remain unresolved.

Canadians harbour overly generous interpretations of historical relations between First Nations and the governments of Britain and France. There is, in the case of the Maritimes, little appreciation for the long-standing armed struggle between British forces and the Mi'kmaq and Maliseet, backed by their French allies. There is even less understanding of the dramatic steps taken by the British to root out First Nations opponents, including bounties for Aboriginal scalps and/or prisoners, raids on Mi'kmaq and Maliseet communities, and extensive military campaigns designed to destroy the Aboriginal resistance. As would happen elsewhere across Canada (and in other countries, including the United States and Australia), food was used as an inducement to peace, offered to those willing to accept government terms and withheld from others who demanded more favourable settlements. Hostility and tensions remained in evidence long after the treaties were signed and, despite the friendly words and presents, British willingness to adhere to the terms and conditions of the treaties remained untested. In fact, even before the 1760–61 agreements had been signed, there were indications that Mi'kmaq and Maliseet rights under the treaties would not be routinely acknowledged.

Soon after these treaties were signed, disagreements erupted over the meaning and significance of the accords. The treaty-making process also left many misunderstandings. As a Penobscot leader said of the 1725 agreement: "Having hear'd the Acts read which you have given me I found the Articles entirely differing from what we have said in the presence of one another, 'tis therefore to disown them that I write this letter unto you."[20] Linguistic barriers between First Nations and the British complicated matters further, adding to the likelihood of misunderstanding between the signatories to the treaties. There is no doubt that the Mi'kmaq saw themselves as stewards of the land. Similarly, there is considerable evidence that the Mi'kmaq and Maliseet did not consider that the peace treaties of 1760–1 constituted formal land surrenders. A Mi'kmaq chief observed in 1749: "This land, over which you now wish to make yourself the absolute master, this land belongs to me, just as surely as I have grown out of it like the grass, this is the place of my birth and my home, this is my native soil; yes, I believe that it was God that gave it to me to be my country forever."[21]

Although disagreements lingered about the full meaning of the treaties, the documents clearly identified the rights of First Nations to continue to use the land and its resources. Unlike questions of sovereignty and ownership of the land, which continue to be hotly contested by some Mi'kmaq leaders, the treaty language was, for its time, quite clear. The 1752 treaty stipulated:

> It is agreed that the said Tribe of Indians shall not be hindered from, but have free liberty of hunting and Fishing as usual and that if they shall think a Truck house needful at the River Chibenaccadie, or any other place of their resort they shall the same built and proper Merchandise, lodged therein to be exchanged for what the Indians shall have to dispose of and that in the mean time the Indians shall have free liberty to bring to Sale to Halifax or any other Settlement within the Province, Skins, feathers, fowl, fish or any other thing they shall have to sell, where they shall have liberty to dispose thereof to the best Advantage.

During the Marshall trial, the persecution arqued that there was a significal break between the 1752 agreement and the assumptions imbedded in the 1760–1 treaties. Still, the Mi'kmaq and Maliseet had reason to believe that their lifestyle could and would continue with minimal interruptions and that they would be assured a reasonable economic base.

The root of the problem rested on fundamentally different assumptions about the meaning of the treaties. Within the British/European tradition, such treaties were about sovereignty, with the agreements transferring effective control of the land and its inhabitants to the British. The British (and, in contemporary court proceedings, the government of Canada) argued that, by signing the treaties, the First Nations became subject to British law. By implication, this agreement left the British free to deal with Aboriginal land and resources as they saw fit. The Mi'kmaq and other First Nations took the agreements, as fit with their tradition, to represent peace accords, promises not to wage war and to share resources. These treaties were not, like later western Canadian agreements, clearly devoted to the Aboriginal people's surrender of land and resources, even though explicit land surrenders were actually required before indigenous lands could be alienated for other purposes. Compounding the problem was another simple reality: in the first years, if not decades, after the agreements were signed, very little changed. The Mi'kmaq and Maliseet continued to hunt, trap, fish, and gather as before, enjoyed substantial use of the traditional territories, and rarely felt anything more than the gentle nudge of imperial authority. Maliseet fishing activities, for example, continued into the early 1900s. From 1800 through to the 1920s, the First Nations experienced further problems with imported diseases. With each influx of new settlers, it seems, additional epidemics raced through the Mi'kmaq population, claiming hundreds of lives in the process and further eroding their ability to adapt to the new economic order.

When the *Marshall* case came before the courts, historical questions, particularly about the role of the treaties and the conditions under which the Mi'kmaq signed the treaties, proved to be of critical importance. The central debate is fairly simple. For some analysts, the treaties were a logical outgrowth of military conflict and represented a forced submission by the Mi'kmaq to the British. Others argue that the Mi'kmaq were in a relatively powerful position in the mid-eighteenth century. According to this interpretation, the treaties met the needs of both the Mi'kmaq and the British and were closer to agreements between equals than accords signed by victor and vanquished. The transcript from the original *Marshall* trial, over 5,800 pages and including some 400 documents, included extended debates about the conflicting historical interpretations. Judges at the Nova Scotia Court of Appeal and again at the Supreme Court of Canada devoted a great deal of attention to this issue, for it was crucial to the Mi'kmaq claim that the eighteenth-century treaties assured them of the continuing right to make commercial use of local resources.

As the lawyers for the Appellant (Marshall) argued before the Nova Scotia Court of Appeal, "in our respectful submission, the Learned Trial Judge overlooks the fact that cementing a trading relationship was the essence of the parties' intention; the truckhouses were an inducement and benefit intended to fix the Mi'kmaq to the British and wean them from any lingering seduction on the part of the French. The right to trade was the meat, and a system of truckhouses was the gravy. If you take away the gravy, you are still left with the meat, not as His Honour would have it, an empty plate."[22] The Crown, of course, disagreed. As the lawyers for the Respondant stated in their brief to the Court of Appeal: "There is some evidence before the trial judge that some Mi'kmaq engaged in the sale of fish subsequent to 1760–61. But the evidence does not disclose that this activity was based on purported treaty rights. It was an activity that could be pursued in common with many other Maritimers. The extent of that commerce cannot be determined on the basis of the evidence. In and of itself, this evidence tells us nothing about the alleged existence of treaty commercial fishing rights. There is no compelling evidence to suggest that the British would have committed themselves to giving such rights to the Mi'kmaq. There was no need to. Moreover, any such preferential treatment would have been contrary to the mandate under which colonial authorities were operating ... Nova Scotia authorities, immediately after signing these treaties, acted under the belief that they had jurisdiction over the Mi'kmaq people. They took action in accordance with that belief, including, but not limited to, the enactment of laws which affected the Mi'kmaq including, but not limited to, the scope of their hunting and fishing activities. At the same time the Mi'kmaq themselves acknowledged the jurisdictional and legislative authority of the Crown."[23]

While the lawyers' words suggested a high level of confidence and authority, the reality is that the historical evidence is very thin[24] and subject to different interpretations. The historians involved, Dr Stephen Patterson, Dr John Reid, and Dr William Wicken, testified at length before the courts, presenting the historical documents relating to the 1760–61 treaties and their predecessors and examining the intentions and assumptions of both the Mi'kmaq and the British leaders. While they agreed on many key points, there were fundamental differences. Professor Reid, according to a summary of trial testimony, did not see the treaties as an act of subjection by the Mi'kmaq. He believed that there was a balance of power in the region and that the treaties "represented a further example of a sympathetic relationship between parties that were coequal." Professor Wicken generally agreed and suggested that problems with translation may have caused misunderstanding between the sides. He argued, further, that the British government desired a treaty and was willing "to give advantages" to the First Nations, and that the Mi'kmaq would not have accepted British regulation of their commercial activity.[24] Dr Patterson, in contrast, held that the historical documents – while unclear in many places – demonstrated that the British government used the treaties to assert its control over the Mi'kmaq. The treaties were designed to end conflict, establish the sovereignty of Great Britain, and make the Mi'kmaq subjects of the Crown.[25]

Debate continues on these issues among historians, as they attempt to piece together the realities of the past from the fragmentary documentary record. Academic differences of opinion, based on the careful reading of the documents and a wide general understanding of the historical context, sat at the centre of the *Marshall* trials and, ultimately, the Supreme Court decision. What is also clear is that, whatever the interpretations subsequently offered by professional historians, the Mi'kmaq did not get a great deal of satisfaction from the treaty process. The Mi'kmaq and the British colonial officials disagreed about the protection and rights granted and, over time, any sense of urgency on behalf of the colonial power dissipated. With the French out of the picture and the Maritime region the recipient of thousands of Loyalist settlers in the late 1700s, the First Nations were quickly relegated to the background. The issue of treaty rights would surface from time to time – typically through Mi'kmaq references to the promises of the peaceful accords – but the official recognition that these treaties conferred specific commercial resource rights on the Mi'kmaq would be held in abeyance until the last year of the twentieth century.

When British settlers arrived en masse in the latter half of the eighteenth century, the Mi'kmaq discovered that the treaties provided little practical protection. The lofty promises of the eighteenth century turned into the forgotten commitments of the nineteenth and twentieth centuries. Even more directly, legislation like New Brunswick's 1844 Act to Regulate the Management and Dispersal of the Indian Reserves in this Province provided governments with the legal means to confiscate lands allocated to First Nations. First Nations groups struggled to hold onto their lands and resources, and found that the newcomers paid scant attention to their needs. A Mi'kmaq delegation speaking to the Legislative Assembly of Prince Edward Island appealed for a grant of land in 1832:

Fathers: When your fathers came and drove away our French fathers – we were left alone – our people were sorry, but they were brave – they raised the war cry – and took up the tomahawk against your fathers. – Then your fathers spoke to us – they said, put up the axe – we will protect you – we will become your Fathers. Our fathers and your fathers had long talks around the Council fire – the hatchets were buried – and we became friends.

Fathers: They promised to leave us some of our land – but they did not – they drove us from place to place like wild beast – that was not just.

Fathers: Our tribe in Nova Scotia, Canada, New Brunswick and Cape Breton have land on which their Families are happy. – We ask of you, Fathers, to give us a part of that land once our fathers' – whereon we may raise our wigwams without disturbance – and plough and sow – that we may live, and our children also – else, Fathers, you may soon see not one drop of Indian blood in this Island, once our own – where is now our land? – we have none.

Fathers, we are poor – do not forsake us – remember the promises your fathers made to ours. Fathers, we salute you.[26]

By the time Lennox Island was purchased for the Mi'kmaq on Prince Edward Island in 1870, the prime real estate had been taken up by immigrant farmers. Throughout the Maritimes, the small reserves allocated to the Mi'kmaq were rarely on serviceable land and were often located, deliberately, away from non-Aboriginal settlements.

Historian Leslie Upton provided a succinct description of the Mi'kmaq reality in the years after the British had asserted their control of the Maritimes and the Loyalist migration had recast the region (now divided into three colonies, Nova Scotia, New Brunswick, and Prince Edward Island):

After 1783 the Micmacs had to accept that they were under the political jurisdiction of three separate governments which responded to the interests of the settlers. The Micmac way of life was totally disrupted by settlement on farm and riverbank. They could no longer support themselves by fishing or hunting or trading. Colonists were concerned about this situation only sporadically, and then only in the context of how the Indians affected the "progress" of the colonies. The new authorities accepted that not even Indians should be allowed to starve and belatedly distributed a grudging relief to those whom progress had pauperized. The occasional attempts to assimilate the Micmacs into the sedentary farm ideal of white society invariably foundered on their preference for the traditional life. They retained their mobility, the most cherished aspect of their past independence, and became peddlers of handicrafts and woodenware. They retained their own blend of Catholic Christianity which clearly marked them off the from the protestant majority among the colonists. They maintained their tribal authority, with its structure of chiefs and captains chosen by election. They remained responsible to each other.[27]

With the entry of the Maritime provinces into Confederation (Nova Scotia and New Brunswick in 1867 and Prince Edward Island in 1873), Mi'kmaq and Maliseet affairs came under federal jurisdiction. (Interestingly, there was a short-lived panic among the Mi'kmaq about Confederation, for rumours apparently circulated that the existing treaty rights would be abolished under the new dominion. Mi'kmaq leader Peter Cope travelled to London to petition the Colonial Office, from which he received assurances that the treaties would be honoured.) The Department of Indian Affairs, formally established in 1880, was not a key federal agency, particularly in eastern Canada, and attracted scant attention and few resources. While exercising little national authority, the department quickly asserted considerable control over the lives of First Nations people, both by legislative restructuring and administrative action. The nineteenth-century pattern of encouraging reserve living and counting on initiatives in education and Christianization to bring the First Nations into the "civilized world" continued unabated, albeit with inadequate funding. The government constructed a major Roman Catholic residential school at Shubenacadie, Nova Scotia, in the 1920s and encouraged parents to release their children to institutional care. The government positioned the school in full view of the railway and highway, so that, in the words of Duncan Campbell Scott, deputy superintendent of the Department of Indian Affairs, "passing people will see in it an indication that our country is not unmindful of the interest of these Indian children."[28] Like other residential schools across the country, the Maritime institute had it share of good teachers and tyrants, and left a mixed legacy among its students. Stories of physical, sexual, and psychological abuse abounded, and many Mi'kmaq families attempted to avoid losing their children to the school. While the classroom experience provided young people with some writing and other marketable skills, graduates typically discovered that they had few options in the still hostile regional marketplace.

The Mi'kmaq and Maliseet people did not simply fade into the forest. Shunned by the dominant society, tightly controlled by a federal government department that sought to "civilize" them, and unsure of their place in a fast-changing regional society, they struggled to hold onto their land and their heritage. Traditional harvesting activities continued, as they do to the present day, to a degree that few non-Natives appreciated. Mi'kmaq and Maliseet worked irregularly in the wage economy, although the collapse of the Maritime economy and the Depression of the 1930s pushed many out of the industrial sector. Their language remained in common use well into the twentieth century, despite efforts by schoolteachers and missionaries to convince them to speak only English. Elders retained prominent positions in their communities, exerting more real authority than parachuted federal officials or First Nations representatives appointed by government agents. Large gatherings of Mi'kmaq continued throughout the region, maintaining ties of kinship and loyalty that predated the arrival of the Europeans. In the forests, along the rivers, and in the ocean, the Mi'kmaq and Maliseet found the resources they needed to feed and support themselves. Ironically, significant numbers of Mi'kmaq men volunteered for military service during both world wars and the Korean War, perhaps finding the army an acceptable alternative to unemployment, a means of attempting to demonstrate loyalty to Canada, or both.

Throughout these years, the First Nations routinely petitioned government officials and politicians for redress, drawing attention to their treaty rights and the need to look again at Mi'kmaq-government relations. Little came from their efforts, for officials had a different agenda. As costs for administering Mi'kmaq affairs mounted, the federal government chafed at maintaining the twenty widely scattered

Mi'kmaq reserves in Nova Scotia. It made sense, to administrators, to centralize the Aboriginal population on two large reserves, at Eskasoni and Shubenacadie. Alex Christmas, president of the Union of Nova Scotia Indians, said of this effort:

Beginning in the 1940s we became the targets of a number of ill-fated social engineering experiments initiated by officials from the Indian Affairs branch. One such experiment was "centralization" whereby Mi'kmaq were forced to leave their communities and their farms to take up residence at one of two reserves designated by Indian affairs. The stated purpose of this exercise was to make it easier for bureaucrats to administer our people at two central locations. But the effect was to take more of our people off the land, deny them their livelihood and force them to live on two overcrowded containment centres.[29]

This experiment failed – Eskasoni and Shubenacadie were too small to handle the influx – and was officially abandoned in 1953. In the general enthusiasm for government intervention in Aboriginal affairs, however, federal initiatives continued.

Most contemporary Maritimers associate First Nations communities with a desperate social pathology, marred by suicides, alcohol and drug abuse, and violence, but seldom recognize that this reality is relatively new. As late as the early 1960s, when First Nations people first gained full voting and drinking rights, Mi'kmaq and Maliseet communities evidenced little of the social turmoil that is now assumed to be commonplace. There were problems to be sure, especially those of ill-health, poverty, and discrimination at the hands of the majority. The communities suffered, as well, from the omnipresent hand of an interventionist government and the loss of control over their children through the school system. But the reserve communities were peaceful places, with strong Aboriginal values and traditions running through the societies.

The major challenges lay in the combination of an overwhelming mass culture (television, radio, and the movies), increased economic marginalization, the mixed benefits of the intrusive federal government, an expanding resource frontier that pushed Mi'kmaq and Maliseet people further off their traditional lands, and the growing identity crisis associated with the uneasy relationship between Aboriginal and non-Aboriginal peoples. The 1960s and 1970s witnessed a rapid transformation of social conditions. Government programs proliferated and, not necessarily in a cause-and-effect relationship, so did tensions within the communities. Many Mi'kmaq and Maliseet moved off reserve and into the towns and cities of the region. Time and time again they experienced discrimination in hiring, housing, policing, and government services. On reserves, cheaply built government housing created ghetto-like conditions for the First Nations people, re-enforcing negative stereotypes and adding to the growing sense of despair.

More generally, the tremendous transitions in this generation highlighted the distance that separated First Nations people from their traditions and customs. Harvesting activity declined, but did not disappear. A small percentage of Mi'kmaq and Maliseet people worked their way through the school, college, and university system and found employment in the mainstream economy, but most found themselves dragged into a cycle of dependency on government handouts. Drug and alcohol problems proliferated, as the young First Nations people of the Maritimes sought to identify for themselves a place in a regional society that shunned and ignored them.

Through the changes that followed the Second World War, the resources of land, river, and ocean in the Maritimes were heavily commercialized. Hydro dams were built across fishing rivers and the provincial governments enforced fishing regulations more aggressively. New markets emerged for hitherto marginal species, such as lobster and crab. The non-Aboriginal communities experienced shocks of their own in the 1980s and 1990s, as overfishing resulted in sharp economic depressions and severe dislocations. Mi'kmaq people, however, saw many non-Native people profiting handsomely from the harvesting of resources off their lands, which only a generation earlier had supported a harvesting lifestyle, and the oceans, which had been much less intensively "mined" before the 1960s. Even though the regional resource economy was often troubled, the returns from their fields vastly outpaced the slow improvements, if any, in Mi'kmaq and Maliseet economic conditions. And, in community after community, resentment and frustration built.

The growing anger of the First Nations in the Maritimes coincided with, and built on, national and international indigenous protest. The politicization of indigenous peoples that so surprised Maritimers in the 1980s and after was part of a global phenomenon, which itself arose out of increased political interest in the rights of minority populations, a rising sense of liberal guilt among majority groups about the poverty of the First Peoples, and fast-developing activism among the indigenous communities themselves. Aboriginal political activism arose from growing frustration with poor living conditions, government interference, racial hostilities, broken treaties and agreements, and continuing legal discrimination. When the American Indian Movement (AIM) burst onto the U.S. scene in the 1960s, with dramatic confrontations with police and inflamed rhetoric about genocide and rampant murder, Canadians recoiled at the excess, which they saw as a radicalized and racialized American political reality. They soon found Canadian leaders uttering similar words and speaking about a history of indigenous dispossession that bore no resemblance to the one they had learned in school about Canada's early days in school.

The Maritimes were the last region in the country to develop Aboriginal organizations, for the first ones did not appear until the 1960s. The Union of New Brunswick Indians (which also incorporated Prince Edward Island) was established in 1967, with the Union of Nova Scotia Indians following two years later. In contrast, the Native Brotherhood of British Columbia had been in operation since 1931. By the 1990s some seventeen separate regional voluntary organizations had been formed to press First Nations issues. Aboriginal women created separate organizations, coming together in the Native Women's Association of Canada in 1974 to push their agenda. Groups emerged in each Maritime province: Nova Scotia (1973), New Brunswick (1973), and Prince Edward Island (1974).

The mix proved potent: deteriorating social conditions on Mi'kmaq and Maliseet reserves, government uncertainty about its role in Indian Affairs, rising indigenous anger, and increased media attention to the desperate affairs of First Nations people. In the early 1960s few Maritimers gave much thought to the realities of First Nations life. By the 1970s most Canadians were well aware of the frustrations and expectations of indigenous peoples across the country. The Mi'kmaq and Maliseet people were not unduly confrontational; groups in Quebec, Alberta, the Mackenzie Valley, and particularly British Columbia attracted most of the attention. But across Nova Scotia, Prince Edward Island, and New Brunswick, Mi'kmaq and Maliseet people were increasingly aware of the expanding Aboriginal protest movement. Combined with government financial support for Aboriginal organizations and a clear awareness of the depth of the problems on their reserves, the indigenous initiative took firm root in the Maritime provinces, ensuring that the First Nations had a substantial, at times loud, voice in regional and national affairs.

The Mi'kmaq and Maliseet people had experienced many profound transformations over the four centuries of contact with Europeans, changes that removed most of the memories of the thousands of years of indigenous occupation that preceded the newcomers' arrival. The land that supported countless generations of First Peoples had itself been transformed, with cities, farms, roads, and other marks of development. And the people who had once claimed all this land for themselves now shared it with several million others, most of whom rarely took notice of the Mi'kmaq and Maliseet heritage. Into the cauldron of history and memory have been stirred the painful realities of modern life, ranging from racial discrimination to substance abuse, creating an urgent desire among the First Nations people for attention to their grievances, a resolution of outstanding claims, and full recognition of treaty and Aboriginal rights.

CHAPTER THREE

Mi'kmaq and Maliseet Frustrations: Social Crises and Government Responses

Understanding the Mi'kmaq reaction to the *Marshall* decision requires an appreciation of contemporary social, economic, and cultural conditions among the First Nations population in the Maritimes. The *Marshall* judgment represented a watershed opportunity for communities that had long been marginalized and ignored in the region. It did more than illustrate the validity of Mi'kmaq claims about their treaty rights; the decision, together with the earlier lower court statements on the *Thomas Peter Paul* case, gave the Mi'kmaq and Maliseet hope. And hope has been in preciously small supply among the First Nations of the Maritimes.

The Aboriginal population in Atlantic Canada remains relatively small, with a total of almost 24,000 First Nations people recorded in 1996 (this number includes Newfoundland and Labrador). To put this figure in perspective, it represents about 4 per cent of the national First Nations population, and slightly more than 1 per cent of the regional population. The majority (66%) of the indigenous people in the Atlantic region live on reserves, a higher percentage than for the country as a whole. The communities are, in turn, quite small. Only two Atlantic settlements have a population of over 2,000 people, with most (18 of 31) falling into the 250–1,000 range. Small in number, widely scattered, and increasingly divided between on- and off-reserve residents, the Mi'kmaq and Maliseet do not represent a sizable or concentrated population.[1]

A description of contemporary conditions among the First Nations, most often a litany of social and economic problems, can easily reinforce existing stereotypes and assumptions. However bleak the picture – and at times the portrait is very disturbing – there are many bright lights that cry out for attention. Mi'kmaq culture, despite many obituaries over the years, remains strong and in evidence throughout the region. Elders continue to play important roles in some communities. Traditional family and group values retain respect, even among the youth who are said to be alienated from their culture. As is happening elsewhere in the country, First Nations people are leading and celebrating a renaissance – in music, storytelling, ceremonial life, traditions, historical knowledge, and harvesting activities. Mi'kmaq-language CD-ROMs, major cultural events, and First Nations schools and sporting teams all bear witness to the resiliency of Mi'kmaq and Maliseet people. Universities, particularly St Thomas University in Fredericton, New Brunswick, and the University College of Cape Breton, offer courses on Mi'kmaq and Maliseet language and culture and frequently host conferences on Aboriginal issues. First Nations artists keep alive the artistic traditions of the past and use new media to express aspects of their culture. And, in community after community, Mi'kmaq and Maliseet workers routinely take their places alongside non-Aboriginal colleagues, providing evidence to offset deeply ingrained stereotypes about indigenous people.

More than any one factor, the commitment and determination of First Nations leaders provide their communities with reasons for optimism. In an era when Martimers routinely decry the outmigration of university and college graduates to more fertile pastures in the United States or in central and western Canada, talented Mi'kmaq tend to stay in the region to seek work among their people. Band chiefs and councillors, many of them facing personal pressures and complexities that greatly exceed the challenge facing most local politicians, stay the course, continuing to work on problems that less committed people would feel compelled to abandon. There is no perfect relationship between Mi'kmaq leaders and their communities: in the spring of 2000, for example, members of the Eskasoni First Nation reserve in Nova Scotia launched a bitter attack on their chief, Allison Bernard, over alleged financial mismanagement, including his salary, and struggles over band council seats and local priorities are commonplace. Mi'kmaq people continue to view their present and their future in local and regional terms. Despite years of hardship and discouraging results from their negotiations and protests, they continue to press for improved programs and new opportunities.

Bernd Christmas is a good example of this crucial Mi'kmaq leadership. Christmas is a lawyer, with a strong interest in Aboriginal economic development in the Maritimes. Born to a Mi'kmaq father and a German mother, he has had extensive involvement with the Membertou Band Council (Sydney, Nova Scotia) and a number of Mi'kmaq organizations. He graduated from Osgoode Hall in Toronto in 1991 – the first Mi'kmaq from Nova Scotia to do so – and worked for a prestigious law school in the city before returning to the Maritimes in 1995. Christmas has been leading the commercial struggle over the *Marshall* decision and Aboriginal rights generally, seeking to ensure that First Nations secure some of the financial and employment benefits from major resource developments in the region. During the intense debates over the *Marshall* decision, Christmas held meetings with fishers from the Northumberland district of Nova Scotia and sought to negotiate the transfer of licences from commercial fishers who were leaving the industry to Aboriginal people. More generally, Christmas and his colleagues have taken the lead in hammering out deals with companies anxious to do business with Maritime First Nations.[2] Bernd Christmas is, moreover, an excellent symbol of the new style of leader in First Nations' affairs, well schooled and well trained, entrepreneurial and ambitious. More than anything, he, and others like him, are willing to use their skills in the interests of their community.

But enthusiasm and commitment have not yet been matched by significant results. Turmoil, uncertainty, and tensions remain the order of the day. First Nations communities continue to experience hardships and despair that are often endemic. Using almost any social or economic indicator, the Mi'kmaq and Maliseet people face prodigious problems. The death rate per 1,000 people is over nine, while for the Canadian population as a whole it is only six. Infant mortality stands at thirteen per 1000, versus eight for the country. Death statistics provide the most graphic illustration of the difference. Aboriginal males can expect to live for sixty-eight years and females for seventy-three; for all Canadians, the figures are seventy-four and eighty, respectively. Fortunately, life expectancy for First Nations people been increasing faster than for other Canadians over the past forty years, an indication, in particular, of improvements in infant health care. A consistently high birth rate suggests that issues will grow in complexity and intensity in the years to come: although it has dropped dramatically since the 1960s, it is still over twenty-two per 1000 population, more than twice the national average.[3] These are not tangential or peripheral problems. The social, economic, and cultural concerns strike at the heart of contemporary indigenous life in the Maritimes and animate and inform virtually all discussions involving Mi'kmaq leaders. The depth of the problems creates a sense of urgency that few non-Aboriginal Canadians feel and results in an intensification of debate, frustration, and anxiety among the Mi'kmaq and Maliseet people.

CULTURE AND LANGUAGE

While non-Aboriginal people typically focus on social and crime statistics as the best indication of problems in the First Nations communities, indigenous peoples more often look at issues of culture and language. Since the nineteenth century, Mi'kmaq people have lived with forecasts of their imminent demise and have heard countless references to themselves as a "dying race." The best tool for survival has been preserving distinctiveness through language and culture. Even those Mi'kmaq who adopted European dress and the English or French language, and adhered to the dictates of the wage economy, often maintained strong cultural connections with their community. And, until the 1950s, most Mi'kmaq and Maliseet people grew up speaking their language – gaining all the knowledge and insight that goes with this understanding.

Conditions have changed dramatically over the past forty years. Greater contact between First Nations and non-Aboriginal people has placed a premium on proficiency in English or French. Compulsory education, particularly in the residential school at Shubenacadie, involved a concerted effort to break young people from the habit of speaking their language. More generally, discrimination against Mi'kmaq and Maliseet people created a serious identity crisis for young Aboriginals, many of whom were pushed and pulled between competing traditions. In addition to these conflicts there is the pervasive influence of popular culture – radio, music, movies, and, in particular, television. Altogether, it is easy to explain the steady decline in First Nations cultural practices and language use.

Matters of language are the easiest to document. By the 1980s very few young people were learning more than a smattering of Mi'kmaq and Maliseet words. Since that time, school and university programs have increased attention to Aboriginal languages, and some youth have been introduced to the language of their ancestors. Occasional use in a classroom, however, or even the full immersion program available in several reserve schools, is not a guarantee of proficiency and continued use. As a result, by the year 2000 only a small percentage of Mi'kmaq and Maliseet people under the age of sixty could speak the language. The implications of declining linguistic competence are profound, for a great deal of cultural knowledge is imbedded in the language and in place names. As these phrases fall out of regular use, so does the connection between the youth and the distant past. Band councils, government agencies, and other groups are all attempting to address the problem – a good indication of the severity of the matter and of the intense desire among First Nations to keep language use alive.

Describing changes in cultural activities and traditions are much more difficult, if only because of the complexity of First Nations society. Many of the communal values and assumptions that underpin indigenous culture remain in evidence, and Aboriginal spirituality has proven to be very resilient, despite repeated efforts by Christian missionaries to undermine traditional belief systems. In recent years, there has been a resurgence in Aboriginal cultural practices, from celebratory feasts to cleansing rituals. At the same time, all cultures evolve and change over time: the fact that some Mi'kmaq and Maliseet traditions have declined in significance while others have increased in prominence is a sign of vitality, not devastation. Given the challenges in the broader Canadian society, it is hardly surprising that many First Nations leaders identify a serious generation gap between elders and youth and decry the limited attention paid to community leaders.

The balance between cultural continuity and cultural change is difficult to identify in the Maritimes. Far more of the traditions and values remain intact than is commonly assumed. Elders continue to play critical roles, family and community responsibilities remain strong, and many ceremonies and rituals are being used, or reintroduced, in the settlements. At the same time, Michael Jordan T-shirts are more common than Aboriginal motifs among teenagers, and the attractions of popular culture often outweigh the desirability of elders' talks and lessons. Furthermore, popular culture has had as much, if not more, of an impact among the Mi'kmaq and Maliseet as in Maritime society at large – and band council meetings and cultural events compete with *Jerry Springer* and *Friends* for the attention of younger people.

Critics of First Nations aspirations often point to the "modernization" of Aboriginal life as a reason to reject indigenous legal challenges and political demands. Non-Aboriginal comments in Tim Horton's shops across the region often include the insistence that Aboriginal hunting rights be exercised with a bow and arrow, and fishing rights with hand-made canoes. First Nations live with the expectation, in some quarters, that they remain completely "traditional" or accept integration into the mainstream. The Mi'kmaq and Maliseet, like other First Nations, have no desire either to retreat to pre-contact conditions or to abandon their cultural and community orientation. Like all societies, indigenous cultures adapt over time, and they do not cease to be "Aboriginal" simply because they have changed. At the same time, leaders are anxious that language and key cultural practices remain in place, and they are endeavouring to shore up these vital props of the Mi'kmaq and Maliseet tradition. Recent experience reveals that this preservation is a profoundly difficult and important challenge.

ECONOMIC REALITIES

The statistics paint a bleak picture. Official unemployment rates among the Mi'kmaq and Maliseet run at well over twice the regional average, and the Maritimes have the highest percentage of unemployed in the country. But the official numbers understate the real problem. Hundreds of working-age men and women have simply stopped searching for work, dismayed by years of failure and the absence of meaningful employment in or near their communities. Outside the band offices and related work (many bands now run their own services and, understandably, attempt to hire First Nations employees), there are few opportunities close at hand.

In Campbellton, in northern New Brunswick, local unemployment is running at over 20 per cent. The announcement in March 2000 that Canadian National was pulling close to two dozen well-paying accounting positions out of the community and relocating them in Montreal sent shivers through the town. It was too easy to add up the cost of this latest loss to the local economy. Across the river in Quebec, the Lestigouche First Nation lives a separate existence. More than just the river and a provincial boundary divide the communities. The Lestigouche band blockaded the bridge joining the towns in 1998 in a protest with government officials, then found itself immersed in a messy internal squabble over band management and finances. The differences erupted in a nasty dispute over staffing, a public debate that had many non-Aboriginal observers questioning the competence of First Nations leaders and wondering what would staunch the flow of money from the reserve's coffers.

This conflict, matched by a similar dispute at Eskasoni in Nova Scotia in 2000, created the impression of rampant corruption and seemingly endless financial resources among the Maritime First Nations. The public airing of internal conflicts, combined with fairly routine First Nation appeals for additional funds – for education, ambulance services, fire protection, policing, cultural programming, community facilities, and the like – has further inflamed the rhetoric of opponents of Aboriginal self-government and federal support for First Nations. The impression they have left is very misleading. Unlike a handful of bands in western Canada, their bank accounts swollen with resource payments, the Mi'kmaq First Nations are far from well off. There have been problems with band finances, to be sure, as devolution of authority to chief and council on some reserves outpaced the band's ability and willingness to manage the new resources. The federal government's desire to stand back from supervisory responsibilities for the funding did not help, for it left these bands without the technical ability and experience necessary to handle the substantial budgets passing through their hands.

The push to Aboriginal self-management through the 1990s has resulted in close to 90 per cent of all direct expenditures on First

Nations being handled by the bands themselves. Welfare and old age payments, employment subsidies, educational grants, and most local services are financed by Ottawa, but administered at the band level. The dollar sums involved are substantial – running into the millions of dollars per year – and the management challenge is formidable. Some First Nations did not adapt to the new responsibilities quickly. Moreover, the immediacy of the issues at hand – hungry children, lousy housing, community emergencies, and the pressures of managing the affairs of friends and relatives – led some bands into ill-planned expenditures. The Tobique Band in western New Brunswick, for example, found itself several millions of dollars in debt and facing government intervention. But again, the sums involved are misleading. Most of the money is committed before it arrives in the bands' hands; they serve primarily as the conduit for federal support to individual families. Moreover, demands for services run so high in the small, often isolated communities that the resources never come close to matching needs. Some movement is possible with funds allocated for economic development, for instance, but the available money falls far short of the immediate requirements.

It is important not to underestimate the impact of the politics of smallness in Aboriginal communities. Given the intensity of the issues, easy access to leaders, and high expectations, it is hardly surprising that internal turmoil is relatively commonplace. Noah Augustine, a key New Brunswick leader, observed:

On most reserves, elections are held every two years. With a population under 500 people, our community is under constant political division. Everybody knows everyone, causing emotions to run high. When an individual commits an action that offends another individual (verbal or physical), that action offends not just that individual, but a whole family or group of individuals. And for every action, there's a reaction. During the peak of election season, the community becomes a time bomb ready to explode. When one lives or works on a reserve, it becomes very difficult to detach yourself from the politics during an election. Everyone becomes involved, willingly or unwillingly. Political issues and incidents absorb every ounce of attention from the community residents to such a degree that it becomes very difficult for one to see through the cloud of politics, unable to reach any goals of achievement.[4]

In the heated cauldron of Aboriginal politics, community life can readily become divisive and complicated.

Despite vast federal expenditures on welfare, job training, and business support programs over the past thirty years, the economic conditions among Maritime First Nations remain appalling. When the high birth rate and the extremely large youth population are factored into the equation, the prognosis for the next two decades is even more distressing. Jobs are few and far between, and most of the available work is unskilled, seasonal, low-paying, and, in many cases, subsidized by government. Some regional companies, including powerhouse corporations like forest giant J.D. Irving, have started special programs to hire First Nations people, but with relatively few tangible results to this point. In most communities, the only substantial group of people with full-time, middle-class jobs work for the band; only a handful find work in the surrounding non-Aboriginal towns.

One group stands apart from this general trend. A small but growing number of Mi'kmaq and Maliseet people have completed college or university in recent years. Demand for trained and skilled Aboriginal people greatly exceeds the supply, both on and off the reserves. These workers, many of whom are employed by the band or hold elected office with the First Nations, enjoy sizable incomes. As is happening across much of Aboriginal Canada, Mi'kmaq and Maliseet society reveals signs of sharp divisions between the small professional class – well paid, mobile, astute, and flexible – and a much larger group of Aboriginal people who depend on seasonal work and government transfers to make ends meet.

Across the region, then, First Nations have enjoyed few of the benefits of on-going resource and industrial development in the Maritimes. Unemployment rates run high, particularly in the winter (when some reserves count over 80 per cent of their working-age population as out of work), and prospects remain dim. Remote settlements face particularly serious problems, as there are often no towns or cities nearby to provide employment for those willing to look off-reserve. First Nations have long been angry about their virtual exclusion from the resource sector, and often argued that they should have special opportunities to harvest trees, fish, and other marketable products from their traditional lands. Until the *Thomas Peter Paul* decision (later overturned) and the *Marshall* judgment, however, access to these jobs rested on the good will of government and the private sector. Some steps had been made – government loans enabled some Mi'kmaq to buy fishing boats and licences and to purchase equipment for use in the forest industry – but gains were small and by no means assured.[5]

Economic distress contributes substantially to Aboriginal activism and frustration. Young women often have established duties within their families and community, and many also have children of their own and are frequently the primary caregivers. For young Mi'kmaq and Maliseet men, the situation is more bleak. The traditional role of harvester and provider has been replaced by government payments, and opportunities have been eroded by non-Aboriginal intrusions into the resource areas and the related decline in First Nations activities. These young men, blocked from meaningful employment and with few prospects for improvement, have been at the forefront of First Nations anger. Often the frustrations have been taken out on themselves and their communities, but, increasingly, indignation has been directed towards forest companies, fishers, mining companies, and government officials, who are accused of using Mi'kmaq or Maliseet land and stripping the men of real opportunities for employment.

The stereotypes held by non-Aboriginal people are far from supportive. The First Nations, this argument runs, are lazy, unmotivated, and only too happy to live off the benevolence of government. While often ignoring the dependency culture that holds portions of the Maritimes in its grip, this argument suggests that the Mi'kmaq and Maliseet have no desire to change from this "luxurious" state of affairs. This picture has been shown not to be true, especially during the first days after the *Paul* and *Marshall* decisions, when young Aboriginal people moved quickly to capitalize on the newly legalized opportunities. Suddenly, the chorus of opposition changed. Far from being too lazy, the Mi'kmaq and Maliseet were too aggressive and posed a serious threat to the future of the fragile resources. Reconciling these conflicting images of First Nations people will undoubtedly take a considerable amount of time.

SOCIAL CONDITIONS

Mi'kmaq and Maliseet reserve communities are no longer the ghettos they were several decades ago in terms of infrastructure. The government funding provided for housing, although far short of that needed, has been more substantial than in the past, and the transfer of responsibilities to the local level has resulted in major improvements in services and facilities. Many settlements now boast attractive schools and recreational centres, and the medical centres are quite well appointed. Major investments have been made in water and sewer systems, and few of the egregious problems that plagued the settlements remain. The external appearance of the reserves often surprises those few non-Aboriginal Maritimers who venture onto them, for the shanty towns of the late 1960s have been replaced by suburb-like villages.

Just as the apparent poverty of the postwar settlements masked the determination and cultural strength of the First Nations of that era, so the improved facilities and homes mask some of the very real social problems in the contemporary communities. Housing stock has not kept pace with population increase, particularly after Bill C-31 (1985) changed the Indian Act rules governing status Indians and, by eliminating gender discrimination, returned tens of thousands of women and children to the federal government's band lists. Overcrowding is endemic, and it is not uncommon to have several families living in the same house. Birth rates remain extremely high, running far closer to figures in the developing world than in the rest of Canada or other industrialized nations. These increasing numbers place inordinate pressure on housing, education, and health services. Sexual activity and alcohol use often start at an earlier age among First Nations than among non-Aboriginal Maritimers. Family breakup is common, and many children are raised by their mothers in single-parent families or with the support of grandparents. Intergenerational conflict is substantial, as elders struggle to understand the pressures of the new age and as young people wrestle with identity conflicts and the pain of racial discrimination.

In the weeks surrounding the turn of the twenty-first century, the Big Cove reserve was wracked by a series of teenage suicides. Analysts quickly rushed in with context – the exceptionally high rate of suicide among First Nations youth, similarities between Big Cove and the more publicized crisis at Davis Inlet in Labrador, and reviews of the swirling social challenges that drive young people to such acts of desperation. None of the analysis caught the depressing essence of these events, which clutched at the heart of the community and claimed yet another set of victims in an unending struggle for stability. Stories of Aboriginal suicide have become so commonplace that they rarely rate more than a day's worth of notice. Nothing, however, so reveals the degree of despair that infects many Mi'kmaq and Maliseet communities as the pattern of self-destruction evident among the young people.

Markers of social despair are abundantly evident among First Nations in Canada. Whatever the social indicator, First Nations will be among the most severely affected. Suicide rates are seven to eight times higher than for other Canadians, as is the incidence of other violent death, particularly among young men. Through 1999, for example, New Brunswick's attention focused on the murder trial of Noah Augustine, the prominent young Mi'kmaq leader accused of killing another Mi'kmaq man. Augustine was found not guilty, to the surprise of many observers, but his once-promising political career lay in tatters. Domestic violence remains a serious problem and is one of the main reasons many women have fled the reserves for uncertain futures in the city. Swirling around all these manifestations of social crisis is a deeply entrenched culture of alcohol and drug abuse, which stubbornly resists efforts to change behavioural patterns. Maritime First Nations (mostly men) often come in contact with the police and the courts through drinking and drugs, though Mi'kmaq and Maliseet arrest and conviction rates are not nearly as high as those in western Canada. From Manitoba to British Columbia, First Nations people represent a staggering percentage of the overall prison population – as many as two-thirds of the prisoners in Saskatchewan in 1990. In Prince Edward Island, New Brunswick, and Nova Scotia, in contrast, First Nations people represent between 3 and 5 per cent of the prisoners. The self-destructive behaviour also shows up in health statistics: a lower life expectancy, high rates of fetal alcohol syndrome (caused by drinking by pregnant women), chronic illnesses related to poverty (including an upsurge in tuberculosis), and alcohol and drug abuse.

While, at times, the scale and diversity of social problems seems overpowering, most First Nations people have not succumbed to alcohol or drug abuse and do not show up on the statistics of social disintegration. But there is no denying the severity of the problems and their seeming intractability. For over thirty years, federal and provincial governments have repeatedly attempted to reverse the social pathology. Counsellors have been hired, special services launched, educational initiatives undertaken, youth programs expanded, and the intervention of elders and community leaders sought. But over the same period of time, by most statistical measures, conditions appear to have stayed as bad or gotten worse, defying all efforts to bring about an improvement.

One oddity runs through the social difficulties of the First Nations communities. Other minority groups facing similar problems and experiencing so little optimism have often struck out against the dominant society. The United States lives continuously with this perceived reality, though interracial violence in the United States is relatively rare. Among the Mi'kmaq and Maliseet, however, this conflict has not occurred. Violence remains largely internal to the community, and examples of First Nations' attacks on non-Aboriginal people are remarkably few in number. Self-destructive behaviour is far more common than bitter outbursts directed at the non-Aboriginal population. Aboriginal people are, in effect, taking out the brutalizing effects of cultural domination on themselves and on each other. This pattern, replicated across Canada, has buffered the majority of the population from the pain and suffering of the First Nations and has lessened the sense of urgency surrounding indigenous social conditions.

That the trauma of indigenous communities has not yet surfaced in interracial conflict remains one of the underpinnings of optimism surrounding the future of the First Nations – however difficult it is to explain and understand.

OFF-RESERVE REALITIES,
STATUS AND NON-STATUS INDIANS

The conflicts inherent in poverty, marginalization, and social despair are but part of the challenge facing First Nations. Additional tensions divide communities and raise doubts about future cohesion. Conditions on the reserves have forced many to leave for non-Aboriginal towns and cities. Across Canada, according to data from 1991, two-thirds of the Native people live off reserve, and over 40 per cent live in urban areas. It is difficult to chart the movement of Mi'kmaq and Maliseet people into urban centres. Some leave the Maritimes and head for centres like Montreal, Toronto, and Vancouver – each of which is home to close to 50,000 First Nations people from bands across the country. According to a 1991 survey, however, close to 10,000 First Nations people had congregated in the Halifax region, with a much smaller group (perhaps 2,000 to 3,000) living in and around Saint John, New Brunswick. Many of the migrants move into towns and cities for only short periods of time, making it difficult to determine the size of the population. What is clear is that the migrations to urban centres are increasing dramatically. Census data for 1951 and 1971 indicate that very few Mi'kmaq people lived in Halifax in these years; the recent figure of close to 10,000 suggests a rapid and recent movement.[6] In each of the Maritime provinces, the number living off-reserve increased dramatically after 1971, climbing from 40 per cent to over 60 per cent in Prince Edward Island, from 31 per cent to 38 per cent in Nova Scotia, and from 29 per cent to over 44 per cent in New Brunswick. Across Canada, the off-reserve population jumped from less than 35 per cent to almost 44 per cent.[7]

The choice is often dictated by economic circumstances: the larger centres present much better job opportunities and, typically, better schools and facilities for children. The migration to the cities, part of a national and international trend for indigenous peoples, creates divisions between on- and off-reserve residents. Under recent self-government agreements, the federal government has passed responsibility for managing a wide range of financial matters to the reserve-based bands. These councils, in turn, have always limited the access to band finances to people who live on reserve, and have fought efforts to extend voting rights and services to individuals who have moved off reserve. When new rights have been identified – as in the case of the *Marshall* decision – the stakes simply grow in importance. The federal government negotiates with duly constituted band councils, not with loosely formed alliances of off-reserve First Nations. As a result, allocations of harvesting rights or compensation were routinely targeted at reserves and administered through band councils, leaving off-reserve people with no benefits from the new arrangements.

The situation facing off-reserve band members is changing rapidly. As a result of the Supreme Court decision in the 1999 Corbiere case,[8] the Department of Indian Affairs and band councils across Canada were granted until November 2000 to change their electoral procedures to permit off-reserve band members to participate. This decision – yet another illustration of the importance of the Supreme Court in determining the structure and nature of First Nations legal and political options – will ensure that off-reserve band members have a much greater say in band governance in the future.

The struggle between on- and off-reserve groups is partly about resources and power, but also illustrates a difference of opinion about what is best for Mi'kmaq and Maliseet culture. To those who support reserve residence requirements, it is imperative that the people stay together to preserve the language and the culture. To scatter to surrounding towns and cities, they argue, weakens the band and the social order. To divide the already inadequate resources with individuals and families who have easy access to the much broader range of services and facilities available in the larger centres simply makes reserve life even less attractive. Off-reserve residents, in turn, argue that many were driven from the reserve, through no fault of their own, and should not now be punished, or that the reserves do not offer sufficient educational and career opportunities for individuals and families struggling to be self-sufficient. To stay on the reserve, they argue, is to risk being drawn into the morass of social despair; towns and cities at least offer greater hope. To be penalized for being motivated and ambitious, they contend, serves only to rob the band of its more forward-looking members.

An even more controversial division runs through the indigenous population in the Maritimes. Under Canadian law, specifically the Indian Act, there is an official distinction between the people with "status" and those without. To be a status Indian, one must be included on the membership lists maintained by the Department of Indian Affairs and Northern Development. Status Indians have access to all the programs and special rights of Aboriginal peoples. Non-status people, who may or may not speak the language and follow indigenous cultural traditions, are not on the lists and do not have these rights and privileges. In most of the country there is a third group, the Métis, who have achieved considerable recognition of separate legal and constitutional status. In the Maritimes, this group does not enjoy much standing with either provincial governments or the federal government.

Non-status First Nations people have no assured standing before governments and the law, but argue strongly that Aboriginal rights and treaty rights should extend to them. Changes to the Canadian Constitution in 1982 gave their effort greater authority, for the constitution included references only to "Indians," not to "status Indians." Status Indians, not surprisingly, have no desire to see their resources and rights shared with a broader constituency and generally oppose non-status efforts to secure First Nations privileges. These complexities create a great deal of animosity. It is possible for one individual, legally status but with little cultural, linguistic, or social connection to a First Nation, to have the legal ability to secure a full range of services and to exercise a variety of Aboriginal rights. Another individual, lacking status but with a strong command of an Aboriginal language and excellent cultural connections, has no comparable rights.

Aboriginal women have been particularly aggrieved by the regulations governing Indian status. Until the passage of Bill c-31 in 1985, First Nations women who married non-Aboriginal men automatically lost their status. Their children also lost all claims to Indian status. The reverse was not true. If a First Nations man married a non-Aboriginal women, she automatically gained Indian status and their children retained their Indian status. Women were disgusted with this double standard and attempted on several occasions to force the government to change. However, Ottawa was not convinced to move until the United Nations Human Rights Commission intervened and, more significantly, the Canadian Charter of Rights and Freedoms came into force. Within ten years of the passage of Bill c-31 the federal government received over 200,000 applications for reinstatement. A report for 1987 indicated that 4,600 applications had been filed in the Maritimes. Of these, over 1,500 had their Indian status restored, but only 476 (31%) were re-entered on band membership rolls. The controversies surrounding this law remain, however, as the children and/or grandchildren of Bill c-31 status Indians stand to lose their status depending on who their grandmother or mother married.

Changes to the law to permit women and their children who had lost their status to be placed on the national membership role did not solve the problem. Women discovered that many band councils were not pleased. This was hardly a surprise, as band councils had resisted their appeals from the beginning and only rarely supported their claims before governments, the courts, and international tribunals. Now, more practical matters stood in the way. Membership in a specific band was determined by the band, and many services, such as housing, were allocated by councils. Consequently, the Bill c-31 women experienced continued discrimination and hardship. Their problems have not yet been fully resolved, and many continue to struggle to find a place on the reserve. These women, if living off reserve, have also been denied the right to vote in band elections, and their children are not assured of access to band schools. Ironically, the women's victory over the Canadian government exposed deep divisions within the indigenous communities.

SPECIAL PRIVILEGES

More than one First Nations leader, confronted with angry denunciations from critics of the "special status" allowed under the Indian Act, has asked the non-Aboriginal speaker if he or she wished to change places. In recent years, particularly as the federal government's determination to address Aboriginal difficulties increased, public criticism of the special programs and benefits offered by the Department of Indian Affairs and Northern Development has mounted The list is substantial enough: exemption from income, sales, and consumption taxes; grants for college or university education; "free" houses; Aboriginal harvesting rights; subsidies for various health and cultural initiatives; and special employment and welfare programs. The federal government has often documented the total value of these payments, and most Canadians consider the expenditures to be fair – if not overly generous – compensation for past injustices and contemporary difficulties.

First Nations, not surprisingly, vigorously reject the notion that the benefits, programs, and services provided by the federal government are either "free" or generous. First, and despite Reform Party/Canadian Alliance rhetoric to the contrary, the various government initiatives are scarcely "generous" in terms of what is provided for individual First Nations. Although much is made of examples of excessive spending, the reality is that many government services, from housing to education, on First Nations reserves are well below accepted national standards. Furthermore, Aboriginal people assert with considerable indignation that there is nothing "free" about what is provided. First Nations, they remind other Canadians, paid for whatever meager benefits they are receiving through treaty settlements and other forms of non-Aboriginal land occupation and resource use. The more critical First Nations observers argue that the various government payments, services, programs, and schemes are simply measures that the dominant society uses to keep Aboriginal people beholden to the Canadian government. The very idea that these programs are even "special" privileges irks First Nations peoples as much as the existence of such services irritates some non-Aboriginal Canadians.

Little attention is paid to the various commitments attached to these arrangements. Given current economic conditions, few Mi'kmaq and Maliseet can find work on their reserves. Those who do work often have to relocate to towns or cities. The houses provided by Indian Affairs, while much better than the slapdash homes constructed in the 1960s, come with a caveat – individual First Nations people cannot get title to the property, arrange normal mortgages to cover the cost of the home, or sell if they decide to move. Harvesting rights are deeply imbedded in Canadian law and practice, and fill an important economic and cultural need in the communities. While critics are quick to highlight cases of abuse, they rarely point out the degree to which the fish and meat gathered under these Aboriginal privileges are distributed widely within the communities.

Very few First Nations people are getting rich on the basis of their Indian status. Although there are occasional examples of abuse – fully deserving of both public attention and redress – the various benefits attached to Indian status provide only a modest return to individuals. Even with the support, programs, assistance, and rights specific to First Nations, the vast majority of Mi'kmaq and Maliseet people earn much less than regional and national averages. Their living conditions bear little resemblance to those of most Maritimers and Canadians. Moreover, the presence of the Department of Indian Affairs in indigenous life has, over the past forty years, created a culture of dependency and despondency that greatly exceeds the often-criticized Maritime reliance on federal government support.

RENAISSANCE

The past thirty years have witnessed much hardship and suffering on First Nations reserves, but this same period has seen remarkable examples of resilience and rebirth. The federal government's decision in the 1980s to look to Aboriginal self-government as an alternative to centralized, paternalistic management transferred a great deal of responsibility and considerable resources back to the reserves. While there have been troubles, communities like Lennox Island (on Prince

Edward Island) and Eel Ground (New Brunswick) have experienced significant improvements. Housing stock has been upgraded, new community facilities built, and numerous First Nations – controlled businesses started up. Band-run schools have expanded Aboriginal programming and encouraged language and cultural training. First Nations sporting teams, continuing a tradition that has been around for generations, compete proudly in Aboriginal and general competitions. While the status of Mi'kmaq and Maliseet language worries elders and community leaders, the availability of teachers from kindergarten through to university provides reason for optimism.

Amid the difficulties – which attract much of the attention – there are abundant signs of rebirth and increased determination. First Nations musicians, many of them mixing Aboriginal and regional traditions, are gaining new prominence. Artists are discovering a growing interest in their work. Mi'kmaq spiritual and environmental knowledge attracts increased attention, and First Nations writers provide new insights into the reality of Aboriginal life in the Maritimes. Community activists, while still fighting Aboriginal campaigns, have been finding common cause with non-Aboriginal groups to broaden their base of support and understanding. And young people, though distracted by the forces of contemporary popular culture, are finding more and more value in the language, customs, and traditions of their elders. It is far too soon to declare the struggle for cultural persistence over, for the weight of non-Aboriginal influences verges on being overwhelming. Still, Mi'kmaq and Maliseet people have lived for generations with forecasts of their imminent demise ringing in their ears; now they see around them promising signs that all is not lost and that there are good reasons to be optimistic about the future.

The growing confidence of the Maritime First Nations can be seen in the leadership. Compared with Aboriginal political figures in the rest of the country, Mi'kmaq and Maliseet leaders are known for being relatively non-confrontational. Their critics, regionally and nationally, claim that the eastern leaders acquiesce too easily to government and lack the sharp edge and aggressiveness of their counterparts from Quebec, the Prairie provinces, and British Columbia. Mi'kmaq and Maliseet politicians have not figured prominently on the national stage, in part because of their more conciliatory approach to public affairs. If they have lost some opportunities by not pressing their cases hard enough, they have generally gained because of their approachability and reasonableness. These leaders face an unenviable task, standing between the outspoken elements within their communities (particularly the young men and the women's organizations), more traditional First Nations people, governments, and the general Maritime population. They find themselves playing a critical balancing act, careful not to overstate their case for the general public but sufficiently assertive to placate critics on the reserve.

Most Maritimers rarely, if ever, visit First Nations reserves. They know about the communities from what they see in the media and from the stereotypes through which they filter information. Most of their impressions of Mi'kmaq and Maliseet culture are based on the difficult years of the 1960s and 1970s, when the reserves looked like Third World settlements and Aboriginal people were truly uncertain about their long-term place within Canada. The last thirty years have seen the pain continue – with the suffering often well recorded in the press – but they have also seen the beginnings of substantial change. Buttressed by changes in federal law and management of Aboriginal affairs, driven by the intense desire of First Nations elders and leaders to break the cycles of poverty and despair, inspired by personal and group accomplishments that pass without notice in the general population, the Mi'kmaq and Maliseet continue to look forward with optimism.

ABORIGINAL RIGHTS

As Mi'kmaq and Maliseet seek to rebuild their communities and reinforce their culture, they have turned aggressively to arguments about Aboriginal rights. Legal victories elsewhere in Canada have strengthened the First Nations' hand and resulted in the recognition of the right to harvest for subsistence purposes. This crucial accomplishment did nothing, however, to address underlying economic difficulties and persistent poverty and unemployment. More radical elements in many communities pressed for an assertion of the indigenous right to hunt, trap, and fish for commercial purposes, long before the *Marshall* case. These struggles were often as much internal as external, as communities sought to find the best means to reinvigorate the local economy.

A 1995 dispute involving the Eel Ground reserve is an excellent case in point. Members of the Micmac Warrior Society were determined to assert their Aboriginal right to fish for salmon and to regulate resource use according to Mi'kmaq custom. Band leaders, led by Chief Roger Augustine, adopted a more conciliatory approach and negotiated a deal whereby they agreed not to permit gill-netting (the net stretched from shore to shore and effectively trapped all fish) of salmon in return for greater control over fishing along a portion of the Miramichi River. This moderate approach saw a classic tradeoff: a surrender of uncertain Aboriginal rights in return for assured control and the resulting economic benefits, in this case $400,000 for development projects. The Warriors occupied the Big Hole Tract, a crucial fishing ground, and warned off both their leadership and the Department of Fisheries and Oceans. The Micmac Warriors, one observer commented in a foreshadowing of the *Marshall* ruling, "wants no truck or trade with the white authorities. Treaties signed three centuries ago give them a right to fish and feed their families in perpetuity, and that is what they intend to do. No concession, even for conservation of the species so that it can be fished in perpetuity, will be considered minor – The Warriors who have occupied the Big Hole Tract fishing lodge are not bent on merely preventing an incursion on native group by federal police. They are looking to undermine all agreements between native bands and DFO that limit fishing rights in any fashion, great or small."[9]

The Eel Ground conflict settled down, although not without political costs for Chief Augustine and his supporters. This volatile situation – punctuated by the sight of fifty armed warriors, of whom Warrior Chief Frank Thomas said: "Our people are ready to die for their rights"[10] – was one of many small, often ignored conflicts between First Nations and governments and, increasingly, within First Nations communities. As Henry Bear, an Aboriginal lawyer from Fredericton, wrote during a 1996 dispute over logging on Christmas Mountain, New Brunswick:

This is another chapter in a true New Brunswick story involving relationships between its people and those of the Mi'kmaq and Maliseet peoples. Relations between Mi'kmaq and Maliseet peoples and non-Aboriginal peoples which have, with some exceptions, been seen as painful and unjust by the Aboriginal peoples. This was because before their very eyes, and even up to the present day, territorial lands have been illegally occupied, converted, and wasted, regardless of Mi'kmaq and Maliseet protests and reliance on these same lands for their economic, social, political and cultural survival. Their ongoing protests to various government bodies were made regarding these illegal encroachments by non-Aboriginal squatters and foreign businessmen, but no action to intervene and protect Maliseet and Mi'kmaq interests occurred until recently, even though the government was and is bound to do so under its promises and guarantees contained in King George's Royal Proclamation of 1763, a document now forming part of the Canadian constitution.[11]

Social and economic despair generates a reaction, and while much of the anger has been taken out internally (revealed in suicide rates and problems with abuse), it is hardly surprising that many Mi'kmaq and Maliseet began to look for solutions outside their communities. For moderate and radical leaders alike, one potential solution lay in the assertion of Aboriginal and treaty rights. And while they might, as at Big Hole Tract, disagree about the tactics and the timing, First Nations share a profound conviction that they possess unalienated and effective rights that have the potential to empower and enrich their communities.

CONCLUSION

First Nations in the Maritimes face conditions similar to those of indigenous people across Canada and, indeed, around the world. The current generation is paying the price for generations of marginalization, as well as the disconnection between traditional and global culture that has arisen through the expansion of the mass media. Mi'kmaq and Maliseet youth need only turn on the television set or the radio to learn how different conditions are in other parts of Canada or the world. They have come to covet the material possessions of the modern age, and they have recognized, painfully, that the broader society has yet to find a place for them within its midst. They do not belong to the world of their ancestors, except by ties of blood, and lack the language skills and traditional knowledge of their elders. They wish for opportunities and work, but find little of either in their communities. And they have learned, often through bitter and direct experience, that they are not particularly welcome in the non-Aboriginal world, where they will be defined and treated in terms of lingering stereotypes. Elders, whose lives were not much different, despair at the lack of optimism among the young people, and know only too well that determined efforts to preserve Mi'kmaq and Maliseet culture have been largely unsuccessful.

It was this world, one of limited hope, frustration, and self-destruction, that was turned on its head by the *Marshall* decision of September 1999. For the first time in the twentieth century – and appropriately with only two-and-a-half months to run in a century that had not been kind to the Mi'kmaq – First Nations in the Maritimes had significant reasons for hope. They had long sought the right to fish, hunt, and log commercially – not just to feed themselves but to generate a living wage. The Supreme Court granted that right in the *Marshall* judgment, sending a burst of hope throughout the indigenous communities. Now, they believed, they had the right to earn a living – and had official recognition that this right was a first order of business for government, not a lesser privilege that would be subordinated to the needs of the non-Aboriginal fishers and population. To most Mi'kmaq, the *Marshall* decision represented a vindication of the elders and leaders, and a reason for true optimism. They could now harvest resources and make a living wage. They could, it seems, break the cycle of dependency without having to leave their communities. They could earn a living, not rely on government handouts for subsistence. And they could do so in a traditional way, by fishing, hunting, and harvesting, thereby rebuilding the skills and values that sat at the heart of Mi'kmaq life.

It is impossible to understand the First Nations' reaction to the *Marshall* decision strictly in legal and technical terms. Few Mi'kmaq rushed off to read the judgment. They soon knew all they needed to know – their right to harvest resources and to sell their work product had been recognized. The enthusiasm that greeted the decision rested not on greed or the prospect for personal benefit, although, inevitably, there was some of this consideration. Rather, it reflected the joy of a marginalized and oppressed group finally given the opportunity to dream again, to believe that the future could be better than the immediate past. For a society on edge, suffused with pain and suffering, the *Marshall* judgment had all the elements of a panacea, a quick solution to the economic and social ills of its communities. More than that, even, the decision held the promise of a very different future, one with reason for hope, built on assured access to resources and backed by the authority of the highest court in the land. After years of being pushed to the periphery, and after decades of cultural and social despair, the Supreme Court decision on the *Marshall* case was the first major sign that the past was simply prologue and that the future held great promise.

CHAPTER FOUR

Prelude to Marshall: *Aboriginal and Treaty Rights in Canada*

The *Marshall* case did not emerge out of thin air. It represented, instead, the latest salvo in a long-standing effort by First Nations to have their Aboriginal and treaty rights recognized and honoured. For many in the Maritimes, the issues of contemporary First Nations rights seemed irrelevant. There were occasional noises from Mi'kmaq and Maliseet people about old treaties that few in the region knew much about. The Innu and Montagnais of Labrador had been fighting for land rights and against military use of their territory. Their protests were often headline news. Quebec provided a steady stream of conflicts and controversies, ranging from the James Bay Treaty in northern Quebec to the Oka standoff in the Montreal area. Ontario experienced a series of conflicts over harvesting rights and logging, but the really intense struggles were in the West and the North. Throughout the 1980s and 1990s, in a seemingly endless series of court cases and negotiations, First Nations demanded – and occasionally received – attention to outstanding grievances.

Little of this conflict seemed to affect the Maritimes. Mi'kmaq and Maliseet politicians lacked the confrontational edge of many of their counterparts, ensuring that Aboriginal issues maintained a low profile. While jurisdictions like British Columbia and the territories struggled with the need to negotiate treaties, First Nations claims in the Maritimes had been settled, so the public thought, in the eighteenth century. Although few Maritimers knew much about First Nations conditions and aspirations, it seemed clear that the Mi'kmaq and Maliseet did not expect the same level of access to forest, fishing, and hunting resources that had become commonplace in the rest of the country. For the First Nations, the situation was different. Pushed by difficult social conditions and aware of the swirling international currents on indigenous rights, local Aboriginal politicians pressed quietly for attention to outstanding issues. The general pattern of non-confrontation left a misleading impression in the region, however, which felt itself buffered by history, geography, and experience from the conflicts that now spread across Canada.

INTERNATIONAL CONTEXT

Canadians like to see Aboriginal issues in a specific national context. Aboriginal and non-Aboriginal alike, they typically explain the ebb and flow of indigenous rights in Canadian terms, tying developments to individual politicians, legal decisions, or political acts. There is nothing unusual in this, for people who follow indigenous rights campaigns in New Zealand, Australia, the United States, and Scandinavia tend to do the same thing. Though there is a specific Canadian pattern to the emergence of Aboriginal rights in the country, it is vital to recognize that national developments emerged in the context of changing international currents and ideas.

Before the Second World War, there was little global interest in the legal and treaty rights of indigenous peoples. Countries around the globe dealt with their indigenous populations as they saw fit, typically by marginalizing them or by removing them from their traditional lands. There was growing academic interest and curiosity about the "primitive" peoples of the world ran high, fuelling interest in such publications as the *National Geographic* and the work of various scientific societies. But in an era when the rights of minorities were routinely trampled in the interests of the majority – from Afro-Americans in the United States to Jews in Germany and Asian Canadians in Canada – it is hardly surprising that the small, scattered, and often powerless indigenous populations attracted little attention.

Shifting intellectual and political currents in the postwar world changed conditions dramatically. The exposure of the Nazi death camps brought home, in a way that a million tiny cuts had never done, the barbarity of racism and institutionalized discrimination. The founding of the United Nations and the expansion of decolonization heightened concern for minority populations. The content of the Universal Declaration on Human Rights challenged nations to revisit policies that discriminated against specific groups, such as the First Nations. More generally, the increased glare of public attention and growing governmental concern for the social and economic conditions of its citizens forced politicians and administrators to look again at their policies affecting targeted populations.

Canada, like other liberal democracies, found it difficult to sustain a critique of the racist policies of other countries, such as South Africa, when it neglected so systematically the needs and aspirations of its own First Nations. In fairly quick order, the protests that had long emanated from the Aboriginal communities found a more receptive ear. Paternalism proved a difficult dragon to slay, however, and the immediate response (in Canada and elsewhere) to the new international agenda was to expand government programs. Residential schools grew in number and size in the North and West, and efforts were made to integrate First Nations into the wage economy. New housing programs, mother's allowance, and a variety of other initiatives sought to offer the benefits of national citizenship to indigenous peoples. Political concern for Canada's poorest citizens ran wide, if not deep, resulting in significant increases in expenditures and programming for First Nations.

Indigenous groups were similarly affected by the processes of political globalization. Before the 1950s they had understood their struggles in local, regional, or, rarely, national terms. Some, like the Maori of New Zealand, had developed effective national political organizations; others, as in Australia, rarely moved beyond highly localized campaigns for attention to their needs and rights. In the new environment, indigenous peoples found strength in the experience and political anger of other groups. The American Indian Movement (AIM), which came to prominence in the 1960s, popularized an aggressive, confrontational style of protest. Indigenous peoples found intellectual succour in the writings of Frantz Fanon (*The Wretched of the Earth*),[1] Che Guevara, and other advocates of decolonization and Aboriginal rights. Tactics ranging from civil disobedience to blockades were borrowed from the civil rights and Black Power movements. And AIM made an effort to spread its message, working with indigenous groups in Canada, Australia, and New Zealand to increase pressure on governments.

In fairly short order, Aboriginal activism increased. There was a peculiarly Canadian twist – one that indigenous peoples in other countries still have trouble understanding. Much of this activism was funded by the Canadian government. The federal government felt the weight of sustained criticism about its Aboriginal programs and responded by closing down the residential schools in the late 1960s and rethinking the high level of intervention in place since the end of the Second World War. The Department of Indian Affairs and Northern Development also funded organizers, Aboriginal and non-Aboriginal, to establish First Nations associations, believing it important for the Native people to have a consistent and professional voice in their own affairs. In many corners of the world, indigenous groups organized and pressured their governments to take action. Most governments did very little; in Canada, the response was more substantial.

ABORIGINAL RIGHTS: FIRST STEPS

In 1960, to provide a benchmark, First Nations people in Canada had many restrictions imposed on them. With a few exceptions, they could not vote or drink alcohol. Almost no indigenous peoples attended university or college, few graduated from high school, and they still faced major limitations on owning land or businesses. Ineffective schools and the restrictions of the Indian Act closed off many potential avenues for personal development and financial success. The Department of Indian Affairs had the authority to remove individuals from the status Indian rolls if it felt they had adapted to the dominant society. Discriminatory practices remained in place, sanctioned by local, regional, or national governments. In several Canadian cities, curfews restricted freedom of movement, and some movie theatres even had special "Indian" seating areas. America had its Jim Crow laws, which rendered African Americans into second-class citizens. Canada had no such formal code, but national practice had much the same effect. At the same time, First Nations people enjoyed few protections of their harvesting rights. They often hunted, fished, and trapped as before, but without the assurance these practices would continue. As non-Aboriginal interest in land and resources increased, they frequently found themselves being punished for continuing generations-old harvesting activities or denied access to resources that had sustained their communities for centuries.

The struggle for Aboriginal rights – of which the *Marshall* case is only the most recent manifestation – moved slowly. A major revision of the Indian Act was completed in 1951, reducing federal powers and eliminating many specific clauses that gave the government authority to undermine Aboriginal culture. Some First Nations men in eastern Canada had been given limited voting rights in the nineteenth century (but only east of Manitoba and only from 1885 to 1897) and these rights were gradually extended to select groups, such as those living off reserve and veterans. On-reserve residents could vote in 1950, provided they surrendered their exemption from income tax. Only in 1960 were all First Nations accorded full federal voting rights. On the provincial level, Nova Scotia appears to have had no formal restrictions on Aboriginal voting; First Nations people in New Brunswick and Prince Edward Island secured the provincial vote in 1963. Changes to the Indian Act allowed First Nations people to drink alcohol, in accordance with provincial or territorial regulations. They were not permitted, however, to be drunk in public. The *Joseph Drybones* case from the Northwest Territories in the 1960s challenged this provision. Drybones was charged with being drunk off a reserve. His lawyers argued that he was denied equal treatment before the law – a non-Aboriginal person who was drinking in similar circumstances would not have been charged. His lawyers argued, successfully, that the Canadian Bill of Rights took precedence over the Indian

Act. The Supreme Court of Canada agreed in 1970, granting First Nations people greater equality before the law.

By the early 1960s the federal government acknowledged that its interventions in Aboriginal affairs had been unsuccessful, and efforts to find a new and better approach expanded. Jean Chrétien, then minister of Indian affairs and northern development, came forward in 1969 with a dramatic proposal, a White Paper on Indian Affairs. Chrétien's plan called for the elimination of special status for First Nations people and the integration of Aboriginal services with those for the general population. The proposal touched off a storm of protest and helped spark the creation of strong, coherent national Aboriginal organizations. The government was forced to back down. Four years later it also had to retreat from its determination not to address outstanding Aboriginal land claims in the face of a near-loss on the *Calder* case before the Supreme Court. In that challenge, the Nisga'a attempted to get the government to acknowledge Nisga'a ownership of their traditional lands and to negotiate a modern treaty. The court split 3–3–1, with the last vote rejecting the Nisga'a complaint on a legal technicality tangential to the main point. Realizing that the federal government might lose another such case, the Trudeau administration reluctantly agreed to negotiate new treaties.

Between 1960 and the mid-1970s, the First Nations had gone from political and legal irrelevance to national importance. Federal and provincial governments now paid greater attention to Aboriginal demands and needs, and a variety of social and economic programs were introduced to address community difficulties. First Nations' legal authority continued to mount. The victories were conceptual rather than practical for the most part. First Nations had managed to get Canadians and their government to acknowledge their rights and their equality before the law, though often this recognition did not match up to Canada's international commitments to human rights and respect for ethnic minorities. There were also the first signs that governments would be forced by political and legal necessity to address some of the many outstanding historical grievances collected by bands and tribal groups across the country. Few recognized in the mid-1970s what a complex, difficult, and costly enterprise had been unleashed.

FIRST NATIONS IN THE CANADIAN CONSTITUTION

First Nations concerns have been debated at length in the country's many constitutional negotiations, which commenced in the 1970s and have continued through to the present. The militancy of First Nations organizations increased in the early years, led by demands from the

Dene and other groups for a recognition of indigenous sovereignty. These demands shocked many non-Native observers, who were startled by the breadth and intensity of the claims. Many Canadians, used to Aboriginal people fading quickly into the background, found the assertiveness ridiculous – but there was no doubting the seriousness that underlay the demands. In the North, where major development projects threatened the existence of communities and where the Mackenzie Valley Pipeline Inquiry under Thomas Berger provided a unique forum for indigenous protests, the idea of autonomy and self-government seemed to make sense. But the various claims were quickly picked up across the country: reduce the power of the Department of Indian Affairs; empower individual First Nations and bands; recognize indigenous rights to co-manage resources; and acknowledge the historical or treaty right of First Nations to fish, hunt, trap, and otherwise make a living.

When the rise of the Quebec separatist movement forced federal and provincial governments to amend and patriate the Canadian Constitution, First Nations seized the opportunity. They presented themselves as a founding people, and national organizations like the National Indian Brotherhood (later the Assembly of First Nations), the Inuit Committee on National Issues, and the Native Council of Canada (later Congress of Aboriginal Peoples) demanded a place at the negotiating table. The label "Indian" increasingly fell into disuse and the title "First Nation" became more commonplace. When constitutional discussions began in earnest in the late 1970s, First Nations lobbied for inclusion. What followed was a political soap opera: First Nations were in, then they were out; Aboriginal groups became more vocal in their criticism and even took their protests to Great Britain; governments backed off (sort of), and courts were asked to rule. The courts did, but only in part. When the federal government and the provinces produced a draft constitution in 1981, Aboriginal rights had been dropped – unleashing a burst of First Nations' protests. After forging an alliance with women's rights activists – women had also been excluded from the document – the First Nations convinced the governments to reverse their position. Aboriginal rights were back in. The dramatic interventions by First Nations people gave the Aboriginal rights agenda a national and international profile. It also produced results.

Although the process of unilateral patriation left many Canadians unimpressed and many more confused, the passage of the Constitution Act and the redrafting of the Canadian Constitution represented a watershed for First Nations. The new legislation included section 35, which stated that the existing Aboriginal and treaty rights of the Aboriginal peoples of Canada were recognized and affirmed, and that, in this act, the "Aboriginal peoples of Canada" included the Indian, Inuit, and Métis peoples of Canada. Rights had been affirmed, but not spelled out. Commitments were made to continue the meetings between First Nations and government representatives on further changes to the constitution, but they failed to produce any substantial results. Still, Aboriginal people – Indian, Inuit, and Métis – had been included in the constitution and their rights were guaranteed. It was a major achievement, and a significant advance from the First Nations' legal position only twenty years earlier.

The battle was far from over. Many First Nations leaders demanded recognition of the right of Aboriginal self-government, a request some provincial premiers found unacceptable. More radical indigenous leaders advocated the assertion of sovereignty over traditional lands, something the governments would not countenance. The last of the three constitutionally mandated meetings between governments and First Nations leadership, held in 1987, ended in a dramatic fashion, with the Aboriginal politicians accusing government officials of bad faith and with sharp recriminations on all sides. The optimism of the patriation process had been replaced with anger and frustration.

Almost immediately after the rejection of Aboriginal aspirations, general enthusiasm for constitutional amendments was revived in the intense national debate over the provisions of the Meech Lake accord, designed to bring Quebec into the constitutional fold. Meech Lake failed in 1990, in large measure due to the interventions of Elijah Harper, a Cree MLA from Manitoba, who prevented the accord from coming before the legislature. Harper, supported by First Nations from across the country, denied a government request for unanimous consent in the Legislature and prevented passage of the bill. The country plodded on through the constitutional morass, generating a new constitutional arrangement in 1992, the Charlottetown accord. Ovide Mercredi, grand chief of the Assembly of First Nations, figured prominently in these negotiations and secured a clause that would have entrenched the right to Aboriginal self-government in the constitution. The Charlottetown accord, however, was defeated in a national referendum in the fall of 1992. While many who voted against the agreement did so because of the provisions relating to Quebec, opposition to Aboriginal self-government figured prominently in the critique. A significant majority of First Nations people also voted against the proposed constitutional changes. Many First Nations claimed that the deal did not go far enough, but non-Aboriginal critics said it went too far. Aboriginal women also joined in the protest against the agreement, arguing that they wanted assurances that the Charter of Rights and Freedoms would continue to apply to First Nations. The federal government found a way to introduce constitutionally protected Aboriginal self-government outside of the amendment process, by signing self-government treaties with First Nations. Because treaties are protected under section 35, self-government gained constitutional authority.

In the aftermath of the Meech Lake fiasco and the searing memories of the Oka standoff, the Mulroney government authorized the establishment of a Royal Commission on Aboriginal Peoples. The commission was charged with investigating the social, economic, cultural, and political needs of Aboriginal people and with recommending solutions to the dilemmas facing First Nations, Inuit, and Métis communities. It did not live up to expectations. The review dragged on longer than expected, with the final report not released until 1996. The new Liberal administration responded fitfully to the numerous recommendations, and the voluminous final report generated very little discussion. Clearly, public interest in sweeping constitutional and political reorganization relating to First Nations had peaked with the patriation of the Canadian Constitution in 1982. Since that time, First Nations people have had to seek other avenues for redress of their concerns.

CONTEMPORARY ABORIGINAL RIGHTS IN THE COURTS

While the constitution-making process gave First Nations issues a stature and authority they had not enjoyed since the eighteenth century, when nation-to-nation negotiations between First Nations and the French and the British governments were the norm, they provided little specific guidance for future relations. Similarly, as public will eroded, as it did in the 1980s and 1990s, the First Nations found that the pressure tactics and demands that had worked earlier failed to stir a response. The acrimonious relationship between Indian Affairs Minister Ron Irwin and Grand Chief Ovide Mercredi in the mid-1990s represented the nadir in a long-uncertain relationship. First Nations sought solutions elsewhere, increasingly in the nation's courts. The judges were left to tackle a series of issues that, many would argue, were best dealt with at the political level. Their technical task has been to interpret the meaning of Section 35 and to determine the scope and nature of Aboriginal rights in Canada.

This process began before the constitutional wrangles of the 1980s and 1990s and continues through to the present. The legal interpretations and judgments have replaced constitutional negotiations as the primary forum for the resolution of the First Nations–non-

Aboriginal relationship in Canada. Without a great deal of public debate and awareness, and slowly accumulating authority over time, court decisions on Aboriginal and treaty rights have been redefining the place of the First Nations within Confederation. And, as Maritimers discovered in September 1999, when the Supreme Court ruled on the *Marshall* case, the court processes can often have sweeping implications for the people and regions involved. Several key judgments, of which the *Marshall* decision is now one, have shaped and defined Aboriginal rights in Canada. These cases are closely followed internationally and figure in court judgments in Australia and New Zealand. A brief summary of the major cases illustrates the nature and the trajectory of Aboriginal rights in Canada.

Royal Proclamation of 1763

The first item is not a court case, but a critical legal document. The Royal Proclamation of 1763 is generally held to be the foundation for historical and contemporary treaty rights and a pivotal first illustration of the British government's commitment to signing land surrender treaties with First Nations before traditional lands were occupied. Following the Seven Years' War with France, the British government found itself in command of a huge expanse of land in eastern North America. The colonists in the south seemed determined to expand their settlements to the west, raising the spectre of further costly military encounters with the Indians. The First Nations worried about the territorial ambitions of the British colonists (the French seeming to be more rooted along the St Lawrence), and skirmishes and battles broke out along the settlement line. Having finally fought the French into submission, the British also wished to consolidate their hold on the continent and to slow the pace of colonial expansion.

The Royal Proclamation sought to limit settlement on the lands specifically "reserved" for First Nations people as their hunting territories: "And whereas it is just and reasonable, and essential to our Interest, and the Security of our Colonies, that the several Nations or Tribes of Indians with whom We are connected, and who live under our Protection, should not be molested or disturbed in the Possession of such Parts of Our Dominions and Territories as, not having been ceded to or purchased by Us, are reserved to them, or any of them, as their Hunting Grounds." The British Crown reserved for itself the right of negotiation with First Nations people over their Aboriginal lands, hoping to protect them from the abuses that characterized land sales in the coastal colonies. In other words, the act of establishing sovereignty over new territories was deemed to be separate from the process of securing a surrender of Aboriginal title. "Dominion" did not equal full control of the land. By this act, the British government recognized the presence of First Nations people in the otherwise unoccupied territories and committed the Crown to negotiating land treaties with them before the land was opened for non-Aboriginal settlement.

While many Aboriginal commentators assert that the Royal Proclamation recognized indigenous sovereignty, the document makes it clear that the British government considered these "Indian Territories" to be fully British. As the proclamation states: "And We do further declare it to be Our Royal Will and Pleasure, for the present as aforesaid, to reserve under our Sovereignty, Protection, and Dominion, for the use of the said Indians, all the Lands and Territories not included within the Limits of Our said Three new Governments [Quebec, East Florida and West Florida], or within the Limits of the Territory granted to the Hudson's Bay Company, as also all the Lands and Territories lying to the Westward of the Sources of the Rivers which fall into the Sea from the West and North West as aforesaid." Nonetheless, the Royal Proclamation set a high standard for the government to follow, for it clearly stated that Aboriginal lands in areas not previous settled by Europeans were to used for and by First Nations people until a proper treaty had been negotiated.

The proclamation was issued shortly after the key 1760–61 treaties between the Mi'kmaq and the British government and grew out of the generally unfavourable experience in the British eastern colonies around the issue of Aboriginal land rights. All along the eastern seaboard there are stories of agreements signed and then ignored, treaties negotiated and not honoured, sales finalized and subsequently not followed. The intervention of private citizens and companies into the process only complicated matters further and added to the difficulties. Although the Royal Proclamation of 1763 did not result in different treatment for the Mi'kmaq and Maliseet, the document does indicate that, at a very early date, the colonial authorities recognized the importance of negotiating land treaties with First Nations and, in advance of settlement, protecting the area of Aboriginal use.

St Catherine's Milling and Lumber Company, 1888

In the years after the Royal Proclamation, questions about the nature and extent of Aboriginal land ownership and resource use only occasionally reached Canadian courts. First Nations people did not see the courts as a particularly advantageous avenue for pursuing their rights and, struggling under a variety of controls and regulations instituted by the Department of Indian Affairs, had few opportunities to test their legal rights. The *St Catherine's Milling* case arose out of a debate between the federal government and the province of Ontario over the control of Crown lands and resources. A treaty (Treaty 3) had been signed between the federal government and the Ojibway in the area at question – the northwest angle of Ontario between Lake Superior and Manitoba – and Ottawa claimed that the land was the federal government's to regulate, while Ontario insisted that the resources belonged to the province. Although First Nations issues were involved in the dispute, they took no part in the proceedings.

The Judicial Committee of the Privy Council, the highest court of appeal in the Canadian legal system at the time, ruled in favour of the province. The judgment asserted that the rights of the provincial government took precedence over any outstanding or existing Aboriginal claims. If the federal government wished to establish reserves for the First Nations, for example, Ontario's concurrence was required. The decision effectively undercut any legal assertion that First Nations rights still "lived" and made it clear that, in the opinion of the Judicial Committee of the Privy Council, Aboriginal rights and claims had been superseded by the establishment of provincial governments.

The *St Catherine's Milling* case effectively removed recourse to the courts from the arsenal of Aboriginal weapons against the Canadian government. Some groups, notably the Nisga'a of British Columbia, still tried. Reacting to what they viewed as bothersome intrusions by First Nations organizations, Parliament amended the Indian Act in 1927 to prohibit the use of band resources to pay for lawyers for the purpose of challenging the federal government. For almost eighty years after the *St Catherine's Milling* case, First Nations did not actively use the courts as a means of addressing outstanding grievances. Only in the 1960s, with a series of small but crucial court decisions, did that begin to change.

Syliboy, 1928

During the Aboriginal rights debates between 1997 and 2000, non-Aboriginal observers often wondered why First Nations had waited so long to press demands under the eighteenth-century treaties. What was typically forgotten was a simple truth: Mi'kmaq and Maliseet people had often raised questions about their treaty, land, and harvesting rights and had petitioned governments on numerous occasions for greater attention to their economic and social needs, in the context of earlier treaties. Before the 1960s, Aboriginal efforts to seek recourse before the courts rarely went very far. Chief Syliboy, a

Mi'kmaq from Nova Scotia, was charged with and convicted of possessing pelts in contravention of the Lands and Forests Act. Syliboy argued that, as an Aboriginal person, he was exempt from the provisions of the act and, further, that he had "by Treaty the right to hunt and trap at all times." As the court reported, "Every now and then for a number of years one has heard that our Indians were making these claims but, so far as I know, the matter has never been before a Court."

The courts did not dwell on the case for very long. Syliboy had been convicted by a magistrate for being unlawfully in possession of furs; Acting County Court Judge Patterson upheld his conviction. Patterson, however, expressed considerable sympathy for the accused: "Such sympathy as a Judge is permitted to have I have with [the] defendant. I would gladly allow the appeal if I could find any sound reason for doing so, but I cannot and must confirm the conviction. The very capable Magistrate who heard the case below has, I am pleased to see, fixed the penalty at the very lowest figure that the Act allows. Even so I venture to express the hope that the authorities will not enforce the conviction."[2] Gentle sentiments aside, the decision effectively rejected Syliboy's contention that First Nations rights under the treaty superseded provincial regulations.

White and Bob, 1965

First Nations people across Canada continued to hunt, trap, and fish for much of their sustenance (as they do today, at a much more extensive level than most people recognize). So long as few non-Aboriginals competed for the same resources or lived in the outlying reaches of the country, these harvesting activities attracted little notice. As non-indigenous development expanded in the 1950s and 1960s, however, First Nations resource use came into conflict with non-Aboriginal users, the growing interest in conservation, and increasingly active wildlife officers. This conflict resulted in more and more arrests of First Nations hunters and fishers – or harassment, as they called it – and increasing disagreement over the extent and nature of Aboriginal harvesting rights. In the mid-1960s the legal tide began to turn, slowly, in favour of First Nations rights.

The British Columbia court case of *White and Bob* involved two First Nations men, Clifford White and David Bob from the Nanaimo Indian band on Vancouver Island, who were charged with hunting in violation of the Game Act. They had shot six deer on land that was not otherwise occupied and were charged with hunting without a permit and hunting out of season. In the mid-nineteenth century

Governor James Douglas had signed a series of local treaties, sometimes called purchase agreements, with First Nations on Vancouver Islands. Although the treaties had not been granted much political or legal power, they did indicate that First Nations were "at liberty to hunt over the unoccupied lands, as formerly." The Supreme Court, agreeing with the British Columbia Court of Appeal, decided that the coastal First Nations had signed a treaty, as defined under the Indian Act. The Court stated further that those rights could not be overturned by an act of the provincial government. Only the national Parliament could act on the matter of the hunting rights as outlined in the treaty. This crucial decision clarified Aboriginal harvesting rights under the Douglas treaties and, it could be argued, gave First Nations the right to fish commercially (as *Marshall* did).

The *White and Bob* case was argued by Thomas Berger, who played a critical role in the evolution of Canadian law on Aboriginal matters. Berger was new to the practice of law and was called into the case by Maisie Hurley, the publisher of *Native Voice*. The judgment served to invest the Douglas treaties with new-found authority. It was also the first case in British Columbia to draw heavily on testimony from social scientists, including University of British Columbia anthropologist Wilson Duff. The *White and Bob* trial and judgment have generally attracted little attention, for they have been overshadowed by more dramatic Aboriginal legal victories in subsequent decades. It was an important decision, however, in that it demonstrated the contemporary relevance of often-ignored nineteenth-century treaties, introduced social science research into British Columbia First Nations court cases, and provided a first glimpse of the important role to be played by Berger in the resolution of Aboriginal legal entitlements. Moreover, *White and Bob* demonstrated that Aboriginal legal and treaty rights remained substantially unresolved and suggested that they would soon become a common feature on the Canadian legal and political landscape.[3]

Calder, 1973

The judicial "revolution" on Aboriginal land and resource rights began in earnest in 1973, with another case argued before the Supreme Court of Canada by Thomas Berger. The Nisga'a from northwestern British Columbia had followed the *White and Bob* case and were pleased with the Supreme Court's recognition of pre-existing and still operative Aboriginal rights in British Columbia. They hired Berger, one of the first BC lawyers to develop any kind of expertise in Aboriginal legal issues, to present their case. They lost their cases in British Columbia, but appealed to the Supreme Court in 1973. The Nisga'a had been attempting since the late nineteenth century, with no success, to secure a treaty with the government of Canada. They had petitioned Ottawa and the British government directly and had earned the enmity of federal authorities for their persistence and professionalism. It was Nisga'a activism, in particular, that convinced the federal government to place restrictions on First Nations hiring lawyers to further their legal arguments.

In the 1960s Frank Calder, a Nisga'a and later provincial politician, asked Berger to take forward the Nisga'a demand that the federal government recognize their ownership of traditional Nisga'a lands. To the First Nation, the issue was painfully simple. They had never signed a treaty, yet the provincial and federal governments acted as though all Nisga'a claims to the land had been eliminated simply by administrative actions. The Nisga'a lost their initial hearings and, over considerable objections both within their communities and among other British Columbia First Nations, took the case to the Supreme Court of Canada. It was a risky endeavour, for a loss at this level could well have written the end of Nisga'a and First Nations efforts to use the courts to secure recognition of their Aboriginal title.

When the judgment came down in 1973, the Nisga'a lost – but they also won. The Court split 3 to 3, with the seventh justice deciding the case on a technical point. One group argued that the Nisga'a had, indeed, had title to their traditional territories, but that title had been extinguished by actions of the British government and the colony of British Columbia before the coastal province joined Confederation. The other three agreed that the Nisga'a had Aboriginal title and argued, in the absence of a formal treaty, that rights to the land and resources had never been surrendered. The Supreme Court made news by accepting the Nisga'a argument that they had exercised full control over the areas before the first Europeans arrived, thereby implicitly by recognizing the nature and extent of Aboriginal governance. Although the Court arguments contained many positive statements, the reality was, however, that the Nisga'a claim had been turned back.

In quick order the legal defeat turned into a political and moral victory. Surprised by the judgment and by a groundswell of public support for the Nisga'a position, Prime Minister Trudeau and Indian Affairs Minister Chrétien agreed to commence land claims negotiations with those indigenous groups (mostly in British Columbia and the territorial North) that had never signed treaties. In April 2000, twenty-seven years after the *Calder* decision and after countless hours of negotiations and debate, the Nisga'a treaty with the federal government secured Royal Assent and became law. The contemporary land claims process in Canada can be traced directly to the *Calder* decision. It radically transformed the legal and moral foundation of Aboriginal rights in Canada, politicizing and publicizing claims and entitlements that had long been ignored by the political and legal system in the country.

Guerin, 1985

Courts in British Columbia were once again asked to address a major Aboriginal issue when Daniel Guerin, chief of the Musqueam, challenged a lease that the Department of Indian Affairs had negotiated on behalf of his band. The land in question, located close to the University of British Columbia in Vancouver, had been leased by the Musqueam to a private golf club. In the 1970s, almost two decades after the lease had been signed, Guerin discovered that the Department of Indian Affairs had withheld vital details at the time of the negotiations with the Shaugnessy Golf Club, resulting in an overly generous deal that did not adequately protect First Nations interests. The federal government had a fiduciary obligation to consult with the Musqueam and to provide them with sufficient information to make an informed decision. At issue, therefore, was not whether the deal was good or bad (and it clearly was unfavourable to the Musqueam), but whether the federal government had faithfully discharged its legal obligations to inform the Musqueam. After a win and a loss in the lower courts, the Musqueam appealed to the Supreme Court of Canada. The Court upheld the initial judgment and awarded the Musqueam a payment of $10 million.

On the surface, *Guerin* appeared to be a relatively benign decision that set right a historical injustice. Chief Justice Brian Dickson, however, offered a critical statement about the status of Aboriginal rights. He observed that the First Nations' "interest in their lands is a pre-existing legal right nor created by Royal Proclamation, by ... the Indian Act, or by any other executive order or legislative provision. It does not matter, in my opinion, that the present case is concerned with the interest of an Indian band in a reserve [rather] than with unrecognized title in traditional tribal lands. The Indian interest in the land is the same in both cases." The Court's decision represented a major advance for First Nations, for it acknowledged that, under Canadian law, all Aboriginal groups had legal rights, as yet unspecified, on both official reserve lands and traditional territories.[4]

The Musqueam struggle has continued. Residents of British Columbia have, over the past two years, watched a bitter and often nasty squabble between the Musqueam First Nation and individual lease holders. The leases for house plots, rented at low rates and signed for ninety-nine-year terms, were up for renewal. The Musqueam had the right to raise these rental rates to "market" conditions, which they proceeded to do. Some people saw their rates jump from a few hundred dollars a year to well over $20,000, a crippling increase that made their homes virtually unsaleable. The renters fought back, demanding less dramatic increases and appealing to government and the courts for salvation. The Musqueam, who had endured many years of below-market rates, found themselves opposed and even vilified for increasing the rents for this highly valued property.

Simon, 1985

The first major Aboriginal rights case involving the Mi'kmaq was resolved in 1985, with the contest focusing, again, on harvesting rights. James Simon, a member of the Shubenacadie band, had been arrested for possession of a rifle and ammunition. He admitted that he possessed the gun and shotgun shells, but argued that the Treaty of 1752, which stated that the Mi'kmaq should have "free liberty of hunting and fishing as usual," provided him with immunity from provincial hunting regulations. In the lower courts, Simon's position was rejected, with the judges claiming that the eighteenth-century treaties no longer had practical authority.

The Supreme Court overturned the lower court decision in resounding terms. The judgment stated, – "Both Governor Hopson and the Micmac had the capacity to enter into the Treaty of 1752 and did so with the intention of creating mutually binding obligations. The treaty constitutes a positive source of protection against infringements on hunting rights and the fact that these rights existed before the treaty as part of the general Aboriginal Title did not negate or minimize the significance of the rights protected by the Treaty." This treaty right had not been extinguished by subsequent government action and "the Treaty of 1752 continues to be in force and effect." The *Simon* case, which related only to subsistence harvesting rights, demonstrated the vitality of eighteenth-century treaties, the continuation of Mi'kmaq harvesting rights, and the protection provided to these rights by section 35 of the Constitution Act.

Sioui, 1990

The *Sioui* case, involving the Wendat (Huron) people of central Canada, tested the contemporary validity of pre-Confederation treaties. The accused were from the Lorette Indian reserve, convicted in lower court of cutting down trees and camping in Jacques Cartier Park. They readily admitted their involvement in the acts, but claimed that they were practising traditional customs and religious rites. The terms of a 1760 treaty between the Huron and the British guaranteed the Huron British protection and the free exercise of their religion, customs, and trade. The government, in contrast, argued that the 1760 document was not a treaty, as understood for the purposes of the Indian Act, and therefore did not have continuing relevance.

The Supreme Court ruled that the agreement was a treaty and that it continued in effect. The Court sided with the Wendat and stated: "The park falls within the class of conservation parks and is intended to ensure the permanent protection of territory representative of the natural regions of Quebec or natural sites presenting exceptional features, while rendering them accessible to the public for the purposes of education and cross-country recreation. This type of occupancy is not incompatible with the exercise of Huron rites and customs." The case demonstrated the Court's willingness to examine the historical and cultural context in which disputed legal agreements arose. The judgment stated: "Though the wording of the document does not suffice to determine its legal nature, the historical context and evidence relating to facts which occurred shortly before or after the signing of the document indicate that General Murray and the Hurons entered into an agreement to make peace and guarantee it. They entered into this agreement with the intention to create mutually binding obligations that would be solemnly respected. All the parties involved were competent to enter into this treaty." The Court also ruled, in an important additional comment, that the fact that a treaty right had not been exercised for a long period did not, by definition, extinguish that right.

Sparrow, 1990

The next major turning point in the First Nations' struggle to secure recognition of their rights to hunting, trap, fish, and gather came in 1990 and again involved both British Columbia and the Musqueam. Ronald Sparrow from the Musqueam reserve was charged with violating federal fishing regulations when he was caught on the lower Fraser River using a driftnet that exceeded acceptable limits. Sparrow appealed, arguing that the Constitution Act of 1982 had, in section 35, recognized "existing Aboriginal and treaty rights" and that his right to fish for salmon for food was an Aboriginal right. Given the sensitivities, on both coasts, about fishing rights and First Nations demands for access to their traditional sources of food, the *Sparrow* decision was watched very closely. Moreover, it was the first substantial test of the authority granted to First Nations under section 35 of the Constitution Act.

The Supreme Court, ruling in 1990, came down decisively on the side of the First Nations, continuing a string of important Aboriginal victories in the highest court. Progress had been slow, but it now took a dramatic turn. The Court ruled that Aboriginal and treaty rights could evolve over time and should be interpreted in a "generous and liberal manner." In other words, the nature of the federal government's commitment was such that the courts should not interpret the rights narrowly. Governments could regulate the Aboriginal use of such resources, but they were instructed to do so carefully, and only with a "compelling and substantial objective." Federal authorities could intervene in First Nations fisheries for reasons of conservation and resource management, but they had first to demonstrate that they were justified in doing so. Further, Aboriginal access to resources was granted a high priority by the Court, coming immediately after conservation and before commercial and sport fishing. The judgment stated that the question of Aboriginal resource needs for subsistence purposes should be addressed quickly. It also made it clear that section 35 had considerable teeth, in that it gave substantial recognition to First Nations rights that had not been explicitly extinguished by treaty.

The importance of the *Sparrow* decision was demonstrated in the *Badger* case in 1996. The Supreme Court ruled that the government of Alberta had not provided sufficient justification for imposing restrictions on Aboriginal hunting. It overturned a lower court ruling and ordered a new trial.

Denny, Paul, and Syliboy, 1990

Three Mi'kmaq men, from Eskasoni and Afton River, were charged with a variety of fisheries offences. The Eskasoni charges related to fishing without a licence for cod and salmon, and possessing salmon illegally. The Afton River case involved using a snare for fishing for salmon. The accused argued that their Aboriginal right to fish for food took precedence over fisheries regulations. The Appeal Division of the Nova Scotia Supreme Court agreed with their position, and stated that "an aboriginal right to fish for food in the waters in question" had "not been extinguished through treaty, other agreement or competent legislation." In recognizing the "legitimate food needs" of First Nations fishers, the court further indicated that this

Aboriginal right to fish for subsistence purposes stood only behind conservation as a priority in terms of resource use. This decision made it clear that Mi'kmaq food fishing rights were recognized by law and took precedence over commercial or sport fishing. The *Denny* decision came in the middle of a trial of fourteen Mi'kmaq charged with illegal moose hunting. That case was dismissed on the grounds that the fishing judgment created "a presumption of aboriginal rights" that made it clear First Nations people had the right to hunt, as well as fish, for subsistence purposes.[5]

Van der Peet, N.T.C. Smokehouse, and Gladstone, 1996

In the continuing legal effort to clarify Aboriginal harvesting rights, the Supreme Court ruled in 1996 on a trilogy of cases involving First Nations from British Columbia. The judgment provided additional clarification of the conditions under which a government agency could justify limiting an Aboriginal right (as spelled out in the *Sparrow* decision) and provided a detailed indication of the tests a First Nations claim had to pass before it would be recognized by the Court. To be accepted, a practice, tradition, or custom had to be integral to a specific First Nations culture and had to constitute a significant aspect of that culture. The activity had to have been in place before the first Europeans arrived in the area, and it could not be marginal or occasional. As a result of the *Van der Peet* "tests," specific Aboriginal rights were to be determined on a case-by-case basis and had to meet the standards set out by the Court. More generally, the Court recognized that harvesting activities carried out for reasons of sustenance, spiritual or ceremonial activities, and social customs could be considered "Aboriginal rights." It also indicated that the trading of resources – if part of the First Nations activity before the Europeans arrived – might constitute an Aboriginal right.

Delgamuukw, 1997

The 1997 ruling on the *Delgamuukw* case ended one of the longest and most complicated court proceedings in Canadian legal history. The Gitskan and Wet'suwet'en First Nations of north-central British Columbia argued that they retained title to their traditional lands, pointing out that they had never signed a treaty with the Canadian government. The first judgment on the case, by British Columbia Judge Alan McEachern in 1990, included a biting critique of pre-contact Aboriginal existence, one that suggested he had ignored the many days of Aboriginal oral testimony presented before him. His decision was laced with pejorative descriptions of Gitskan and Wet'suwet'en culture and lifestyle, and he argued that the actions of the federal and provincial governments had effectively extinguished Aboriginal rights in the district. They could still continue traditional fishing, hunting, and gathering, but they had no other major rights to resources. First Nations and their supporters across the country were furious. A series of appeals, interrupted by a long hiatus as the First Nations attempted to reach a negotiated settlement with the governments of Canada and British Columbia, ended when the Supreme Court ruled on the case in 1997.

The judgment is both sweeping and not altogether clear. The Supreme Court ordered a new trial, overturning the initial McEachern decision, but also urged the parties to seek a negotiated rather than a judicial settlement. The Chief Justice concluded his decision with the words: "Let's face it. We're all here to stay." The Court indicated that Aboriginal oral testimony and oral tradition merited considerable attention in law and that it should be taken into consideration when assessing First Nations cases. The judgment also specified that the Crown had an obligation to consult with First Nations on matters relating to traditional territories and to negotiate with them in good faith.

The key elements in the decision related to the Aboriginal right to traditional lands. The most significant element of the judgment ruled that First Nations' rights to the land is a protected right under section 35 of the Constitution Act of 1982. The justices recognized the Aboriginal right to harvest traditional resources, extended to the use of resources for contemporary purposes, but indicated that it was not a clear and unregulated right. The use of the territories and resources could not be such as to destroy the lasting relationship between the First Nations and their lands, for example. First Nations, they ruled, could not simply assert Aboriginal title to a particular resource or territory. Rather, they had to prove that they had "exclusive" use and occupancy and, perhaps, continual use and occupancy. In the excitement generated by a generally favourable court decision, First Nations did not pay a great deal of attention to this latter element of the ruling. The standard set down in *Delgamuukw* is a considerable one, and the burden of proof of exclusive and continual use rests with the First Nations. Given overlapping territorial and resource claims, and disputes between Aboriginal groups about traditional lands, specific groups might find it difficult to achieve the level of proof required by the Supreme Court.

CONCLUSION

The 1999 *Marshall* decision, then, continues and builds on a pattern of Supreme Court jurisprudence on the matter of Aboriginal land, treaty, and harvesting rights. The cases described – *Syliboy, White and Bob, Calder, Guerin, Simon, Sioui, Sparrow, Denny, Van der Peet,* and *Delgamuukw* – represent the major (but by no means the only) signposts along the Aboriginal rights trail since the 1960s. While non-Aboriginal Canadians have reacted strongly, and often unfavourably, to Supreme Court rulings on First Nations cases, little thought is generally given to the enormous amount of time, money, and effort put into these court challenges by the communities involved. The Gitskan and We'suwet'en spent several million dollars preparing and defending their case. Although it was cast as a major victory, it did not resolve their initial claim, and it ended by ordering a new trial and recommending renewed negotiations. What has happened is that, very slowly, a small body of law has developed on the issues of resource, treaty, and inherent Aboriginal rights. Some lawyers argue that Canadian case law is incredibly thin and that the courts should be flooded with dozens, if not hundreds, of case that would, over time, flesh out, clarify, and formalize the legal rights of First Nations. To date, however, the number of key cases remains relatively small, though each one has substantially redefined the nature of Aboriginal legal rights in Canada.

For First Nations in the Maritimes, more facts remained unknown than known, and more legal issues untested than resolved, more questions unanswered than settled. The earlier cases had made some things clear, however. Unresolved Aboriginal claims to land and resources had to be addressed by the Canadian government. Pre-Second World War II treaties retained their legal validity under section 35 of the Constitution Act of 1982, although the precise nature and authority of those treaties continued to be contested by governments. Oral testimony could not only be used by First Nations in their court cases but should be granted respect and attention. Aboriginal harvesting rights for subsistence purposes – granted *de facto* but not clearly understood in the early 1960s – had been accepted across the nation as a second call (after conservation and management) on traditional resources.

Before the *Marshall* decision, Maritimers did not known how this combination of Canadian law and Aboriginal activism would apply in their region. Beginning in 1997, with an unexpected court victory involving Thomas Peter Paul, and escalating two years later with the Supreme Court decision on the *Marshall* case the area was about to discover the contemporary significance of eighteenth-century treaties and the immediacy of judicial rulings on Aboriginal rights. Given the pattern of court decisions beginning in the 1960s, there were strong indications of First Nations expectations and the leaning of the Supreme Court of Canada. Hindsight, however, is much sharper than the ability to forecast. Few people in the Maritimes in 1997 anticipated what was about to happen in the region.

CHAPTER FIVE

Thomas Peter Paul and the Mi'kmaq Logging Dispute

With the exception of the *Simon* case, First Nations Aboriginal and treaty rights have not figured prominently in Maritime political life. The gradual expansion of Aboriginal rights before the law had slowly clarified the status of Mi'kmaq and Maliseet harvesting. First Nations people had, with or without legal sanction, continued subsistence-based hunting, fishing, and gathering activities, occasionally finding themselves at odds with government regulations. Conservation and wildlife officers, for their part, tended to take a flexible approach to the enforcement of hunting and fishing rules when First Nations were involved. Provided the breaches of the law were relatively minor, not deliberately provocative, and involved the harvesting of resources for family and community use, they were generally dealt with informally, although non-Aboriginal complaints about abuses were common. As the legal authority of Aboriginal resource rights increased, so did Mi'kmaq and Maliseet assertiveness and confidence. Much like other First Nations across the country, they could see a clear, if slow, trajectory in the appeals to the courts on matters of Aboriginal and treaty rights. The words and promises of their more demanding leaders, including those who offered visions of the nation's acceptance of Aboriginal sovereignty and full Aboriginal self-government, were ringing more true with each passing year. It was time to test the increasingly complicated but promising waters of Aboriginal and treaty rights in the Maritimes.

The controversy began in May 1995, when Thomas Peter Paul and two others were arrested for harvesting the prized bird's eye maple, on land licensed to Stone Consolidated (Canada) Inc., with the intent of selling it at a profit. A number of the Maliseet on the St Mary's First Nation reserve felt, as did Aboriginal people across the country, that they retained an Aboriginal right to the land. As Tim Paul later recalled: "Up until we started getting this thing going, we had a hard time passing the laugh test when we told them we owned the land – even on the reserve ... And I always worked gathering ash and that kind of stuff with my father and grandfather. We were always sneaking around the woods – and I mean sneaking. We had to literally sneak around the forest back then." Tim and Nicholas Paul, alerted to the growing legal acceptance of Aboriginal rights, approached lawyer Cleveland Allaby with the idea that they had a treaty right to the land. Their first forays into the woods, aimed at the bird's eye maple, resulted in occasional police scrutiny but no arrests. They continued their small-scale logging, while the men kept pressing to get the police to lay charges. As Tim Paul explained: "We just got done working. We were sweaty. We got the biggest bird's eye we ever had. It took us hours to get it by the road. As soon as we got it there, they all came in. Man, they had cameras and lights and dogs. They were 'get on the ground' and hollering and screaming and terrorizing us."[1] Thomas Peter Paul, not Tim Paul and his crew, was ultimately the one charged with logging without a permit – government officials often avoid charging First Nations people who have self-selected for a confrontation on legal issues – but the Aboriginal community had been in the bush, pushing for recognition of its rights, for quite some time.

Many of the court cases that have proved to be major turning points in Aboriginal law involved long and complicated hearings. Typically, elders testified at length about oral recollections and community understandings. Each side in the struggle brought forward learned experts – historians, anthropologists, geographers, and others – who could interpret historical documents, recreate pre- and post-contact realities, and otherwise provide the court with the context and knowledge necessary to render a meaningful judgment. Thomas Peter Paul brought no such arsenal of experts, and neither did the Crown. The case was handled, in its early phase, away from the glare of publicity and without the detailed arguments that so often accompany these matters. (The *Delgamuukw* case, in contrast, continued for 374 court days, involved hundreds of hours of court time, and included the testimony of dozens of expert witnesses on both sides.)

Paul is a status Indian from the Pabineau Reserve in northern New Brunswick. He and his lawyers argued that he had the right to harvest the trees under existing treaties. The distinction in this case is a critical one. Earlier Aboriginal and treaty rights cases focused on the appropriateness of First Nations people harvesting resources for their personal and community use, what the courts defined as subsistence or "traditional" purposes. Thomas Peter Paul wanted to make money, much like any commercial logger who had the right to cut timber on Crown land. The difference was that Paul had no standard harvesting licence; rather, he claimed he could cut the trees based on the powers conveyed to him and his community under the treaties signed between the British and the Mi'kmaq and Maliseet. William Dummer, lieutenant governor of Massachusetts Bay Colony, had endeavoured to bring the New England area (including the Maritimes region) under the protection of treaties and, thereby, to end hostilities between the First Nations and the British. The treaty that drew the Maliseet and Mi'kmaq into the fold, signed at Annapolis Royal in 1726, is called Mascarene's Treaty, after Nova Scotia's treaty commissioner, Major Paul Mascarene.[2]

The decision, rendered by provincial court judge Frederic Arsenault of Bathurst, was delivered on 28 August 1996. It was an unexpected victory for Thomas Peter Paul, Nicholas Paul, and two other defendants. Arsenault argued that the treaties clearly authorized commercial harvesting and that treaties took precedence over provincial legislation. Nicholas Paul observed: "Aboriginal people were always making a living from the land in one way or another. Anything less than the decision we got here just maintains the situation where Aboriginals are allowed to survive and not thrive when it comes to our rights to resources. One thing I hope will arise from this case is that the province not use a criminal system to deal with us. I mean we were treated like criminals throughout this whole thing. We were just exercising our rights as we saw it."[3]

There was no doubt that Thomas Peter Paul and his associates cut the trees. What was at issue was whether the First Nations had a treaty right to harvest trees for commercial purposes. In reviewing Mascarene's Treaty, Judge Arsenault turned to the phrase "that the Indians shall not be molested in their Hunting, Fishing and Planting Grounds nor in any other their Lawful Occasions." He interpreted this concept very widely, arguing that because the right to harvest trees without a licence existed in 1725–26, it carried forward to the present. The Crown had argued that First Nations' logging interfered with existing tree farm licences. Arsenault rejected that suggestion. He accepted the argument that the treaty conferred a commercial right, and not just a subsistence right, to harvest. Furthermore, he decided that the mere existence of Crown timber licences did not, of and by themselves, extinguish Aboriginal claims to the land. In other words, these two rights could co-exist.

The Crown quickly appealed the lower court decision, and the appeal was heard by Justice John Turnbull of the Court of Queen's Bench in March 1997. Turnbull was disappointed with the material presented to him, for he was being asked to settle what was fundamentally a historical argument without a great deal of detail. Neither the defence nor the Crown provided substantial evidence on the historical questions. Searching for additional information, he may have turned to the files of the 1993 case, *R. v. McCoy*, argued before him earlier. The *McCoy* case involved a Maliseet man, Leslie McCoy from the St Mary's Band, who was charged with hunting illegally – using a light to hunt at night. McCoy claimed that the 1725 Treaty (Dummer's Treaty or the Treaty of Boston) exempted him from provincial wildlife regulations. The Court of Appeal overturned the lower court decision to acquit McCoy and found him guilty of the offence as charged. When Turnbull presented his arguments in favour of Thomas Peter Paul (upholding the acquittal), he made substantial reference to historical documents and information that had not been presented in the original *Paul* trial.

In a classic and increasingly common illustration of the judge as historian, Turnbull's decision, handed down on 28 October 1997, referred to a 1693 Abenaki treaty, which the Mi'kmaq did not sign but which included the phrase "Saving unto the said Indians their own Grounds, & free liberty for Hunting, Fishing, Fowling and all other their Lawful Liberties, & Privileges, as on the Eleventh day of August, One thousand six hundred and ninety-three."[4] By Turnbull's reading, this statement meant that the Mi'kmaq and Maliseet were "owners" of the land, in the European sense. His review of other treaties, including Dummer's and Mascarene's, focused on the question of whether the First Nations subsequently surrendered the right. War (military conquest), sale, or future negotiations could eliminate the ownership rights – but the judge could find no evidence of such a surrender of rights and privileges.

Turnbull's judgment touched off a media storm. Thomas Peter Paul became an instant regional celebrity, the man who had proved that Mi'kmaq and Maliseet people had the right to harvest timber for commercial purposes. The Arsenault/Turnbull judgments sent shock waves around the Maritimes. By arguing that the Aboriginal right to cut trees for profit could co-exist with Crown timber licences, and that First Nations had the right to earn a living in the forest without attending to provincial regulations and timber grants, Judge Turnbull exceeded almost everyone's expectations. First Nations, rushing to capitalize on the judgment, saw no reason to apologize for potential dislocations to non-Aboriginal companies and communities: "We can't turn a blind eye at this point," said Tim Paul. "I mean we have suicides in communities and we've got reserves that are bankrupt. Where we own land that's worth $2.8 billion a year, none of that should be occurring."[5]

Not everyone reacted the same way. Maliseet and Mi'kmaq claimed a huge victory and laid plans to go into the forests to effect it. Ironically, one of the first uses of the right granted by Turnbull came on January 1998, when Robert Levi, Indian Island chief Peter Barlow, and others cut down three truckloads of timber to send to victims of the vicious Quebec ice storm that had cut out power to much of the province.[6] Tim Paul saw the decision as the first step towards a huge settlement: "In the end, someone is going to have to pay up and I mean big time. Myself, I'm looking to at least for every man, woman and child $2-million a head. That's minimal."[7] Such rhetoric hardly soothed fears across New Brunswick. Provincial governments worried about forest companies, the implications for conservation, forest revenues, the security of tenure granted to the land the stability of communities dependent on the forest sector. The forest companies and their employees seethed in anger and frustration, for the prospect of having several hundred First Nations people harvesting trees upset cutting and conservation plans and threatened to play havoc with markets for forest products. Although the companies kept a low public profile, they initially declared their intent not to deal with First Nations people cutting with a standard licence – only to discover that the Mi'kmaq and Maliseet found ready markets for their products in Maine and Quebec.

The controversy lasted through 1998. Turnbull's decision was appealed to the New Brunswick Court of Appeal (involving Chief Justice William Hoyt, and Justices Robert Ricer, Patrick Ryan, Wallace Turnbull, and Ernest Drapeau), where hearings took place in February 1998. Interveners, including Juniper Lumber, J.D. Irving, the Union of New Brunswick Indians, Big Cove First Nation, and the Attorney General of Canada, submitted briefs and sought leave to present oral arguments. The matter, according to University of New Brunswick law professor and Aboriginal rights expert John McEvoy, rested on disagreement between Judge Arsenault and Judge Turnbull over the basis for their decisions.[8] Because of the testimony and evidence presented at the earlier trials, the Court of Appeal focused on the interpretation of history and the law, and did not have to dissect a complicated trial record.

On 26 February 1998 Thomas Peter Paul arrived at the New Brunswick Court of Appeal for his third trial. He had spent the previous few days in the forest, cutting down bird's eye maple and selling the logs, most often south of the border. He knew that this trial was probably not the final step and that the case would eventually make its way to the Supreme Court of Canada. He had secured financial assistance from a variety of sources, including the Native Loggers Business Association and the New Brunswick Aboriginal Peoples Council (representing off-reserve and non-status Indians), to sustain his defence.[9] Crown prosecutor Keith McCormick asked for a review of Judge

Turnbull's decision: he argued that Turnbull's use of evidence not presented by either the defence or the prosecution was unorthodox, and contended that this case was not one of Aboriginal title. Further, he contended that the judge had decided the case along lines not argued during the trial. The Court of Appeal judges hinted at their central concerns, questioning the use of evidence and the reasons for judgment, and debated with counsel the utility of Aboriginal oral testimony and the details of specific treaties relating to the commercial use of resources.[10] Oral submissions from the interveners were not accepted and, after seven hours of testimony, the trial ended.[11]

The Court of Appeal ruling came down in late April 1998. The judgment was harsh and direct: "The evidence here does not establish that the commercial harvesting of timber was a practice, a tradition or custom that was an integral part of the respondent's culture." The court also found fault with Judge Turnbull's use of evidence not presented in trial: "There is neither authority for making such extensive use of historical material under the guise of judicial notice nor for using such material without giving notice to the parties." The judges further stated that "because there was an ambiguity in the words used in the treaty and no evidence to resolve that ambiguity, both [judges] were left to resolve the problem by engaging in conjecture which cannot result in the realistic interpretation of the treaty." The case was returned, subject to appeal to the Supreme Court, to the provincial court for sentencing.[12]

Turnbull's judgment had been summarily overturned. The First Nations' days in the woods were over, if only temporarily, as an appeal was launched to the Supreme Court of Canada. Tense days followed. Mi'kmaq and Maliseet loggers had had their first real taste of independent income from the forest, and many clearly intended to stick around. Jan Nash, a Maliseet from Doaktown, had just invested heavily in his skidder and now faced financial hardship. He reacted bitterly: "The white people, you can't seem to satisfy them. They want it all." Tim Paul reflected – "I don't see any violence occurring unless it's brought on by the government themselves. If people defend themselves, well, what do you expect them to do? But they don't want to fight. They just want to earn a living." Betty Ann Lavallée of the New Brunswick Aboriginal Peoples Council thought, "Oh my God, I'm going to have to bury somebody." Arthur Bear of St Mary's First Nation said it more succinctly: "I tell you, it's a big hurt."[13] Thomas Peter Paul, declaring that he did not feel at all guilty, said of the decision: "It feels like they yanked the plate of food away from us. For the province to put them [his fellow loggers] back on welfare – they should be proud of themselves."[14]

First Nations reeled, in sorrow and in anger. Aboriginal groups met on reserves around the province, pledging to maintain their resistance and refusing to meet with the provincial government. Protesters, some four hundred strong, carrying signs that read "Our ancestors don't have a court of appeal" and "Our land, our right," gathered on a government woodlot outside Fredericton to cheer Aboriginal loggers as they cut down trees in defiance of the Court of Appeal ruling. Noah Augustine, the most outspoken critic of the decision, launched one of his strongest attacks on the government, the courts, and the Irving Corporation, urging a boycott of the company for refusing to buy timber from First Nations people.[15] It was a quintessentially Canadian protest, with the police escorting the Aboriginal protesters through Fredericton and standing watch over the rally to ensure that trouble did not break out.

In early May a cavalcade of Aboriginal protesters in Big Cove registered their anger at both the Irving companies and Natural Resources Minister Alan Graham, generating echoes of support from around the province. Arthur Bear of St Mary's pledged: "We are behind the loggers 100 per cent. But we will not sit down with the province. They [the St Mary's band] told me not to sit down but to fight for our land."[16] Speakers at a rally at the Young Eagle Recreation Centre vowed to resist the provincial government and ridiculed Premier Ray Frenette's offer of 200 acres of cutting land. Loggers vowed to stay in the woods, but they soon discovered that they could not sustain their protests. The willingness and ability of the provincial government to seize equipment and charge Aboriginal and non-Aboriginal loggers, while at the same time reoffering to negotiate deals with the First Nations bands, shifted the game back into the provincial court. Noah Augustine told a cheering crowd – "We have Aboriginal loggers who are out there who are willing to put their lives on the line. When I told that to the premier's office, they all looked at me as if I were joking. And I said again, and I was raising my voice on the phone yesterday [with Premier Frenette]: 'You don't understand where our people are coming from!'"[17]

Frenette appealed directly to the First Nations, offering them the opportunity to return to negotiations and to secure a settlement that suited the needs of both Aboriginal people and the province. Turnbull's ruling had provided jobs, opportunities, optimism, and confidence in the legal system; the Court of Appeal ruling threatened to strip away the employment, destroy First Nations companies, and erode Aboriginal support for discussions with government. The province, for its part, favoured band-to-government negotiations, offering to sign deals with each of the fifteen First Nations. Frenette urged the First Nations to settle their internal differences, which threatened to undermine possible negotiations, and to come to the table prepared to strike short-term agreements. That, in itself, created a problem, as the government preferred to deal with the band chiefs and councils, leaving the New Brunswick Aboriginal Peoples Council banging at the door and requesting a seat at the table. The loudest protests came from logging organizers, who demanded that the band chiefs stay away from the negotiating table and assist, instead, with the assertion and protection of their declared treaty rights.[18] Aboriginal leader Brian Francis summarized the resistance to the negotiations: "I think the province needs advice on how to deal with natives. They don't understand the Indian way. They are too structured and too formal and native people are not comfortable with that and will not accept it. It's like they're going by the book when native people don't go by the book. When native people believe that they have a right, they don't believe that that right can be negotiated or sold away."[19] Noah Augustine, who captured headlines and attention, if not province-wide support, with his articulate and emotional appeals, repeatedly challenged the provincial government. Over and over again he repeated his determination to maintain the struggle: "I am not going to let them pull and pluck that spirit that just came into our communities. No way. Never, never, never ... They better start backing off. If they don't back off, there's going to be trouble."[20]

Band leaders counselled caution and urged continued reliance on the courts and, should those fail, negotiations with governments. More radical elements urged a continuation of harvesting and found themselves in tense standoffs with logging crews, government officials, and the police. Defiantly, First Nations loggers near Minto, working for Thunder East Corporation, responded to the ruling by heading back into the woods. Rumours swirled about that Warrior Societies in Nova Scotia (estimated to be 1,000 strong in the Maritimes) and Quebec were sending supporters to back up the loggers. Lloyd Johnson of Millbrook First Nations worried: "It scares me because these people are serious. Those that are prone to violence from Nova Scotia will go up to New Brunswick and join in the effort. I have no doubts about that one. Somebody's going to get hurt."[21] That Mi'kmaq interests and activism would spread across the region was no surprise. As Butch McDonald said from Eskasoni in Nova Scotia: "It's Micmac territory. Whatever affects the Micmacs and Maliseets in New Brunswick affects us all in the Maritimes. We don't have boundaries. They don't exist to us."[22] Warriors established a camp near Richibucto to support loggers from Big Cove and made it clear they had no intention of backing down. Chief Robert Levi of

Big Cove was particularly outspoken in declaring his intention to support Aboriginal loggers, warning the provincial government to leave them alone. As he wrote in an open letter to the premier: "Be hereby instructed that no other agencies or authorities, be it federal, provincial or otherwise, shall molest, harass or otherwise hinder members of the Big Cove First Nation engaged in this pursuit."[23]

The province, facing considerable province-wide pressure to enforce the law, stepped up the seizure of equipment and the detainment of offenders. Noah Augustine issued a statement to government officials: "Native loggers will remain in the woods and continue harvesting operations based on the treaties and if there's any harassment with the loggers or any interference with their markets, all negotiations or all discussions will cease immediately."[24] The government could not and did not back down, although seizures and arrests were strategic rather than systematic, designed more to demonstrate the state's ability to enforce the law than to bring Aboriginal harvesting to a halt. Compliance with government orders improved slowly but steadily, with officials careful not to gloat or celebrate as First Nations left the forest. Still, as private companies endured additional blockades and work disruptions, they secured court injunctions to keep Mi'kmaq and Maliseet protestors off their land and away from their equipment.

Non-Aboriginal observers reflected on the conflict and wondered openly about Judge Turnbull's pivotal ruling, resoundingly rejected by the Court of Appeal. As the Fredericton *Daily Gleaner* editorialized: "Justice Turnbull described himself as an 'activist judge.' We find this a startling admission for an appointed judge who is expected to be impartial. We were struck by the extreme politeness of the Court of Appeal in rejecting the flawed research and decision of Justice Turnbull in the Thomas Peter Paul case. We are not persuaded to be so polite. The decision of Justice Turnbull has created turmoil, anger and the possibility of violence in the forests of New Brunswick."[25]

At the same time that the *Paul* case was working its way through the New Brunswick court system, a similar treaty-based case was under way in Nova Scotia. Very few people paid much attention to the charges against Donald Marshall Jr at this point, but Marshall's lawyer, Bruce Wildsmith, and the Aboriginal organizations backing him, had prepared themselves for a long and intensive legal struggle with the Crown. Wildsmith assembled his team of experts, including historian William Wicken, collected oral testimony to buttress their arguments, and conducted a thorough and professional investigation of the documentary record. The Crown was undergoing similar preparations at this time, replicating a costly and time-consuming process.

Legal observers had, after the Court of Appeal verdict, recognized the limitations of Thomas Peter Paul's situation – and insiders knew that the Marshall team was assembling a stronger case. Wildsmith recommended to Aboriginal leaders that they drop the *Paul* appeal to the Supreme Court, where the evidence suggested it was going to lose, and throw their support behind Donald Marshall Jr's legal effort. Such combinations are not unusual in the field of Aboriginal law, for the collective First Nations' goal is to secure favourable court decisions and to advance the law in ways that reinforce Aboriginal rights. The process is similar to the one used during the civil rights era in the United States, when key African-American organizations coordinated their court actions so as to husband resources and increase the likelihood of success.

Some First Nations leaders had decided, however, even before the Court of Appeal judgment came down, that if Thomas Peter Paul lost, they would carry their appeal to the Supreme Court. Many believed, simply, that their case was just and that they would prevail. They hoped that the Supreme Court would grant leave to appeal and provide them with an opportunity to expand their arguments in favour of Aboriginal treaty rights. Native loggers pledged another $70,000 for the defence fund, on top of the $100,000 or more spent to take the case to the Court of Appeal. With a tinge of bitterness, lawyer Cleveland Allaby observed: "J.D. Irving has $3 to $4 million to fight this. Juniper Lumber another $1 million, plus you're fighting all the weight and might of the federal and provincial governments. Thomas Peter Paul is just a little guy. How fair is that?"[26] As late as May 1998, with the clock ticking towards the date for a final appeal, it was not clear how the First Nations would pay for the Supreme Court challenge. Donations continued to flow in, and plans were afoot for a fund-raising concert by Aboriginal musicians.

In mid-June Allaby announced the decision to take the *Paul* case to the Supreme Court. Rather than a simple appeal, he opted for the unusual tactic of requesting that the Court accept the *Paul* issue as a reference case – a request for a clarification of a key point of law. Debate flourished again about the merits of pushing the case forward, with a gathering consensus among experts in the field that the *Paul* trial lacked sufficient evidence to sustain or justify a Supreme Court hearing. Arguing that the Court of Appeal made "substantive errors in its application of the concept of judicial notice," Allaby asserted that "the prejudice to the applicant and the ongoing need to develop guiding principles in Aboriginal law require that this matter be heard by the Supreme Court of Canada."[27] The province argued, through Keith McCormick, that the *Paul* case did not raise issues of sufficient merit to require the Court's time. J.D. Irving Ltd also submitted a brief, arguing that "if Aboriginals continue to harvest illegally on Irving Crown land, it may be difficult if not impossible for Irving to harvest its total allowable annual allocation of timber." Like the Crown, Irving lawyers John Rook and Mahmud Jamal criticized the trial documentation: "This is simply not an appropriate case to be before this honourable court. The evidentiary record prepared by both parties was woefully inadequate to address the serious and far-reaching constitutional questions posed by the applicant."[28]

When the case finally reached the Supreme Court, it enjoyed but a brief few moments of attention. The Court denied leave to appeal on 5 November 1998, a determination which meant that the decision of the Appeal Court would stand and that Thomas Peter Paul and his attorneys would not have an opportunity to argue their case in Ottawa. Following Court tradition, no reasons were given for the judgment. Allaby was philosophical about the loss, pointing out that the case had forced the provincial government to open Crown lands to Aboriginal loggers. The sense of resignation was palpable. Leon Sock of the Mawiw Tribal Council (which represented Burnt Church, Big Cove, and Tobique) mourned the decision: "When did the first white man set foot on Micmac territory? That's how long we've been fighting. We're patient people, but some people ask us a little too much." Bruce Wildsmith, who was also representing Joshua Bernard, a Mi'kmaq facing similar charges, asserted that this case had a better chance before the Supreme Court, should it get there, because the evidentiary base was much more substantial.[29] The Supreme Court denial was a quick and unspectacular end to legal proceedings that had rocked New Brunswick to its core.

The *Thomas Peter Paul* case ultimately proved to be something of a legal flash in the pan. The short-term victory that derived from the decisions of Judges Arsenault and Turnbull did not survive full judicial review. Many in the Maritimes heaved a deep sigh of relief, believing that the issues were now resolved. Governments knew otherwise, for there were other cases, perhaps stronger on fact or arguments, winding their way through the courts. Officials also knew that the newly empowered First Nations would not slink quietly back to their reserves, surrendering quietly to the inherent legitimacy of the law. The *Paul* case had enlivened and reinvigorated First Nations in the Maritimes. It gave them, before the law, what they felt was always there as a historical and moral right – the opportunity to earn a living wage from the bounty of their traditional lands. The Supreme Court might have slammed the door on one applicant, but there were others standing in line. Next up, in a return of a familiar face on the landscape of Canadian Aboriginal politics, was Donald Marshall Jr.

As the key cases wound their way through the courts, other First Nations people found themselves defending Aboriginal rights claims. In a controversy that foreshadowed a bitter standoff in 1999, eight members of the Burnt Church First Nation were charged in the early 1990s for operating a commercial fishery without appropriate licences. Burnt Church had secured the right to fish in Lobster Fishing Area 23, but continued harvesting lobster well after the season officially ended. The case came before provincial court judge Andrew Stymiest in July 1993 and inched slowly forward, continuing until final arguments were heard in March 1998. Both sides brought forward their experts: Dr Stephen Patterson, whose testimony would prove pivotal in the *Marshall* judgment, testified for the Crown. Judge Stymiest reviewed the evidence and arguments in light of the *Paul* decision.[30] There were numerous other court challenges, most relatively minor in nature, and many were stayed, pending a resolution of the *Paul* and *Marshall* decisions before the Supreme Court. To a degree that few in the region recognized, the regional court system was becoming a polite but forceful battleground in the on-going struggle over Aboriginal rights.

The New Brunswick Court of Appeal decision against Thomas Peter Paul tipped the balance from the First Nations to the province and the private sector logging companies. Paul had waited until almost the end of the period allocated for launching an appeal. Before doing so, Judge Arsenault began sentencing proceedings, only to suspend them on 15 July 1998 when Paul decided to appeal to the Supreme Court. Crown prosecutor McCormick touched off a courtroom debate when he argued that Paul should be sentenced, the appeal notwithstanding, because the man had "unclean hands" and had continued to log after the Court of Appeal ruling. In response, Allaby protested vigourously: "Mr. Peter Paul has never done anything that would fly in the face of the decision of the court, or in the face of the law. Mr. Peter Paul is an honourable, honest man. It is a preposterous proposition to assume that Mr. Peter Paul is engaged in the removal of wood that has been illegally harvested, that he is somehow tainted or somehow a criminal, and somehow should not be entitled to the same benefit of law that anyone else would enjoy."[31] Sentencing was adjourned, pending the Supreme Court's decision on the appeal.

Paul's difficulties continued in November 1998. The sentencing hearing scheduled for 20 November was postponed again, when Allaby failed to show up. Allaby said he had a back problem and sent Bathurst lawyer Martin Siscoe in his place, but Simcoe did not know enough about the case for the session to proceed. McCormick was less than pleased: "I get paid whether I'm here, in Fredericton, Campbellton, so I can't say my time is wasted. But the taxpayers have had to pay for a car rental and a hotel. This is not only discourteous, but unfair." McCormick also noted that Allaby had told him earlier that he did not plan on attending the hearing.[32] The following week, on 25 November, Judge Arsenault decided that the public interest in the case had been served and that Paul's conviction did not warrant additional punishment. He was released without penalty. As Arsenault commented, "This case has served to establish the law, that in itself has been of some service to the citizens of New Brunswick. As a result of the whole process, the law has been established." The judge also indicated his clear intention to adhere to the Court of Appeal ruling on Aboriginal harvesting.[33]

The importance of the *Thomas Peter Paul* case extended far beyond the courtroom. For over a year the question of Aboriginal commercial logging rights held the province of New Brunswick in its grip. This conflict awoke Maritimers to the disruptive potential of court rulings on treaty rights and set the stage for the response to the *Marshall* ruling.

What makes the *Thomas Peter Paul* case particularly interesting is the fact that it was sprung on the Maritimes with little warning. The court hearing was remarkably short, with little testimony and few witnesses and documents. The decision was not widely anticipated, as relatively few people were aware of the case. Compared with major challenges like *Calder* or *Delgamuukw*, First Nations organizations had given Thomas Peter Paul little help. When the initial judgment came down, and particularly after the ruling by Judge Turnbull, the Mi'kmaq and Maliseet people were caught unaware. The decision promised a major extension of Aboriginal treaty rights and, in one quick swoop, both reinvigorated the eighteenth-century treaties and commercialized First Nations harvesting in the Maritimes. In no time at all, the First Nations paid attention.

The Aboriginal reaction was easy to anticipate. Judge Turnbull ruled that First Nations had a treaty right to harvest timber on Crown land and to sell the logs for commercial profit. The Mi'kmaq and Maliseet leadership hailed the judgment as a vindication of their long-standing argument that they deserved the right to harvest resources for commercial and for personal benefit, and that this Aboriginal right had been ratified by the treaties. Leaders immediately declared their intention to capitalize on this right and, individually and in groups, Mi'kmaq and Maliseet people prepared to enter the woods. The response in Aboriginal communities was joyous. The decision provided an opportunity for employment and profit, and for wealth to flow onto the reserves, since logging was one of the few economic activities readily accessible to the First Nations communities in the Maritimes. The reaction was strongest in New Brunswick, for it was a provincial court ruling, but Nova Scotian Mi'kmaq paid close attention and readied their chain saws as well.

The scale of Aboriginal harvesting in New Brunswick was significant. By early February 1998 over 250 Mi'kmaq and Maliseet loggers, some eighty to one hundred crews, were cutting trees on lands licensed to logging companies, including Avenor, Stone-Consolidated, Repap, Eagle Forest Products, J.D. Irving, St Anne Nackawic Pulp Company, Juniper Lumber, and Fraser Paper. Noah Augustine exalted: "This is the greatest opportunity and most excitement I have ever seen in native communities. What people have to understand is that we're dealing with oppressed communities. This is the first real significant opportunity for native people to earn a respectable living, provide for their families and contribute to society and feel that independence. It's an amazing thing – it's almost like a revolution in a way."[34] For First Nations men like Claude Polches of St Mary's First Nation, the court victory was enough to convince him and four friends to buy a skidder and head into the forests. Rejecting the idea that Aboriginal people were abusing the land, Polches argued that they simply wanted a chance to make a decent living. Resistance from the large companies – J.D. Irving was often singled out in Aboriginal complaints – dampened the sense of accomplishment: "I think with Irving, it's more an issue of control. He can't control us cutting. He could have took that load of mine and put it in his mill. Those trees are making him money, and giving me work, so why can't he take them." The logs were sold into Maine.[35]

The *Thomas Peter Paul* decision was an burst of optimism in a world of economic despair. As the *Telegraph Journal* noted in an end-of-year review: "Economic self-sufficiency appeared to be a tangible reality for natives. Thomas Peter Paul became a hero overnight to the province's many-times disillusioned native population and logging outfits sprang up like violets in springtime."[36] Aboriginal people had claimed for decades that they only needed a chance, a small but reasonable opening, and they would show their competitive zeal and their work ethic. Judge Turnbull did not open the door a crack; he threw it wide open and left it off its hinges. First Nations in New Brunswick were euphoric. They rushed into the woods, sometimes ill-prepared and often without much knowledge of commercial forestry.

Some First Nations loggers signed quick deals with forestry companies from Maine and Quebec and with equipment suppliers. Tim

Paul thought these deals made sense: "I know a few boys that are signing lumber contracts with companies in Quebec. They're supplying [Natives] with all the equipment and they'll ship the wood out to Quebec. It's all going to head out and you know why? Because Irving and all these other lumber companies don't want to deal. They're living in denial. They think Aboriginal people are just sitting back and doing nothing about this stuff. I'm afraid the wood is going to be heading right out of the province."[37] Several found an easier way to capitalize on their Aboriginal right, hiring non-Native people to cut the wood on their behalf. A few bands organized collective logging activity and planned a more deliberate strategy for capitalizing on the authority. Bold statements were made about Mi'kmaq and Maliseet "ownership" of the forestry, and many pledged that Aboriginal concepts of stewardship and conservation would ensure the protection of the resources. A few charged ahead with no thought of the consequences, cutting trees in high-profile areas and angering non-Aboriginal residents in the area. In several instances, for example, they cut the timber between the highway and lake- and river-front cabin properties.

Despite the protests, these were heady times for many First Nations in New Brunswick. Logging brought personal prosperity and, for the first time in living memory, the promise of equality with non-Aboriginal neighbours. Randy Brooks of St Mary's First Nation contemplated a community transformed by the mere opportunity for better times: "It has improved our self-esteem and more and more people are getting off welfare and using their own money from logging. There were too many people with idle time. They were just waiting around for a welfare cheque ... People here no longer have to be turned away from a job because they are Indians." At Big Cove, a community sadly known for its high suicide rate, Young Hawk commented: "The only place you see people now is in the woods or the bank. The people don't have time to fool around with drugs and alcohol these days."[38] These stories were repeated around New Brunswick, strengthening Aboriginal resolve.

Other provincial residents recoiled in various degrees of surprise, shock, and dismay. While the First Nations had their supporters, the critics grabbed the air time. Loggers worried about their jobs and incomes, logging companies expressed nervousness about their harvesting licences, and communities dependent on logging wondered if the court decision presaged a shift in economic power from their towns and villages to First Nations reserves. As the *Telegraph Journal* editorialized: "These competing concerns have clashed almost from the day Judge Turnbull handed down his decision. Some non-native mills have refused to buy wood that was cut by natives on Crown land. Natives have hired non-natives to help with harvesting, a provocative precursor to broader commercial enterprise. The provincial government has laid charges of illegal cutting against non-natives hired by natives. And, most recently, natives have begun legal proceedings that would evict one of the largest forest companies, J.D. Irving, from Crown lands which the natives believe they now own."[39] Opponents of special status for First Nations had a field day and roundly criticized the court for its judicial activism. More generally, debate raged about whether the unexpected and unusual decision by Judge Turnbull would withstand judicial review. Aboriginal issues were hotly debated across the province, with the temper of New Brunswick running about half and half on the issue. As had happened in other jurisdictions, urban residents appeared to favour an extension of Aboriginal rights, while rural folks, the ones most directly affected by the new regulations, opposed the Turnbull decision.

Tempers flared in the forest in particular. Along logging roads and often deep in the forest, First Nations and non-Aboriginal loggers squared off over harvesting rights. Nasty words, filled with thinly veiled threats, shot back and forth. First Nations blockaded company access to assigned forest tracts. Perry Perley, hereditary chief of the Maliseet turtle clan, for example, ordered J.D. Irving off Crown land, claiming that these territories were Aboriginally owned; he also demanded RCMP protection from what he claimed was "harassment and intimidation."[40] The police were routinely called out to keep the sides apart and to adjudicate highly emotional screaming matches. The provincial Department of Natural Resources did not know exactly how to respond, and found itself attempting to enforce provincial regulations while staring at a clear judgment in favour of the First Nations. For a few tense weeks, the forests of New Brunswick seethed with anger, frustration, and uncertainty.

Critics scorned First Nations harvesting practices and wondered aloud if the logging activities of 1998 represented the reality of Aboriginal environmentalism. Early in the controversy, Noah Augustine asked for patience: "What we're seeing differs little from any other situation one might point to where socio-economically disadvantaged peoples scramble to take advantage of opportunities – in the rain forests of Brazil, for example, or in the heavy industries of struggling economies in eastern Europe or China – environmental issues always take a back seat for a time. In our case, I believe this will be a short time and I have every confidence that native people of New Brunswick will do what is responsible environmentally in the long run. Don't judge us too harshly for today."[41]

Aboriginal leaders kept a surprisingly low profile, reflecting in large part the effort needed to coordinate activities within their communities. Groups like the Union of New Brunswick Indians, however, rarely addressed the issue in public, creating an opening for more outspoken members, such as Tim Paul and Noah Augustine, to present the Aboriginal position. These statements, and the tone in which they were delivered, tended to be more confrontational and provocative than the style of established leaders like Roger Augustine and Second Peter Barlow. Noah Augustine criticized the established leadership: "With all due respect, I totally disagree with how they're handling this whole logging issue because it isn't just an isolated event – it's part and parcel of a movement that's taking place right across Canada with Aboriginal people asserting their rights. We're lacking focused leadership because nobody is offering that right now."[42] Roger Augustine, former chief of the Union of New Brunswick Indians and a respected national leader, said of the younger Noah Augustine: "I think he'd better live a little more before he makes those kinds of comments. There's a good reason behind the silence of the chiefs on the logging issue and it should be respected: They were elected to represent not only loggers, but also the people who are against harvesting trees and that's something they have to keep in mind. To take advantage of their silence is wrong because the chiefs are honourable people doing great work in their communities."[43] Grand Chief Phil Fontaine of the Assembly of First Nations attended a meeting in Fredericton in mid-May to lend his support and, to the dismay of some in attendance, urged a return to the negotiating table.

The government of New Brunswick was caught in a difficult spot. Ray Frenette had only recently succeeded Frank McKenna as premier of New Brunswick, and a leadership race was under way to replace him. The interim leader clearly did not need a major irritant on his desk during the transition period. To his credit, and that of the Liberal government, the problem was tackled quickly. Under the direction of Aboriginal Affairs Minister Bernard Thériault, the government ordered a review of provincial initiatives for First Nations people – a mini-royal commission, with a very short time frame for research and reporting – and arranged for Gerald La Forest, a former Supreme Court judge, and provincial court judge Graydon Nicholas, the first Mi'kmaq appointed to the bench in New Brunswick, to lead the investigation. Realizing the potential impact of the *Thomas Peter Paul* judgment, the province appealed the case to the New Brunswick Court of Appeal. Simultaneously, it began negotiations early in April 1998 with Mi'kmaq and Maliseet bands to secure short-term deals designed to bring order to the industry. In the wave of enthusiasm that followed the decision, truckloads of logs were heading out of the province, denying wood to the sawmills and jobs to the workers. Well-established conservation plans lay in tatters, as First Nations ignored company and government arrangements for selective harvesting. Moreover, as tensions rose and the number of conflicts increased, the government worried about the potential for violence in the forests. There were also the growing legal complexities: Did First Nations people have the right, for example, to hire non-Native people to cut and move trees on their behalf? It was clear that the province faced a formidable problem.

The provincial government's favoured approach – negotiating with individual bands – revealed the weak spot in the Aboriginal position. While some First Nations simply wanted a blanket recognition of their rights, many did not trust the band chiefs and councils to make a proper and fair allocation of timber-cutting rights and revenues. This concern was particularly strong among off-reserve and non-status First Nations people, who had no access to band-based opportunities. Thomas Peter Paul, the man at the centre of the controversy, said of the government's plan: "Why should the bands administrate who's going to cut and where? I mean if they are into the business, who do you think is going to get the cream of the crop? The band administration. I'm going to carry on the way I am."[44] Opponents of the government's plan to negotiate with band councils formed the Micmac Maliseet Council, consisting of groups not party to the provincial government's negotiations with twelve band councils (as it was at that juncture). The group included representatives from Big Cove, Burnt Church, Tobique, traditional/hereditary chiefs, the New Brunswick Native Loggers Business Association, the Mawiw Council of First Nations, and the New Brunswick Aboriginal People Council. The stated goal was to produce a united front and to force the provincial government to make substantial concessions.[45] The government, however, was not prepared to budge.

The Frenette administration opted for short-term, one-year agreements designed to buy time for all parties to the dispute. Time and again the more strident members of the First Nations leadership rejected and even ridiculed his position, and each time he restated his willingness to negotiate with band governments and to ensure them a portion of the provincial timber allocation. He adopted a conciliatory approach, avoiding the hardline positions and confrontational style that has often characterized Aboriginal-government relations in Canada. In British Columbia, for example, the long-serving Social Credit government of Bill Bennett and Bill Van der

Zalm routinely rebuffed First Nations requests for negotiations, and the province endured many roadblocks and standoffs. Even Mike Harcourt's New Democratic Party administration encountered numerous difficulties with First Nations demands. The goal in New Brunswick was to negotiate deals with individual First Nations which, collectively, allowed for approximately 5 per cent of the total permissible timber harvest for the province. Not everyone was happy. The bands demanded a higher percentage of the forest, logging companies thought the offer was too high, and many First Nations asserted that they would never sign away their treaty right. But they did. Slowly, one by one, the bands signed on with the provincial government. They realized, quite simply, that their communities would lose economic opportunities if agreements were not signed quickly. The deals were not overly generous, but they recognized the authority of the First Nation to manage a percentage of the total harvest while respecting provincial conservation regulations and existing licences.

When the *Paul* decision first came down, logging companies indicated that they had no intention of buying timber from First Nations. They saw a great injustice in having to attend to provincial forestry regulations when Aboriginal loggers were, in their eyes, running amok in the woods. Watching loads of valuable timber cross the borders into Maine and Quebec angered them more, as they saw money and profit leave New Brunswick – even though non-Aboriginal loggers also exported logs out of the province. There were a few angry outbursts in the early days of the controversy, but the major companies kept their protests behind government doors. Led by J.D. Irving Co, the largest forest products firm in the Maritimes and a cornerstone of the Irving family empire, the companies kept pressure on the government, but avoided public statements that might well have inflamed the situation. J.D. Irving even took the unusual step of hiring Roger Augustine, former chief of the Eel River Bar First Nation, to advise the company on Aboriginal matters – a decision that left Augustine open to criticism among the First Nations, but, for a short time, brought a new perspective into the firm. As negotiations proceeded with the provincial government, the forestry companies came more on side and declared their willingness to work with individual First Nations and Aboriginal logging companies.

Those companies that had worked with the First Nations, including a number of firms from outside the province, reassessed their position in light of the Court of Appeal ruling. Afraid that the provincial government would start seizing logging equipment and supplies, the companies quickly removed most of their gear. This, withdrawal, in turn, forced the First Nations logging companies to lay off their workers.[46] The government had the weight of law and the tools of enforcement. The clear illegality of First Nations logging on Crown land scared away potential partners and deprived the Aboriginal companies of their primary markets. Although First Nations could recall wistfully what had been, it was obvious that the enterprise was lost, at least on a large scale.

Attracting even less attention were company efforts at reconciliation with the First Nations. Eel River Bar, for example, maintained solid relations with the town of Charlo throughout the controversy and negotiated an agreement with Avenor, a lease holder in the area, that permitted Aboriginal cutting on licensed land, provided it was delivered to the company. The firm did not work in hardwood, and offered to let the band cut whatever stands of hardwood it wanted once it had located a buyer. For Tim Dedham, a Mi'kmaq economic development officer for Eel River Bar, such arrangements were essential to keep band members working, to provide revenue for band services, and to avoid the conflict that threatened to poison relations in the rest of the province.[47]

The defeat for Mi'kmaq and Maliseet rights in the Court of Appeal had been a major setback. The Supreme Court's subsequent decision not to hear the case only reinforced the degree to which Judge Turnbull's ruling was determined to be legally incorrect and Aboriginal aspirations had been dashed. Where, in the early days, it had been non-Aboriginal loggers threatening violence and worrying about their livelihoods, now it was First Nations that were angry about the reversal. As one New Brunswick editorial observed, "warnings by certain leaders ... came without accompanying pleas that violence be avoided, and as such they are every bit as irresponsible as were the earlier warnings. Genuine leaders do not stand back and shrug when tensions threaten to rise to the exploding point; genuine leaders don't resign themselves to the hand of fate just because that hand is clenched into a fist."[48]

Conflict brewed, as well, within the First Nations communities. Individual loggers voiced distrust of band leaders and worried that deals negotiated with First Nations bands would not be shared equitably or fairly within their communities. Frenette favoured government-to-band negotiations, and offered a share of the annual timber cut provided that the First Nations worked in approved areas, selected in consultation with private companies, and sold their harvest exclusively to Crown licence holders. Individual loggers responded with bitterness to the government's negotiations and rejected the offer of a small percentage of the overall provincial cut.

An initial offer of 200 acres per community was spurned by Stewart Clement of Big Cove, who brushed off the suggestion, saying, "I think we cut that much just this morning."[49] The Micmac-Maliseet Coalition, representing loggers who wanted to exercise their Aboriginal rights, attempted to secure a deal with the provincial government, as did individual First Nations bands. The government eventually improved the offer, offering First Nations a total of 5 per cent of the provincial allowable cut (125,000 cords). Under the offer, Aboriginal loggers could cut on licensed Crown land, provided they paid a stumpage fee (payments generally paid to the provincial government for cut timber) to licence holders and sold their timber to the appropriate licence holder. The stumpage fees would, in return, be handed over to the First Nation. At one point in the early summer there was also some discussion of purchasing MacMillan Bloedel's share of the Eagle Forest Products mill in the Miramichi on behalf of the First Nations.[50]

As negotiations proceeded with the New Brunswick minister of natural resources, Douglas Tyler, First Nations loggers remained in the forest and the provincial government responded in kind. Loggers operating without proper licences were detained and their equipment was seized. On a selective basis, charges were placed, particularly against non-Aboriginals who were acting with First Nations. Arrests, seizures, and enforcement angered Aboriginal leaders, including Noah Augustine. Although he was not part of the cadre of elected First Nations chiefs and politicians, Augustine attracted young Aboriginal loggers who "saw the native logging dispute as an elixir for the problems of life on New Brunswick's native reserves." Augustine jumped from being a small business owner (Great Earth Consulting) to the head of the Native Loggers Business Association and the Micmac-Maliseet Coalition. His articulate, media-savvy, hard-driving, and confrontational style suited the evolving situation. He got more attention than any other Aboriginal leader, including Thomas Peter Paul, but his effectiveness was uneven.[51]

Through the spring and summer of 1998, Augustine was a key figure in the dispute. His passion and conviction were clearly in evidence: "From a personal point of view, we are not wrong or without rights in our battle to secure a future for our children and future generations. We are people with nothing to lose as almost all has been lost to us."[52] Reacting to the government's decision to seize equipment, Augustine pulled few punches: "I am just totally amazed at what has happened here because of the dishonesty coming out of these senior government officials. This is what really shocks me. It is total dishonesty when they tell us the night before that there will be no enforcement ... We're fully aware of the high tensions, the Warrior Society members coming around. That's why in a situation like this you can't aggravate it with this type of action."[53] The government worried, with justification, that the arrest of another Mi'kmaq or Maliseet person might well provide the occasion for one more potentially successful court challenge involving Aboriginal rights to resources. Despite these worries, prosecutions continued – while the government and the First Nations both looked for a suitable case to test the Aboriginal rights issue before the courts.

By the end of September 1998, Noah Augustine was out of the political picture, fighting a desperate battle to free himself from murder charges involving Bruce Barnaby, a member of the Red Bank community. Although he admitted a role in the death, he was acquitted of the murder charge. Augustine was not the only key figure in the logging dispute to run afoul of the law. On 1 October 1998 Thomas Peter Paul was charged with being in possession of marijuana for the purposes of trafficking and with uttering threats to his wife. Police found 8 kilograms of marijuana buds and plants at his home on the Pabineau First Nation reserve.[54] He was found guilty, ironically before Judge Arsenault, and sentenced to concurrent one-year sentences on the charges of possession and production of marijuana for the purposes of trafficking. He claimed, in an original twist on the Aboriginal harvesting theme, that he grew the plants to pay for the logging equipment. The now-famous charges had left him unable to pay his bills: "After being shut down in the woods I'm jammed up with big bank payments – The government is definitely not helping us out, we need to help ourselves. That was a way out for me. I knew it was wrong, but it was a way not to ruin my name at the bank, not to ruin my life. There's no other resource. We're not allowed to cut wood. What resource do we have but illegal activity? What can they expect from native people?"[55]

Thomas Peter Paul also found himself back in court on charges relating to harvesting and possession of illegally harvested wood. As he said in early November, "I have some equipment working on reserve, but my plans are to go back at it, on Crown land. I wish [the Department of Natural Resources] all the luck in the world to find me." If stopped again, "I'll fight it." he said. "I don't know if I'll fight it the same way, but I'll fight it."[56] By the time his case reached the courts in January 1999, his was one of thirty to forty other charges then in process throughout New Brunswick. At the same time, he discovered that the Crown prosecutor had filed a motion to appeal his release on the original charge, arguing that he wanted "to establish what the criteria are for release without penalty, and this is as good a case as any to do it."[57]

First Nations warnings proved not to be idle threats. In June 1998 members of the Warrior Society, in army fatigues and with their now widely recognized red flag, stopped work on three J.D. Irving sites in Kent County. The blockade arose out of a meeting at Big Cove, where leaders debated the gap between the provincial government's 5 per cent offer and their demand for more than 25 per cent of all Crown land in New Brunswick. With emotions running high, and with memories strong of the government's seizure of First Nations' equipment, the meeting decided that direct action was necessary. As Brian Francis of Big Cove said: "The native loggers felt that they had to do something. Basically what we are saying is if the natives can't be part of the industry then we are going to try and stop the industry." Over one hundred Aboriginal loggers, and many more supporters, asked non-Native workers to cease operations. No violence ensued, and protest organizer Noah Augustine repeated that their main goal was simply to get the provincial government back to the table. For their part, J.D. Irving representatives called on the police and the government to protect the companies' and workers' right to continue logging operations.[58] The protests escalated, spreading to other J.D. Irving sites and to those of Repap New Brunswick as well. Gary Augustine of Big Cove reiterated, "If the native loggers can't cut, then no one can." Repap applied for and received a court injunction, barring subsequent blockades of private logging operations. The Micmac Warrior Society, having clearly realized that it could only push the issue so far, agreed to honour the injunction.[59]

In the midst of the protests, individual First Nations struck deals with the provincial government. It was, at one level, a repeat of the long-standing problem facing band governments. Does a First Nation accept a reasonable but limited deal offered by government or does it hold out for a potentially large, but also potentially smaller, deal as a result of a court decision? The province of New Brunswick offered the First Nations 5 per cent of the allowable cut, available on a band-by-band basis. Lawyer Cleveland Allaby had a few choice words on the offer: "I laugh at the joke that the province is flouting, that they're negotiating cutting with Aboriginals. That's the worse piece of drivel I've ever heard in my life. Five per cent and that's it? Where's the negotiation? It must be Stalinist Russia, it's the only place I've heard of negotiating like that!"[60] In early June 1998 the Tobique First Nation became the first to settle with the province of New Brunswick, with Woodstock Chief Pat Francis leading his community to the bargaining table at the same time. The agreements gave an assured harvest of logs, provided those logs were sold to provincial licensees, and a source of discretionary income for the band. Chief Robert Levi of Big Cove continued to press for a much broader deal – he proposed a minimum of 15 per cent of Crown land and the construction of three native-run saw mills – but his plan found little favour with government. The Tobique agreement brought most of the other bands to the table and, in relatively short order, deals were inked. By November 1998 ten of the fifteen bands had interim agreements – and three of the bands (Tobique, Burnt Church, and Eel River Bar) had used up their allocations.[61] They were one-year agreements, designed only to carry over the issue for another year while the government, the courts, and the First Nations wrestled with the implications of Aboriginal logging rights.

A central twist in the New Brunswick logging saga involved non-Aboriginal loggers. First Nations argued that, since they had an Aboriginal right to log, they could hire non-Aboriginal people to work for them. This interpretation greatly expanded the initial understanding of Aboriginal rights, as an income and employment opportunity, into a full-scale commercial option. The idea that a single First Nations person could hire one or more work crews to cut trees, all under the rubric of Aboriginal entitlement, worried government and industry alike. In May 1998 lawyers Peter O'Neill and Harvey Urquhart found themselves defending ten non-Native men charged with logging illegally. Judge Denis Lordon of the provincial court was clearly uncomfortable with the attempt by the lawyers to argue an Aboriginal rights case, largely on the basis of the now-overturned *Thomas Peter Paul* decision. As Crown prosecutor Keith McCormick argued, "Although the Aboriginal people may hire whomever they want, that won't help the defendants unless those Aboriginal people can transfer their immunity from the law, assuming they have any, to the people they hire. That is the real issue."[62] The answer, provided by governments and the courts, was that non-Native people were not able to use the shield of Aboriginal immunity to protect them from prosecution. Through the summer of 1998, additional cases worked their way through the courts. In one, charges against Craig Tompkins were dropped and his father's truck was returned. It had been seized when Tompkins was attempting to deliver a load of logs cut by Reg Paul of Woodstock to a mill in New Limerick, Maine. The judge determined that Tompkins was not expected to ask if the logs had been cut legally and, hence, his vehicle should not be held.[63]

The *Thomas Peter Paul* case also provided the province with an extended illustration, if one were needed, of the determination of off-reserve and non-status Indians in New Brunswick. Negotiations with band councils virtually guaranteed that off-reserve status Indians would not share in the benefits of negotiated agreements. The Aboriginal Peoples Council, representing both off-reserve and non-status Indians, sought without success to be included in the talks, which continued to focus on band councils. When the agreements were struck in 1998, the settlements squeezed the Aboriginal Peoples Council out of the picture. The council registered a human-rights complaint against the provincial government, claiming it had "deliberately and maliciously" discriminated against off-reserve First Nations. It announced its intention to carry the battle all the way to the United Nations – a bold declaration that worried few officials.[64] Unfortunately for the New Brunswick Aboriginal Peoples Council, the government had long since decided that its primary obligations rested with the band governments and it retained its focus on negotiations with reserve governments. The Nation of Acadia Métis, an organization that claimed 5,000 members, likewise claimed to represent a "forgotten people" and pressed the provincial government to include it in logging and fishing negotiations. The Métis had their test cases too, including charges against a Richibucto harvester caught with more than his quota of clams.[65] But like the Aboriginal Peoples Council, the Acadia Métis enjoyed little success in their efforts to secure guaranteed access to resources.

Efforts to get the provincial government to negotiate with the Micmac-Maliseet Coalition failed, even after Camille Thériault replaced Ray Frenette as premier. Requests for high-level meetings and a moratorium on the detainment of loggers and the seizure of equipment went unheeded. So, too, did demands from the Native Business Association that Aboriginal people be allocated 30 per cent of Crown land for logging purposes. At the same time that the provincial authorities were being pressured by non–First Nations people to take action against illegal logging, the half-way measure of seizing equipment and postponing charges seemed a politically expedient solution. It certainly got the attention, and raised the ire, of many First Nations people.

The province-wide initiative culminated in a dramatic proposal, tabled in late June 1998, by the Micmac-Maliseet Native Loggers Business Association. Dropping its demand for 30 per cent or more of the harvest, it instead requested 5 per cent of all softwood, 3 per cent of hardwood, "open and unfettered" access to Crown lands, management rights over selected areas, exclusive sales to New Brunswick mills, and a joint regulatory board. In return, the province was expected to drop all outstanding charges and return all seized vehicles and equipment. Noah Augustine offered: "This is too reasonable for the government to ignore. This is a compromise." Individual loggers, hurt by the Court of Appeal decision on the *Paul* case, had urged a settlement, lest they lose the entire 1998 season and face personal financial problems as a result.[66]

If there was a time to settle, that time had passed. The provincial government had long since shifted its negotiations to agreements with the bands, and they were proceeding well. Doug Tyler, natural resources minister, rejected the "compromise" proposal out of hand. Noah Augustine showed up for Tyler's press conference, challenging the minister and venting his displeasure at the failure to extend discussions. Augustine continued: "We're looking for some kind of orderly arrangement that would allow these guys [Native loggers] to continue working while negotiations continue. Just because Doug Tyler has decided to reject our proposal doesn't mean the native loggers are not major players. They are."[67] For all the confident assertions, the reality was that the independent loggers had overplayed their hand and had failed to realize soon enough that the band chiefs could and would negotiate without them. The attempt for a province-wide accord, driven in large measure by off-reserve First Nations, faded and died.

The provincial government could afford to turn its back on the large and noisy coalition because it continued to conclude deals with individual First Nations. Once the template had been set, the arrangements varied little from reserve to reserve. The deals, designed to serve for 1998 while longer-term agreement were negotiated, offered a set allocation of timber and made the band eligible for federal and provincial assistance programs. As each deal was signed, pressure increased on the remaining bands, lest they lose a share of the annual cut and miss out on the opportunity to provide work and revenue for their community. Complaints continued, quite loudly at times, but momentum had definitely shifted in the government's favour.

New Brunswick companies realized their responsibility for securing a lasting peace in the forest. The major firms backed down from their initial reluctance to purchase wood from First Nations loggers and began negotiations with band councils to integrate Aboriginal workers into their operations. J.D. Irving held discussions with First Nations groups throughout New Brunswick and Nova Scotia and set a corporate objective of establishing, at a minimum, one fifteen-member crew per community, assigned to reforestation and thinning work. By the spring of 1998 an agreement had been reached with the Tobique First Nation, establishing a precedent that the firm wished to extend throughout the region.[68] J.D. Irving also hired the men from the tiny, thirty-six-person Fort Folly reserve and assigned them to silviculture operations in the area.

Involving First Nations in the management of logging operations was no assurance of peace in the forest. The case of the Listiguj First Nation, located north of Campbellton in Quebec, provided an illustration of potential difficulties. Jijug Enterprises Inc., a Mi'kmaq-owned company, had harvested on Crown land in cooperation with the Quebec government. After a bitter local election in 1998, the band council no longer recognized Jijug, which shifted its operations to other Crown lands, without first securing permission. Ronald Jacques, the newly elected chief of Listiguj, negotiated a deal similar to the earlier one with Jijug and determined that the logs would be cut by community members and the profits distributed by the band. The wood would be processed "most likely" at a sawmill owned by Mr Jacques. Meanwhile, the Quebec government moved to stop unauthorized logging. The combined actions angered people associated with Jijug and resulted in roadblocks, intense bitterness in the community, increased factionalism, and a very sad demonstration of the potential weakness of local autonomy.[69] The tensions within First Nations communities, and between reserve and off-reserve, status and non-status Aboriginal people, suggested that similar problems could well surface in New Brunswick.

The *Thomas Peter Paul* ruling did not survive for long, but the impact lingers. The provincial government continued its negotiations on shared logging resources, and the idea of providing Mi'kmaq and Maliseet people with a percentage of the provincial harvest survived the Court of Appeal judgment and the Supreme Court's decision not to hear a further appeal. Several crucial lessons had been learned through the conflict. The public discovered that First Nations people were clearly ready to work and truly desired the opportunity to be employed close to their communities. The forest companies paid attention and, without legal compulsion, expanded programs to train and hire Aboriginal workers. First Nations came to realize, rhetoric aside, that few were ready for full-scale and long-term forestry operations and that there was much to learn about running a successful logging company. The government of New Brunswick learned about the disruptive power of court decisions – a salutatory warning about taking future cases lightly – and the desirability of negotiated settlements to sticky legal and treaty issues. Overriding all these factors, New Brunswickers came to recognize that the pattern of ignoring Aboriginal rights was over and that, by legal or other means, the Mi'kmaq and Maliseet people were determined to secure their share of the province's opportunities.

It is difficult to imagine the New Brunswick logging industry reverting to its former state. On the heels of the Supreme Court rejection of the *Thomas Peter Paul* appeal, the Liberal government under Camille Thériault made a remarkable offer. Although clearly freed from an immediate obligation to do anything, Minister Tyler used the occasion to offer an olive branch to the First Nations. He was, he said, prepared to negotiate twenty-five-year logging deals with the First Nations, giving them substantial and secure access to timber resources and providing communities with the beginnings of an economic base. "When we chose this path," he observed, "we knew there would be no turning back. We will not change course. Regardless of what the courts say, the native people are now a participant in the forest industry of New Brunswick, and that's not going to change." He also recognized that the deals of the previous summer had been problematic – he called some an "utter disaster" in terms of band management – but he recognized the social and economic challenges that undercut the ability of bands to handle the new responsibilities. "I never miss an opportunity to tell a native leader, 'This is a great opportunity. Don't let it slip through your fingers.' But I won't tell them how to do it – that's up to them to work out."[70]

Band chiefs and councils who negotiated 5 per cent deals with the province often found themselves the subject of ridicule and abuse. Chief Robert Levi, an outspoken critic of the provincial strategy, reluctantly accepted a deal in December, becoming the twelfth of the fifteen New Brunswick bands to reach an agreement. Local residents drew up a petition protesting the deal. Opponents alleged that the council would take the money and allocate it among family and friends.[71] The Big Cove agreement differed from the earlier eleven accords in that it was to run for twenty-five years, with a $3.8 million cash settlement up front.[72] And so it continued around the province, with accusations, complaints, painful decisions, and community divisions replacing the excitement and determination that had marked the forestry dispute in earlier times.

The difficulties were severe: overly rapid cutting of allocations, assignment of timber cutting privileges to non-Natives, allegations of favouritism and nepotism in the allocation of logging rights, and suggestions that the money received was not well spent on community needs. On the Kingsclear reserve, twenty-one band members received a share of the First Nations allocation; of these, around fourteen quickly resold their harvesting rights to non-Aboriginal people. While a few Aboriginal loggers paced the work over the winter, ensuring a measure of employment, the outsiders cut the timber quickly and moved on. The band council, charged with allocating the cutting rights and ensuring the distribution of benefits, stood accused by its own members of having done a poor job.[73] Wayne Nichols, director of the Maliseet Forestry Industry on the Tobique reserve, observed sadly: "As the [interim harvesting agreement] was recognized ... band members wanted wood, wood, wood and money, money, money. They were all profiteers. They forgot their traditional values of sharing and building something that would be economically viable."[74] The New Brunswick government, gritting its teeth on occasion, accepted the sometimes painful realities of Aboriginal self-government and left the challenge of dealing with the problems to the band governments.

The final debates about the Thomas Peter Paul logging dispute coincided with the release of the La Forest–Nicholas report on Aboriginal affairs in New Brunswick. The report highlighted the persistent problem of Aboriginal unemployment and poverty, and urged the government to negotiate in good faith and with urgency with the First Nations about matters of collective concern. The legal battles over logs and fish had, by the end of 1998, obscured the research and analysis of La Forest and Nicholas. Their report, which had been launched with considerable fanfare, attracted little attention. The province was moving into an election year. First Nations appeared to favour continued court challenges. Difficult negotiations over logging rights, resolved only when the Court of Appeal and the Supreme Court rejected the *Paul* case, revealed the inherent risks involved in moving along that track. New Brunswick was bruised and, on all sides, somewhat traumatized. There was little appetite anywhere in the province for the hard work of reconciliation and bridge-building recommended by the task force report on Aboriginal issues.[75]

The *Paul* interregnum empowered First Nations in ways not seen since the nineteenth century. Tim Paul said in 1998, reflecting the heady confidence of the period: "We will develop our own strategies, our own planting and our own road building. Once that is done, then we sit down and discuss the rest of the 22 million acres that is the Province of New Brunswick."[76] Entrepreneurs headed into the woods, loggers invested in new equipment, and bands set up logging companies. A particularly aggressive group established the Native Loggers Business Association of New Brunswick and invited their counterparts from Nova Scotia and Quebec to join. Leaders of the logging effort spoke of developing environmentally sensitive plans and establishing both export efforts and cooperative financing deals. The business group often worked apart from the fifteen New Brunswick chiefs, particularly during negotiations with the provincial government, and they were eventually pushed aside by the band-to-government discussions.[77] Throughout the 1997–98 logging season, however, Aboriginal loggers dreamed of a larger industry, employing hundreds of Mi'kmaq and Maliseet people, reinvigorating reserve economies, and providing proof of the power of eighteenth-century treaties and the resilience of Maritime First Nations.

There is no doubt of the magnitude of the change. Well over 90 per cent of the industry continues much as before, and companies have seen the integrity of their licences and permits reinforced, not weakened in this process. But First Nations secured a foothold in a sector of the economy that is crucial to the future vitality of their communities and the province as a whole. Moreover, they have gained an opportunity to prove – to themselves and to the community at large – that the age-old stereotypes about Aboriginal work habits and commercial attitudes do not hold. As Tyler observed in June 1998: "I really sense from both the native community [and] the province of New Brunswick ... that ... the population really believes there is an opportunity here for the native community to become involved with industry. I think that is very significant. That has never happened before and the challenge is to define what that involvement is."[78] For many First Nations leaders, the current agreements provide an opening, a foot in the door. From this base, they assert, they will gain the skills, the equipment, and the commercial expertise necessary to tackle the private sector. They confidently assert that, in short order, they will compete on an equal footing with non-Native firms, expand their operations on a commercial rather than Aboriginal rights basis, and broaden the economic base in their communities. This enterprise, in turn, will reduce dependence on government transfers and provide a heightened level of confidence and purpose to the Mi'kmaq and Maliseet communities.

The impact of the *Thomas Peter Paul* case was not limited to New Brunswick, although the struggle played out in the province. Mi'kmaq in Nova Scotia similarly tested their treaty right to cut trees on Crown land and, in 1998, twenty-two Aboriginal loggers found themselves on trial. Most came from Hants County and entered the woods in the aftermath of the Turnbull decision on the *Paul* case. William Nevin, one of the men charged, said: "Fishing, hunting, logging, that's what I like to do. This is our mother earth here, that's where we all come from and someday we will be back there." Non-Aboriginal loggers were less reflective in their descriptions of Aboriginal harvesting. Harlen Redden of Conform Ltd accused the First Nations of "high grading" and poor harvesting practices; he also noted that the total impact of Aboriginal cutting was minimal, constituting about the same as one mechanical harvester.[79] Backed by the

Union of Nova Scotia Indians and thirteen Nova Scotia First Nations, the loggers sought to have their cases assembled into a single trial which, unlike the *Paul* situation, involved the presentation of substantial quantities of oral and written testimony on First Nations logging and other resource activities.[80]

The Nova Scotia government took a hands-off approach on the issue, for the small number of Aboriginal loggers, estimated at around twenty in April 1998, did not represent a major threat to the forest or the industry. Premier Russell MacLellan broke the silence that month when Mi'kmaq foresters moved into the Bornish Highlands ecological reserve on Cape Breton Island. Even at this time, his approach was conciliatory, asking for a meeting with Mi'kmaq chiefs to discuss the issue. The Union of Nova Scotia Indians declared its willingness to meet with the premier, and restated its determination to decide the issue itself: "The Aboriginal people would decide how we're going to exercise our Aboriginal treaty rights. It shouldn't be the Premier. He got no right to tell us how to exercise our rights."[81] Controversy and conflict were minimal, compared with New Brunswick, as the province awaited the appeal of the Turnbull decision.

Ken MacAskill, minister of natural resources for Nova Scotia, was anxious to avoid further conflict. Pleased that the Mi'kmaq loggers agreed not to continue cutting in the ecological reserve, he used the occasion of the Court of Appeal ruling against Mi'kmaq and Maliseet treaty rights to restate his government's willingness to provide First Nations with specific parcels of land in return for assurances of peace in the forest. As he reflected: "Personally, I find it more satisfactory to at least hear people out before using enforcement. Let's not forget the Oka crisis – we don't want anything like that in the woods in Nova Scotia."[82]

In 1998 the *Thomas Peter Paul* case was heralded as a major victory. A year later, First Nations viewed it as a critical defeat. Clearly, it was neither. The court case did not establish – as the *Marshall* decision did – a well-defined Aboriginal commercial right to harvest. Instead, and perhaps more positively, the *Paul* case tested the First Nations of New Brunswick, the provincial government, the forestry industry, and the people at large – and found them up to a remarkable challenge. The court decision could well have been an occasion for long-term conflict and bitter confrontation; less dramatic judgments have had this effect in other parts of Canada. Instead, the government response was forward-looking, innovative, and reasonably long term. The public supported an initiative – the allocation of timber rights to First Nations – even after the legal imperative was lifted and the decision to negotiate with Mi'kmaq and Maliseet people did not survive as a point of political contention. The logging industry in New Brunswick kept its words and emotions in check, worked through the government to ensure continuity of tenure, and pulled back from an initially confrontational stance with the First Nations. For their part, the First Nations leadership overcame strong resistance in their communities to the idea of negotiated settlements, kept up the pressure on governments after the Court of Appeal robbed the Turnbull decision of its power, and sought to capitalize on the commercial opportunities presented by the new arrangements. While only time will tell if the opening was large enough to make a difference and to reorient Aboriginal economies, the First Nations clearly stepped with enthusiasm into the breach.

The New Brunswick First Nations logging issue of 1998–99 was a major victory, but not for any one side. In a situation quite uncharacteristic of indigenous rights conflicts across Canada and around the world, the participants in the New Brunswick situation pulled back from confrontation, stepped outside and around the parameters established by law, and sought a resolution that served the best interests of all participants. One year later, in 2000, the provincial government continued to negotiate timber allocations to First Nations, albeit with one-tenth the publicity and fanfare of the previous year's accords. There appears to be general agreement among all parties that negotiated, band-specific settlements provide an important foundation for future relations. And there is growing evidence, coming from the forests, the sawmills, and the shipping yards across New Brunswick, that meaningful commercial relationships between First Nations and other New Brunswickers provide a strong foundation for future economic ties.

The defeat of the Liberal government in the summer of 1999 and the election of Premier Bernard Lord and the Progressive Conservatives did not destroy the earlier work completed by Premiers Frenette and Thériault and Natural Resources Minister Tyler. The challenge of negotiating agreements with First Nations fell to Brad Green, who was given the dual portfolio of attorney general and minister responsible for Aboriginal affairs, and Jeannot Volpe, minister of natural resources. The government stayed on the track of negotiating logging rights within the 5 per cent limit, a ceiling that the court defeats forced most First Nations to accept reluctantly. The *Marshall* decision, however, reopened the old debate, particularly from the First Nations perspective. Robert Levi of Big Cove, demanding "nation-to-nation" negotiations with Volpe, joined other Maritime First Nations in interpreting "gathering" to include logging. He told the province that the earlier agreement on logging was scrapped: "But we would like to sit and work as partners and try to figure out what is acceptable in terms of Marshall. No more deals. Nation to nation, government to government – this is how we're doing it." Testing the government's resolve, some First Nations, including Big Cove, continued to log in defiance of provincial policy – although official directives to mills not to purchase logs cut on unlicensed lands and occasional seizures of loads of logs proved a significant disincentive.[83]

None of these crucial political and administrative steps would have been taken without the initial decisions in the *Thomas Peter Paul* case. Judge Turnbull's judgment, in particular, has been sharply criticized for its use of evidence and the logic of the ruling. But this case reveals, better than most, that even a case that is subsequently overturned can spur substantial action. Governments, the general public, and business have often been quick to dismiss Aboriginal aspirations; the courts have proved to be the single most important means of getting them to take notice. Only after the *Calder* case, which the Nisga'a lost, did the federal government open the door to comprehensive land claims negotiations. And only after the Turnbull decision did the government of New Brunswick rethink its approach to Aboriginal logging. In the process, the province appears to have learned a great deal about the similarities of the agendas of government, business, and First Nations and about the opportunities for cooperative action. From legal conflict, and even defeat in the courts, the prospect of a new economic, social, and political relationship can emerge.

The final words on the *Thomas Peter Paul* case properly rest with the First Nations. Francis Simon of Big Cove resented the work of the band councils in negotiating deals with the provincial government. The court victory, however shortlived, he said, meant

that we were able to make a living the way our ancestors had intended. Many of us had a great Christmas, for we had access to an income that could not be deprived from us by the band councils, who seem to be in dire need of controlling everything that goes on in this reserve. It gives a person a nice feeling when your children actually see you work for your money. My son who saw me work also wants to work. If the council keeps me on welfare then I suppose it is his destiny to remain on welfare, maybe even choosing suicide as a method of escape ... I choose to exercise my right to make a living in the forest industry, to make a better example for my son, who deserves better. I am waiting for a court ruling that gives me my right back. I thank Thomas Peter Paul for opening our eyes. So if you see me cutting, please know the reason why.[84]

CHAPTER SIX

The Marshall *Crisis* and East Coast Confrontations

To get a good flavour of public opinion in the Maritimes, it is useful to spend some time in Tim Horton's. The coffee and donut shops are ubiquitous in the region, vastly outnumbering McDonald's and other fast-food outlets – and it is here that Maritimers gather to talk. Since 1997 Aboriginal rights has been the hot topic. The words are less generous than in 1997 and the anxiety level clearly higher. The combination of the *Thomas Peter Paul* judgment and counter-judgment and the *Marshall* decision has clearly unsettled the region. Long-standing certainties have been overturned. Once quiet First Nations are now aggressive and confident. Words of bigotry and fury resonate across a part of the country better known for tranquility and a powerful sense of community.

The debate is by no means one-sided. Comments on CBC radio talk-shows, admittedly attracting a more engaged segment of the regional population, often run more than 50 per cent in favour of accepting and extending Aboriginal rights. Even among the fishers there is a substantial sentiment that acknowledges the legitimacy of First Nations claims and hopes for a quick resolution. And, perhaps most significantly, the provincial governments of New Brunswick, Nova Scotia, and, to a lesser extent, Prince Edward Island realize that the court judgments have permanently altered the status quo. Solutions are eagerly sought, and opportunities to discuss short- and medium-term arrangements are generally accepted quickly. "If there's a couple of rowboats out there with a couple of traps celebrating their rights, we don't have a problem with that," one official was quoted as saying.[1] Unlike British Columbia, where key radio talk-show hosts, led by Rafe Mair, captured the agenda and a substantial portion of the collective imagination on Aboriginal rights, there are no media personalities stirring the public sentiment on this issue, and the Irving-owned newspapers and others in the region have adopted a conciliatory tone.

It is wrong, then, to suggest that the court decisions have pulled the scab off Maritime racism and unleashed a vicious backlash against the Mi'kmaq and Maliseet people. There have been tensions in the past, particularly over the Aboriginal food fishery, but relations have generally been calm. It is also wrong to assume, in the aftermath of the dangerous confrontations and angry words of the fall of 1999, that the frustrations and uncertainties of the non-First Nations population in the region have disappeared. Maritimers remain nervous about the *Marshall* decision, and little has been done to assure them that governments have the matter well in hand. Largely private negotiations between the federal government and individual First Nations move the agenda slowly towards a settlement, but the public has little sense of the broader picture that will emerge once agreements are in place. In this situation, with other cases moving through the courts and frustration building again among fishers and First Nations, public anxiety remains high.

Troubles began in the immediate aftermath of the *Marshall* decision. Natives in Nova Scotia and New Brunswick rushed to put traps in the water, anxious to capitalize on the fall 1999 season. Critics claimed they were plundering the resources. Aboriginal people responded sharply, pointing out that the 1,000 traps used by the Burnt Church First Nation represented the work of only three-and-a-half commercial lobster fishermen.[2] Non-Aboriginal fishers had already pulled their traps in some areas, in keeping with Department of Fisheries and Oceans regulations, and bitterly resented the unregulated harvest. Conflicts sprang up along the coast, ranging from yelling matches on wharves throughout the region to vigilante violence at Burnt Church, New Brunswick. As Michael Belliveau of the Maritime Fishermen's Union declared, "The commercial fishermen in that area who rely on that stock are being asked to shoulder 300 years of grievance of the native people."[3] John Riley, the chair of the Fisheries Council, did some regional calculations and did not like the sums: "In Nova Scotia, there are about 6,000 native families. I don't know what the court meant by a reasonable livelihood, in its decision, but if it's in the order of $30,000 to $40,000, you're talking about a couple of million dollars on an annual basis and the current industry doesn't have the capacity. That represents over 30 per cent of the entire landed value of the Nova Scotia fishery."[4] Government leaders warned repeatedly that violence would not be tolerated, but few politicians showed up on the wharves to meet with the fishers face to face.

As the cacophony of voices echoed throughout the Maritimes, the dispute quickly lost touch with the reality of the situation. Arguments that the Aboriginal commercial fishery would soon eviscerate the coastal industry were wrong-headed and exaggerated. Most estimates of the impact of the *Marshall*-supported First Nations catch called for only a marginal increase in the total harvest. On earlier occasions, the federal government had secured a niche for Aboriginal fishers by buying out non-Aboriginal commercial operations on a market-value basis. While some major, long-term issues remained unresolved – several decades will pass before there is a clear understanding of the full economic and industry-specific impact of the *Marshall* decision on the east coast fishery – the hysteria of the moment did not mesh with the short-term implications. Few Maritime First Nations were ready for a sizable expansion of fishing operations, even under *Marshall*, and the state of the lobster industry was such that a modest increase in harvest would carry neither ecological nor market risk. The simple fact that First Nations had secured legally, constitutionally protected access to the commercial fishery appeared to be the touchstone in this case, and the hostility and anger among the non-Aboriginal fishers would not soon die down.

The lobster fishery posed great difficulties. The industry is well organized, with each region enjoying a specified open season to ensure that local fishers have ready access to a market. When, as happened in 1999, Aboriginal fishers hit the water in "closed season," they were challenging management and economic rules, not conservation considerations. The system was designed to prevent the market from being flooded and to keep lobster prices high. Under the Aboriginal Fisheries Strategy, bands had negotiated their way into the fishery beginning in 1993. Burnt Church, for example, had an annual quota of some 135,000 kilograms of lobster. Although the system had been in place for the better part of a decade, some non-Aboriginal fishers, particularly in the Burnt Church region, were still hostile to the "special" status these people enjoyed in the fishery.

The Maritime lobster season is organized by region within specific dates. From 30 April to 30 June, lobster fishing is permitted off the north coast of New Brunswick, north of Prince Edward Island, and in the waters between PEI and Nova Scotia. The fishing grounds between Prince Edward Island and north-central New Brunswick are open from 9 August to 10 October. Waters off the northeast coast of Cape Breton Island can be fished from 15 May to 15 July. Fishers can harvest lobster between eastern Cape Breton and the Nova Scotia mainland from 10 May to 10 July, and the area immediately to the north from 19 May to 20 July. The waters off the northwest tip of continental Nova Scotia are open from 29 April to 20 June, and the two lobster zones immediately to the south (off the east coast of central Nova Scotia) from 19 April to 20 June. The area off the southwest and southern coastline of Nova Scotia is open from the last Monday of November to 31 May, and the upper Bay of Fundy can be fished for lobster from the last day of February to 31 July and from 14 October to 31 December. The New Brunswick coast of the Bay of Fundy is open from 31 March to 29 June and from the second Tuesday in November to 14 January. Open season in the area around Campobello Island, New Brunswick, runs from the second Tuesday in November to 29 June. This arrangement, as noted earlier, addresses conservation needs and ensures that Maritime lobster fishers are not all bringing their product to market at the same time. (See Appendix B)

Observers wondered, from the beginning, about the nature of non-Aboriginal protests over the fishery. In 1995 a report of the Fisheries Resource Conservation Council (a federal agency) warned of over-harvesting. Industry people rejected the suggestion and refused to cut back. Later, lobster fishers argued for more flexible regulations and larger catch limits. Now, in a critical about-face, they contend that a relatively small First Nations fishery would wreak havoc on the industry and suggested that *Marshall*-based harvesting would destroy the resource. And the number was, indeed, small. Estimates in mid-October claimed that the First Nations had set about 12,000 traps – a tiny figure compared with the almost 2 million traps dropped annually by the commercial fishermen.[5]

Public interest in the conflict obscured the more cooperative approaches adopted by some Mi'kmaq groups. The Mi'kmaq of Conne River, Newfoundland, stayed out of the escalating controversy, determined to protect the fish farming, logging, and guiding that sustained their small community.[6] In other communities, hands reached across the cultural divide. First Nations and non-Aboriginal fishers at St Mary's Bay, Nova Scotia, based on several years of professional negotiations, calmed emotions and worked towards sustainable solutions. In doing so, they continued the work of the Bay of Fundy Fisheries Council, established by fishers to ensure the long-term survival of the fishery in the area. The shift away from federal control to community-based management provided a structure that readily – although not always easily – accommodated Aboriginal aspirations, even before the *Marshall* ruling. The coincidence of community-centred decision-making and ecologically sensitive approaches to resource management meshed easily with Aboriginal concepts.[7] Well into the heat of the conflict, Aboriginal fishers reported continuing good relations with non-Aboriginal people. Bernd Christmas of the Nova Scotia Assembly of Mi'kmaq Chiefs said: "There's tremendous goodwill on the part of the fishing community to work with us. What we're getting is that people want to sit down with us and dialogue."[8] Aboriginal leaders even offered to meet directly with the Maritime Fishermen's Union, only to have their invitation rejected.

Cooperation would not be the hallmark of Maritime fishing after *Marshall*, and the federal government found itself with an extremely difficult political and administrative challenge. The task of handling the *Marshall* fallout fell to Herb Dhaliwal, a second-term cabinet minister from British Columbia and minister of the Department of Fisheries and Oceans. A Vancouver politician of East Indian descent, appointed in the summer of 1999, Dhaliwal positioned himself as a man of business, but he had had little time to put his strategy in place. He wanted to add value to Canadian fishing, develop new markets, and increase efficiencies in the industry, all the while adhering to a conservationist agenda. He talked of developing markets for new species, expanding the network of fish farms, encouraging fishers to work with more than one species, and broadening the base for traditionally seasonal fish-processing plants.[9] These goals would become issues for his second year in office.

By almost any reckoning, Dhaliwal mismanaged the file from the beginning. In the aftermath of the *Marshall* decision, he called on people to "exercise patience and restraint," commenting on 20 September: "We are working with other federal departments to analyze the implications of the decision. As soon as we have completed our preliminary review, we will engage in dialogue with Aboriginal communities, provincial governments and other stakeholders in the fisheries."[10] He then went into seclusion with his department officials for several days. When he did emerge, he again asked for calm and insisted he would enforce conservation regulations as a top priority. In a profound understatement that only irritated observers, he noted on 23 September: "There is no doubt that there will have to be some changes in the management of our Atlantic fisheries to reflect this agreement and our relationship with Mi'kmaq communities."[11] Dhaliwal assigned the task of making sense of *Marshall* to a senior administrative group, continued to ask for calm, and promised action in the near future. Most critically, he postponed a personal trip to the Maritimes for a full two weeks. Meanwhile, fishers begged for clarification and action, the First Nations laid plans for a full-scale Aboriginal fishery, tensions escalated and tempers flared.

In December 1999 internal documents revealed that the Department of Fisheries and Oceans did not have a contingency plan for dealing with the Supreme Court decision. In August, a month before the judgment, the department indicated to the minister that "approaches for addressing the substance of the decision will be developed after the decision is rendered." The briefing note continued: "Because of the range of possibilities for the decision, contingency planning is difficult. The immediate message will be that the decision is being reviewed and will emphasize the importance of conservation and responsible fishing." Mike Belliveau of the Maritime Fishermen's Union sadly bluntly: "We hold them responsible for the fact that the thing exploded up here in New Brunswick. They don't grasp what we've being dealing with for a number of years. They don't grasp the intensity of commercial fishermen's feelings around this thing where they're being asked to give up a portion of their livelihood in a context where they're not clear where it will end." Peter Stoffer, New Democratic Party critic, was more blunt: "This is madness, pure madness. Take about your pure disaster. That's Communications 101."[12]

As one New Brunswick observer wrote, "Like an unskilled parent who gives in to a child's temper tantrum, the Department of Fisheries and Oceans waited until violence occurred to bring the minister here to meet face-to-face with leaders in the fishery. Why the delay? It lends the appearance of rewarding lawlessness. Or is it more evidence that only when a riot breaks out does distant Ottawa become truly what Mr. Dhaliwal claims to have been since the September 17 Marshall ruling: preoccupied by the Atlantic fishery."[13] It was a disappointing performance, to be sure, and one that stirred, rather than calmed, the waters in the Maritimes. As the *Telegraph Journal* editorialized: "Knowing that non-native fishermen were growing impatient, that clashes occur often in Miramichi Bay, and that the native fishery has been a source of friction in the area for nearly a decade, Mr. Dhaliwal should have put as many enforcement officers on the wharves and on the water last week as were necessary to keep the peace. He didn't and a confrontation that could have been prevented now threatens to divide the area beyond the succour of reason. The free-for-all Mr. Dhaliwal said he wouldn't permit has already begun."[14] Rod Allen of the *Times & Transcript* had harsher words: "I was surprised to learn they [non-Aboriginal fishers] are not all that disappointed with what they feel are new Fisheries Minister Herb Dhaliwal's apparent lack of preparation for the Supreme Court judgement, his slow-footed response once it was announced and his cowardly decision – once it was finally made – to wait 30 days before closing the native lobster fishery on the Miramichi and Sou-west Nova Scotia. They're simply not surprised, considering he is no different from any other federal minister who continues to get his advice from the same old bureaucracy."[15]

Dhaliwal's subsequent actions were an improvement. After a week of inaction, the Department of Fisheries and Oceans announced that conservation regulations would be enforced. The minister also began, some two weeks after the Supreme Court decision, to hold meetings with fishers and First Nations. He continued to plead for calm, and asked for time to develop workable solutions. Dhaliwal placed his confidence in negotiations and mediation. In mid-October he assigned a seasoned negotiator, James MacKenzie, the chief federal negotiator for Labrador land claims, to the task of finding a workable solution. MacKenzie was joined in November by Gilles Thériault, a former executive director of the Maritime Fishermen's Union, who was named as assistant federal negotiator. Chief Lawrence Paul of the Atlantic Policy Council of First Nation Chiefs said of MacKenzie's appointment, "We are very pleased." Mike Belliveau of the Maritime Fishermen's Union was less sanguine: "I think a negotiator is obviously going to need pretty substantial financial backing for whatever he does because the way the fishery has evolved, it is all limited-entry fishery."[16] The intended resolution focused on band-by-band fishing allocations – a mirror of the New Brunswick strategy in the logging dispute – designed to allow First Nations to fish without upsetting local fishers. It was also clear that, given the sweep of the *Marshall* decision, consideration had to be given to the inclusion of other species (snow crab, smelt, etc.) in the agreements. The medium-term solution offered by the Department of Fisheries and Oceans was more of the same, reinforced by the purchase of lobster and other licences from non-Aboriginal fishers and grants to First Nations to allow them to purchase boats and otherwise benefit from the expanded Aboriginal harvesting right. Six months on, Dhaliwal's reputation had been rebuilt somewhat, but his handling of the episode damaged his political reputation and that of the federal Liberal Party in the region. Conflict avoidance, rather than the development of a viable, long-term solution to the matter of Aboriginal rights, appeared to be Dhaliwal's primary objective.

The public response to Dhaliwal's performance was largely critical. Initially, there was support for his effort to bring a more businesslike perspective to the fishery: as one industry representative said, "The age of building fish plants only so local people can earn enough weeks of work to get pogey cheques are long gone, and he just might be the guy to bring a little bit of sense back into it." After *Marshall*, Dhaliwal became the focus of intense criticism. One fisheries worker, Mireille Cormier, claimed: "He wasn't ready for such an important position ... Why weren't they prepared for that [conflict over the *Marshall* decision]? Where was the leadership."[17] Certainly, the mild-mannered cabinet minster had not taken charge of the first major test of his administration of the east coast fishery when he released his long-awaited statement on 1 October 1999. He said he wanted an interim agreement, which would remain in place while a long-term settlement was reached. He offered no apology for the delay in responding, arguing that it had taken time to digest the Supreme Court decision. And he said that government policy would be dictated by four principles: conservation, fairness, transparency, and partnership. He concluded philosophically: "Every challenge is an opportunity. The opportunity here is for all of us to demonstrate some of the values that make this country great: our tolerance, our generosity, our willingness to work together, and our respect for the law and the Supreme Court."[18] To emphasize his point, he added later, "I will not allow a free-for-all on the water."[19]

The minister's announcement touched off an angry response by off-reserve and non-status Indians. Dhaliwal indicated that he would work initially only with reserve governments, holding out the hope of latter negotiations. On the lobster issue, as with logging, groups like the Aboriginal Peoples Council attempted to be part of the negotiations. The continued insistence by governments on band-to-government discussions effectively barred the off-reserve, non-status, and Métis groups, some of whose members nonetheless insisted on exercising their Aboriginal right to harvest resources commercially. In some quarters, this approach also revived a debate about the appropriateness of working through elected band councils. Millie Augustine attempted to organize a New Brunswick campaign to force the federal government to negotiate with a coalition of Aboriginal peoples, not with elected chiefs and their councils. As she noted, "Based on past performance, we don't trust our native governments."[20] Non-status, off-reserve, and Métis people continued to intervene, hoping (and failing) to get a seat at the negotiating table. In October close to one hundred members of the Nation of Acadian Métis went to Ottawa in an attempt to get attention. Richard Hopper argued: "They've forgotten about us. We're the off-reserve, non-status Indians, but we have just as much right to hunt and fish as our cousins living on reserves. The reserve chiefs only represent a fraction of the people who claim native heritage. I'm a direct descendant of the people that signed that treaty and I want my rights. The provincial government wants to ignore us, but we're not going to go away. We're going to fight for everything we're entitled to."[21] It was an emotional appeal, but once again these groups found themselves on the outside looking in.

Non-Aboriginal fishers, who had demanded a complete halt to Aboriginal harvesting, were also furious: "We're regulated to death and by not regulating natives on the same basis as we are is complete racism. If they have the right to fish, they must fish within the regulations we have." Michael Belliveau was clearly annoyed: "The waiting time is over, the meeting times are over. There's a long history of fishermen and fishermen's families. To ask them to step aside just like that, I don't know what world some of these guys are living in." Nova Scotia premier John Hamm had hoped for a cooling-off period and was likewise disappointed that the federal government had not done more.[22] As Zoel Breau of the Maritime Fishermen's Union commented bitterly: "The lobster will be gone soon. We should place two lobsters in a zoo somewhere, so that people can see what we once had."[23] The union declared that it would boycott any meetings until the Aboriginal boats stopped fishing.

Maritime anger was not limited to the minster and, from the outset, expressions of frustration escalated throughout the region. Early in the conflict, non-Aboriginal Maritimers, including Premier John Hamm of Nova Scotia,[24] appealed to the prime minister to prevent a "potentially explosive situation" by suspending the Aboriginal right to hunt and fish until the decision could be considered and plans made. The Maritime Fishermen's Union petitioned Jean Chrétien on this account, drawing attention to the "confusion and consternation" running rampant through the Maritimes.[25] Even though politicians like Elsie Wayne, the populist, outspoken, and often off the wall MP for Saint John, weighed in on the issue, demanding that the federal government use the notwithstanding clause in the constitution to overrule the Supreme Court, Dhaliwal rejected the suggestion. MPs' offices in the region were swamped with demands for action, and politicians faced dozens of inquiries from worried constituents. A meeting at Yarmouth, Nova Scotia, on 26 September 1999 attracted over seven hundred angry and anxious lobster fishers, who gathered to complain about the *Marshall* ruling and to consider heading out onto the water to compete with the First Nations. Although tempers flared, the meeting agreed to give the federal government a week to resolve the issue. On 28 September Dhaliwal said, "Suspending the judgement is not within my mandate, but I will raise it with my cabinet colleagues."[26] To most observers, the government's response was cautious, conciliatory, and hopelessly inadequate.

Anger raged across the Maritimes. Seafood processors worried about the industry's future.[27] Charles Moore, writing an opinion piece for the regional press, reacted strongly to reports of a 6,000 pound haul of lobster by a single boat: "As for goodwill and patience, I wish Mr. Dhaliwal lotsa' luck in selling that brand of dog food to non-native fishermen with hundreds of thousands of dollars invested in boats and gear, now obliged to sit ashore seething as natives land thousands of pounds of out-of-season lobster, to sell for prices seasonal fisherman can only dream of." Moore quoted a fisher from Nova Scotia saying, "Nobody wants [violence] but we've all got guns." And another: "I don't want to see anybody get hurt ... but I'm not going to be a second-class citizen either."[28] Harold Therieault, president of the Bay of Fundy Fishermen's Association, noted: "There's fear here and anger. I was even getting threats myself. Everybody's so dependent on this lobster fishery here. This fishery survived because it was so well taken care of. But we've seen so darn much underground, black market work going on, by both native and non-native people. What I am hoping for is that we can work out solutions."[29]

At the same time, the non-Aboriginal fishers asked processing plants to boycott the Native harvests, hoping to choke off the market and quell demand.[30] The Maritime Fishermen's Union threatened to ask members to stop selling lobsters to any plant buying from Mi'kmaq fishers, and announced that it had "suspicions" about who might be buying the First Nations' catch.[31] Complaints mounted. Kevin Cassidy, a veteran fisher, argued: "It's too many traps in molting season and nobody else fishes this time of year because you try to let the lobster grow so you have something for next year. Lobster can't last and if you fish them year round they're going to disappear after a while." His colleague from the Miramichi Bay region, Wilmot Loggie, concurred: " I hope the government has sense enough to step in and do something or our livelihood is pretty well over."[32] Belliveau declared: "It's a dog's breakfast. We shouldn't be asked to stand aside while our moderate livelihoods are put to ruin."[33] Demanding that the government stop the Burnt Church fishery, Loggie said: "I think they are waiting for someone to get hurt. You get a group of 1,000, 2,000 men together, there's no telling what could happen." Fighting words hardly calmed the waters, and threats to burn boats, destroy traps, and otherwise disrupt the Aboriginal fishery proved an ineffective means of bringing the First Nations to the table.[34]

The federal government tried to get Mi'kmaq leaders to pull their communities' fishing boats off the water, counting on Aboriginal good will to buy the government time. Most went along, convinced that a good deal lay in the offing and worried about the steady escalation in the anger and frustration of the non-Aboriginal community. Aboriginal frustration remained high. As Chief Lawrence Paul observed, "The non-Indians don't want to share. But due to Supreme Court decisions, the rules of the game have changed and they'll have to share, whether they like it or not. I think the bottom line on the whole thing is not conservation, it's not about saving fish stocks, the bottom line is greed."[35] Elsewhere, officials asked Mi'kmaq fishers to abide by established communal licence provisions and regulations, a request that most simply laughed off. Communal licences for specific quotas are allocated to entire communities, not to individuals, and it is up to the community to decide how the harvest is distributed. A few bands – Yarmouth, Burnt Church, and Baie des Chaleurs – refused to back down, however, and continued to fish for lobster. The Department of Fisheries and Oceans had no other strategy at hand, and regional officials knew that the First Nations leaders were in a difficult spot. Department spokesman André-Marc Lanteigne observed: "It is difficult. It is a tough thing to ask. They just had these new rights and for us to ask them to get out of the water for a cool-off period ... But it is the only thing we could do at the time."[36] Stopping Aboriginal people from fishing in the midst of Supreme Court-induced euphoria was a difficult task, and communities like Burnt Church revelled in the income and promised independence.[37]

Coastal communities were, in the fall of 1999, experiencing a euphoria similar to that which had engulfed New Brunswick First Nations bands following the *Thomas Peter Paul* decision. Some communities participated actively in both periods of judicial liberation, with loggers heading to the forests after the *Paul* decision and fishers heading onto the ocean for lobster after the *Marshall* decision. The excitement was palpable along the Atlantic coast, for the Court ruling granted First Nations a clear, constitutionally protected right that also held considerable commercial potential. Communities long-squeezed by high unemployment and low incomes celebrated the opportunity to earn a decent and potentially sustainable income. Non-Aboriginal critics who had earlier complained about First Nations dependence on government "handouts" now expressed deep concern and anger over the prospect that the same Aboriginal people would fish too much and too hard, cutting into their earnings and providing what they saw as "unfair" competition. Among the First Nations themselves, the response to *Marshall* paralleled the reaction to the *Paul* judgment, and young men in particular readied themselves for a quick and decisive move into the industry.

Efforts to contain the crisis continued, on First Nations reserves, at fishers' meetings, and in negotiations with the government. On 29 September Donald Marshall Jr joined the fray, asking the chiefs to pull the boats from the water and urging them to negotiate with government officials. Marshall himself was no firebrand and did not relish the limelight that followed the Supreme Court decision. He re-entered the fray only reluctantly, shying away from most public gatherings, news conferences, and political discussions. Whether he wanted it or not, however, Marshall now commanded considerable personal respect, both for his two difficult tussles with the Canadian legal system and as a symbol of the attainment of long-lost treaty rights in the region. When he did attend public events, he was applauded strongly by First Nations people and their supporters. With very few exceptions (including one potentially awkward and difficult confrontation with non-Aboriginal critics in a bar near his reserve), he did not engage in open debate with opponents of the Supreme Court judgment. "We waited this long," he said. "I think we could wait a little longer."[38] Aboriginal leaders gathered at meetings of the Atlantic Policy Congress to determine strategy and build support for a strong Aboriginal position. Realizing that containing the more assertive bands and fishers might result in criticism of their leadership, the chiefs took a cautious approach, celebrating the Supreme Court victory, restating their newly gained rights, and demanding that government adhere to the requirements of the decision. After a meeting at the end of September, First Nations and government officials agreed to set up a task force to deal with the matter, with the vital caveat that Aboriginal fishers did not have to stop harvesting lobsters.

Protests swelled, in number and intensity. One hundred angry fishers gathered at the offices of Liberal MP Charles Hubbard (Miramichi) and demanded action: an ominous telephone message left on his answering machine said simply, "If Mr. Hubbard doesn't do anything, blood is going to be shed." Small, random acts of vandalism occurred around the region. Burnt Church remained the centre of the controversy, with close to one hundred (one-tenth of the population) fishers from the community on the water.[39] Belliveau, the leading spokesman for the Maritime Fishermen's Union, could barely contain his growing frustration: "This isn't a couple of motorboats out there with some poor bastard trying to make a living. This is big business. We don't want our quarrel to be with the natives, we want the federal government to come up with a rational interpretation of this ruling – but we have to close the bay in the meantime. There is no other way to look at it." According to local estimates, the Burnt Church fishers had pulled in over 130,000 pounds of lobster in only thirteen days – compared with a licensed haul of some 600,000 pounds for the May–June period. The gradual onset of winter weather slowed the harvest, which flourished in large measure because the First Nations harvest had centred on the inshore fishery, where lobsters were comparatively easy to catch.[40] Fishers continued to protest, to little avail, complaining about both the unlicensed harvest and the fact that Mi'kmaq fishers did not have to adhere to federal fisheries guidelines. Reports that the Department of Fisheries and Oceans had ordered fisheries officers to ignore Aboriginal transgression unless truly flagrant only inflamed passions more. Non-Aboriginal solidarity was far from complete. Stories surfaced from several fishing areas, including Miramichi Bay, that non-Natives were assisting First Nations with their harvests. The region inched towards confrontation.

The media, meanwhile, had arrived en masse in the Maritimes, drawn by the familiar Canadian tale of Aboriginal versus non-Aboriginal resource use and by the less common national sight of potential violence and intemperate comments. Camera crews showed up routinely on wharves, much to the irritation of Aboriginal and non-Aboriginal fishers alike. Reporters rushed down to Maine to interview the Passamaquoddy and then back to Burnt Church or Yarmouth for the latest fishers' rally. By early October several television crews were onsite, ready to report news of the rapidly unfolding events. In short order, they had interesting images to report to Canadians.

The *Marshall* decision made the Treaty Day celebrations at Province House in Halifax on 1 October particularly poignant. Donald Marshall Sr had revived the tradition of Treaty Day in 1986, referring to a clause in a 1752 treaty which called for an annual gathering of Mi'kmaq and non-Aboriginal government leaders. The 1999 meeting, which attracted 150 observers, celebrated the *Marshall* decision and was highlighted by calls from Aboriginal leaders, including Alex Denny, grand captain of the Mi'kmaq Grant Council, and Lawrence Paul of the Assembly of Nova Scotia Mi'kmaq Chiefs, for more substantial government reaction to the *Marshall* decision and Mi'kmaq treaty rights.[41] The celebrations and the growing regional controversy sparked wide-ranging discussion of the possibilities arising out of the Supreme Court decision. As Joe B. Marshall, a faculty member from the University College of Cape Breton, said, "I'm going to feel pretty damn proud this Treaty Day." Professor Marshall reflected on the court's phrase "a moderate income" and offered the opinion that it might extend to about $80,000 a year. Others talked about the possibility of demanding compensation for the many years when Mi'kmaq fishers were denied access to the commercial fishery. As Chief Paul concluded, "The day I'll celebrate is the day that we no longer have to go to court to enjoy the treaty rights guaranteed by our forefathers. I'll celebrate when society at large comes to grips with the rights of our people. To date, that hasn't happened."[42]

On 3 October non-Aboriginal fishers struck in a dramatic pre-dawn Sunday attack on Mi'kmaq lobster traps in Miramichi Bay. An armada of some 150 boats from Neguac and Escuminac hit the water, destroying as many as 3,000 traps. The fishers appear to have pulled up next to buoys, raised the lobster traps, let the lobsters out, vandalized the gear, then thrown it back into the water. After the attack,

Aboriginal and non-Aboriginal people gathered on the wharf, screaming abuse at each other and pushing and shoving in frustration. The RCMP stepped in and separated the groups before serious fighting broke out. When the RCMP and the Department of Fisheries and Oceans investigated the unlawful attack, they declared their intention to lay charges once sufficient information had been gathered. Edward Francis, a Mi'kmaq Warrior, threatened, "We will do exactly the same thing to them in May (when the regular lobster season opened.)."[43] A non-Aboriginal boat carrying a CBC Newsworld crew was greeted by an angry group of Mi'kmaq, who believed that the boat had participated in the attack on the traps. At least two Mi'kmaq men were injured in the various scuffles.

The situation worsened quickly. Vandals broke into the Burnt Church reserve school and messed the principal's office. Angry mobs, perhaps one hundred strong, descended on fish processing plants in Aldouane, Pointe Sapin, and Richibucto. They attacked computers, overturned vending machines, and tried to break into the coolers. The dozen or so employees in one of the plants fled in the face of the unruly fishers, who proceeded to ransack the buildings. Attacks spread throughout the area. Vandals damaged a shed on a nearly wharf and, allegedly, threw captured live lobsters back into the ocean. Trucks owned by non-Aboriginal people were torched in retaliation. Two Aboriginally owned pickups were also destroyed. A truck carrying several Aboriginal people was rammed by a van, and two of the passengers were confined to hospital, one in serious condition. An empty cottage on the reserve near the wharf was also torched, a poignant symbol of the disintegrating relations between Mi'kmaq and non-Aboriginal people. A few days later, an Aboriginal religious structure was also destroyed by arsonists.

Throughout the Burnt Church area, tempers stayed at a fever pitch and police patrolled nervously, worried about the next outbreak. The men justified their actions. André Martin of the Escuminac Wharf Committee claimed: "We're just here to protect our rights. We're here to make a living. If we don't protect our rights, Baie St. Anne is over. Miramichi is over, New Brunswick is over, and we may as well get out of Canada. We got nothing left."

In Nova Scotia, angry fishers gathered in a Yarmouth gymnasium. While the meeting agreed to give more time to the federal government, some participants wanted immediate action: "There's no room in the fishery," one man yelled. "Let's get the gear out of the water. I'm going to cut gear off now."[44] Many local residents were mortified by the escalation of violence and the bitter words that swirled around the region. A clearly shaken Camille Cormier, a fisher from St Louisde-Kent, said: "It doesn't look good for the future. I think someone's going to get killed. It's too bad. It's a shame."[45] Mi'kmaq people feared for their safety and looked with suspicion on former friends and neighbours in the areas. Anne Dedam offered an all-too-poignant description of what had changed in their area: "We were getting along until this happened. Now when you drive up to a stop light and see a non-native, you get the finger."[46] Donald Marshall Jr, furious at the turn of events, could scarcely contain his anger: "If the Supreme Court, or if Canadians, don't accept what happened, well that's too God-damned bad. We've been treated wrong a long time and we'll always be treated wrong."[47] Fishers on over 150 non-Aboriginal fishing boats united at Yarmouth, Nova Scotia, in a protest over the First Nations fishery. Fists flew, and the police had to step in to make several quick arrests. The unruly crowd destroyed First Nations traps, then worked its way to a nearby Aboriginal home, where only intervention by the RCMP prevented further violence.[48] It was a nasty scene, and could easily have been much worse.

The Mi'kmaq prepared to defend themselves and their property. The morning after the destruction and vandalism, on 4 October 1999, Mi'kmaq Warriors had surrounded the wharf at Burnt Church with flags and teepees and had effectively occupied the facility. The First Nations returned to the ocean, albeit with fewer traps. Attacks on the school frightened many Mi'kmaq parents, a sizable number of whom opted to keep their children at home and away from the fray. On a broader level, Atlantic Mi'kmaq chiefs gathered in Halifax to discuss the option of establishing a month-long moratorium on fishing, a move designed to resolve the crisis and to raise the stature of the Aboriginal community. Their critics, the non-Aboriginal fishers, took their cause on the road, travelling to the Department of Fisheries and Oceans office in Moncton.[49]

Dhaliwal played his now-traditional role, asking for calm, demanding a short-term agreement, and promising to close the fishery if no deal was forthcoming. He increased surveillance by RCMP and Fisheries Department officers and reiterated that violence would not be tolerated, but he moved the agenda forward slowly. Government policy remained as muddied as before, as the prime minister and his minister of fisheries and oceans offered different opinions on the question of asking the Supreme Court to suspend the decision until a deal could be worked out. Chrétien, always acutely sensitive to public condemnation, responded vigorously to claims that his government had "blown it." Defending himself and his administration, he offered an explantion that could well be the most precise summary of the political principles animating his government: "In public administration there is always new problems coming up to the surface, and you take one problem at a time and you resolve it one step at a time."[50]

Dhaliwal agreed to meet with non-Aboriginal fishers, some three hundred of whom gathered outside the Fisheries office in Moncton. The federal government remained the focus for their anger, and they once again demanded immediate action. They argued that First Nations were welcome into the fishery, provided they operated according to the same rules and did not displace existing licence holders without compensation. A half-hearted attempt by the fishers to push their way into the building failed, as RCMP officers and others kept their protest under control.[51] Dhaliwal turned to his formidable task with determination, shuffling between the non-Aboriginal and First Nations groups. He quickly convinced the Maritime Fishermen's Union and the Prince Edward Island Fishermen's Association that he meant business, and managed to soothe the tempers among the commercial fishers.

The minister's approach to the First Nations also produced results. The Acadia First Nations, based near Yarmouth, Nova Scotia, had been the focus of considerable controversy. Local non-Aboriginal fishers complained loudly about the "threat" to their industry and threatened to pull the Mi'kmaq traps from the water if the First Nations fishers proceeded. Anxious to avoid a bitter confrontation, the Acadia First Nation decided in early October to adopt a thirty-day moratorium on fishing. This action was welcomed by all sides in the dispute, and pulling the boats quickly pleased the Yarmouth non-Aboriginal fishers. Even here, however, signs of tensions abounded. The apparently intentional scuttling of a non-status Aboriginal's fishing boat seemed to have been related to the spreading controversy, although the accusation was unproven.[52] In mid-October the Yarmouth controversy flared yet again. The burning of the home of a non-Native fisherman – which the police said was not related to the lobster conflict – stirred passions. Shoving matches followed, with Non-Aboriginal fishers declaring their determination to dredge the bottom of the ocean of First Nations lobster traps.[53] Said Don Cunningham, a fish plant owner, "They're frustrated [the non-Aboriginal fishers] and they want to do something. Even it it's only coming to Yarmouth and gathering to show the public that the fishing industry means something."[54] A potential clash was averted when Mi'kmaq leaders agreed not to set any traps and called off planned demonstrations in the area.[55]

Parker Barse Donham, a columnist for the Halifax *Daily News* and resident of Cape Breton, was irritated by the Yarmouth outbursts:

"That Yarmouth should be a centre of the protest was ironic. The town sits smack in the middle of Lobster Fishing Area 34, the richest lobster fishery in the world, with landings of $149 million – an average of $152,010 per boat – in 1998. Yarmouth is also a hotbed of illegal fishing – an activity frowned upon in most other parts of Atlantic Canada. Fishermen in LFA 34 can legally set up to 400 traps, 50 per centre more than any other district. Informed observers estimate they set another 25 per cent in illegal traps. It works out to 100,00 illegal traps in the Yarmouth area along compared to 5,000 Mi'kmaq traps in all of Nova Scotia."[56]

The confrontation at Burnt Church appeared to have surprised and chastened the protestors, who were somewhat mollified by the news that Dhaliwal had agreed to come to the Maritimes to meet with them. Non-Aboriginal people, fearing retaliation from the First Nation, petitioned officials for action and protection. Said one woman from New Jersey, near Burnt Church: "My husband has been threatened. This isn't about fishing anymore. This is about two communities."[57] The failure of political leaders to come to the site of the conflict to address both sides in the dispute remained an oddity. During the conflict, Atlantic premiers sent messages from their meeting with New England governors, calling for calm and urging the federal government to move, though they did not condemn Dhaliwal for acting too slowly. The unwillingness of any provincial or federal leader to respond personally to the crisis added to the sense of distance and isolation. Non-Aboriginal fishers, in particular, wondered who, if anyone, was on their side. The provincial premiers did, however, phone the prime minister and the minister of fisheries and oceans to demand action.[58] More to the point, a little after the fact, the RCMP brought an additional thirty-five officers to the Neguac detachment to patrol the community.

Apart from the political meetings, non-Aboriginal and First Nations people from Burnt Church began the difficult process of rebuilding relations between the communities. A prayer service was held on 7 October to draw the people together, and local non-Natives, such as David Warmer, organized a closed-door meeting in an endeavour to overcome the bitterness: "We have a long, long healing process to go through to just get back to where we were."[59] Small acts of kindness and reconciliation provided a vital, but at this point inadequate, counterbalance to the more public demonstrations of antipathy. More than fifty non-Aboriginal community members met with RCMP officers and local members of parliament, seeking assurance they would be protected and the hooligans controlled. On 7 October a small group gathered at St David's United Church to pray for reconciliation. Gkisedtanamooqk, one of the Burnt Church reserve's spiritual leaders, offered prayer and hope for reconciliation.[60] It was a start.

The region waited, and the people around Burnt Church prepared for the next stage in the struggle. Worry hung in the air. Mi'kmaq Warriors patrolled the wharves and the reserve. Police maintained their presence. Aboriginal and non-Aboriginal watched each other with distrust and disdain. Someone brought a generator onto the wharf to keep the coffee flowing – what one person called the "Mi'kmaq Horton's." People whose friendship had bridged the cultural divide now stared awkwardly at each other, not sure of how the community as a whole regarded them. The end of the violent outburst had not brought Burnt Church back to its former state. "There was always a little bit of racism here," Robert Sylliboy noted. "It wasn't blown out of proportion but behind your back, you could hear 'you dirty Indian, go back to your reservation. We don't need you here.' Now it's not behind your back, it's to your face."[61] Non-Natives living at Burnt Church – off the reserve – fretted. The old order, where people worked, lived, and played together, was gone. The police investigations into the violence at Burnt Church continued, and those involved in the rowdiness feared imminent arrest – although few were repentant about their actions. The Fisheries Department had had seven boats on the water during the attacks on the Mi'kmaq traps and each carried at least one RCMP officer, armed with a camera. Everyone knew that years of healing would be needed to restore old relationships – provided violence did not erupt once more. Those who thought that the conflict was about lobster were probably wrong; it was more about relationships and the capacity for Aboriginal and non-Aboriginal people to coexist. The people of Burnt Church had learned, bitterly, that the prospects for the future were poor indeed.

The critical meeting in Halifax between the minister of fisheries and oceans and the thirty-five Atlantic First Nations chiefs, supported by Aboriginal leaders from across the country, took place on 6 October 1999. Although discussions were tense and disagreements repeatedly surfaced, they did agree to a voluntary thirty-day moratorium. The decision came only after Dhaliwal left the meeting. According to reports from the session, it was Ben Sylliboy, grand chief of the Mi'kmaq Grand Council, who convinced the chiefs of the need for a break in the confrontation. The chiefs asked for a freeze on all fishing – Native and non-Native – while a suitable deal was negotiated.[62] Fishers' representatives were called to a meeting on 9 October in Truro, Nova Scotia, to discuss the delay of the opening of the lobster season. The fishers were not pleased with the prospect of surrendering the first part of the harvest that brought them between $20,000 and $30,000 a year. Suggestions that fishers be compensated for any loss was quickly rejected by the minister.[63]

The First Nations reaction, particularly from Burnt Church, was far less pleasant. Gaylen Paul told the community: "I ain't listening to anybody. They don't want to listen to the people, to hell with them." Millie Augustine was even more angry: "If they agree to the moratorium, that's fine, but we're not going along with it. They went there and promised to stand up for our rights. They betrayed us."[64] Fishers at Burnt Church, hustling to replace their damaged traps (they ordered 1,000 at $70 each), declared their intention to return to the lobster fishery, screaming their defiance at First Nations chiefs who they described as "sellouts." Glen Thompson of Rexton captured the intensity of the feeling:

We have had enough of waiting and talking and sitting at the back seat of the success bus. This land is our land and we are reclaiming it: taking it back from the thieves who took it, in the name of our ancestors who are buried here and in the name of our young people. We can all see that the great white race and all its pillars are falling apart. Justice in our land is for just-us (the whites). We've had all the hate and prejudice we can handle. The boiling pot is boiling over. We don't want to be part of a failed system or to bow to a foreign queen. We have our own elders and children who bear the blood of the red man. The Mi'kmaq and Maliseet nations shall prevail. No white master will command our lives again. I publicly denounce the Queen of England ... I am no longer a subject of the Queen. And I urge all Mi'kmaq to do the same.[65]

Tempers relaxed over the coming days, aided by the onset of colder, wetter weather in the north and the willingness of even more aggressive chiefs, such as Robert Levi of Big Cove, to urge their fishers to pull their boats off the water. Getting the community on board was difficult. Levi and Grand Chief Ben Sylliboy spent three hours arguing with 560 members of the Big Cove reserve about the need to avoid confrontation – and even then could not guarantee that all the fishers would leave the water.[66]

But the Maritime reaction continued to defy easy categorization. With non-Aboriginal fishers urging the government to let their season continue, anxiety rose in Nova Scotia, for even a short-term closure threatened to devastate the local economies.[67] Fishers from the Bay of Fundy gathered at a meeting in Nova Scotia on 9 October, cheering calls for the resignation of Herb Dhaliwal. At the same gathering, Chief Brian Toney, from the Annapolis Valley First Nation, earned a standing ovation when he attended the fishers' meeting and demanded that the Fisheries Department not impose a moratorium on the fall fishery.[68] Even at Burnt Church, not-so-secret "secret" meetings between the department and local leaders attempted to iron out a workable solution for their region. Such promising steps were offset by continued outbursts. Cyril Gehue of Big Cove declared: "We have been dealing with the white man for 200 years and where has it gotten us? There's going to be no deal. We stick to the treaty. We are tired of dealing." To punctuate his statements, he laid an Acadian flag over a lobster trap and set it on fire.[69]

Dhaliwal's federal political colleagues did not cover themselves with glory. Robert Nault, minister of Indian affairs and northern affairs, had kept his head down through the early weeks of the controversy. When he finally spoke up, many in the region wished he had kept silent. Nault's first foray into the dispute included the bold statement that the *Marshall* decision likely extended beyond ocean fishing rights. In a surprisingly impolitic statement in mid-October 1999 – one that earned him an immediate rebuke by his provincial counterparts–Nault suggested that the Supreme Court judgment was open-ended and might include other natural resources available in the region: "The treaties were ways of sharing the resources, and now what First Nations are saying when they go to court is that we would like to share in those resources so we can create economies. This is about equality really. We are talking about equality and opportunity in economic terms. It is about jobs. That is what this is all about ... The impact of the Marshall case likely will not be confined to fish and it will likely not be confined to Atlantic Canada."[70] New Brunswick Aboriginal Affairs Minister Brad Green described Nault's intervention to be "at odds" with the provincial position on logging rights. "The last thing we need at this point in time is comments to be made that don't take into account what effect they may have" he continued. "To prejudge what the result will be creates problems, particularly for the provincial government of New Brunswick."[71] As a negotiating ploy, Nault's observation was spectacularly inappropriate; as a measure for building federal-provincial cooperation, it could not have been more ill-timed.

The twists and turns continued, with Dhaliwal announcing on 10 October 1999 that he would permit a limited Mi'kmaq fishery for Burnt Church (600 traps) and Shubenacadie (Indian Brook), Nova Scotia (800 traps). The Burnt Church community had earlier rejected a Fisheries offer of a new wharf, education and other assistance with the fishery, and a 300-trap limit, and were angry about the suggested reduction. Women and children paraded in the community, demanding government support for the treaty and the *Marshall* decision. Indian Brook chief Reg Maloney stated, "Generally, people don't like the idea of us being dictated to or regulated like that."[72] As debate swirled among the Mi'kmaq, grudging acceptance of the government's limit became apparent, along with their determination to secure a long-term deal that actually met their needs and honoured their rights. Conditions around Burnt Church calmed down considerably from the tense days of the previous weeks. Fisheries moved very slowly to enforce the regulations (issuing tags and explaining the rules), enough First Nations pulled their traps to bring the community close to the quota, and the presence of several dozen police officers made it clear that violence would not be tolerated.

Dhaliwal himself seemed to become more comfortable with the task at hand, establishing limits on both Aboriginal and non-Aboriginal fishers, and more determined to stay the course. He credited his "Eastern view" (coming from his Sikh background and his earlier experiences in India) with helping him to understand the intensity of the Mi'kmaq–non-Aboriginal conflict. He remained the focus for considerable abuse – most people in the region appeared to blame him for the controversy and the violence – but seemed more settled in his position. He continued in his quiet way, advocating negotiation and promising long-term deals, while restating his determination not to tolerate violence.

First Nations gathered to discuss alternatives and to restate their interpretation of the *Marshall* decision. Back in Ottawa, Dhaliwal faced a blistering attack in the House of Commons, where the government was accused by the opposition parties of mismanaging the affair. The lengthy debate allowed all parties to lambaste the now well-known minister and demonstrated only that there was no consensus in Parliament about what should be done. On 13 October the Maritime chiefs formally repealed the voluntary moratorium, a decision Dhaliwal called "disappointing because I think it was a tremendous gesture on their part and it would have been tremendous goodwill. There were a lot of communities starting to work together and there was a lot of cooperation developing because of the goodwill shown."[73] Back at Burnt Church, the First Nations criticized the minister, accusing him of ignoring their legal rights. But, to less fanfare, Aboriginal and non-Aboriginal fishers gathered to discuss ways of integrating First Nations into the harvest. The most popular idea was for the federal government to purchase existing licences and allocate them to bands. This approach, advocates observed, created space in the fishery, but ensured that individual non-Aboriginal fishers retained their livelihood.[74]

The end of the moratorium created new tensions. Non-Aboriginal fishers headed into the waters off Yarmouth on 15 October, determined to smash Aboriginal lobster traps and threatening to close down the fishery. Fisheries Department negotiator James MacKenzie rushed to the site, hoping to head off another Burnt Church–type confrontation. The sight of several hundred fishers and their supporters gathered on the wharf at Yarmouth looked ominously familiar, and the department was anxious to avoid a repeat of the earlier conflict. There was a little pushing and shoving and two arrests, but the demonstration was generally peaceful. Still, tempers were high and frustrations with the government peaked again.[75] Early meetings did not proceed well – the first offer presented by the federal government was quickly rejected by fishers who gathered in Yarmouth on 19 October to consider their options – but by the end of the month the issue had started to settle down. Fisheries officials and the RCMP were also back on the water in Miramichi Bay, removing Aboriginal traps that exceeded the established 600 limit for Burnt Church, although the seizures were handled with tact. Chief Robert Levi turned the situation around, declaring that he was "on the warpath" and demanding that the RCMP protect his community members. Levi had grounds for concern, including the alleged ramming of an Aboriginal fishing boat by a non-Native vessel.[76] Government officials and fishers knew that the issue had only been postponed. All the issues would arise again when the spring lobster season opened in May 2000, but Dhaliwal felt that the negotiations and interventions had at least bought some time.

Fisheries initiatives did not quiet the Mi'kmaq chiefs, who gathered again on 12 October 1999 to discuss whether they should continue with the moratorium, their anger directed at Dhaliwal for imposing limits. They completed their reversal the following day, angry that the federal government had limited the Aboriginal fishery, yet allowed the commercial harvest to continue. Among the topics under dispute was the government's decision to issue communal licences – covering the entire reserve – when the First Nations demanded that the government recognize the right of individuals to harvest resources for commercial purposes. Ben Sylliboy, the grand chief credited with bringing the deal together, said of Dhaliwal: "So today, I don't like talking to a man with a forked tongue."[77]

The regular commercial fishery in Nova Scotia, threatened with suspension, was permitted to proceed – a decision that many attributed to the intervention of Chief Brian Toney of the Annapolis First Nation. Gary Hurley of the Fundy East Fishermen's Association applauded Toney's work: "We sure owe thanks to the First Nations in this area for their support. They didn't need to come forward and support us but they did."[78] Many observers credited First Nations leadership, quite appropriately, with containing the demands of more radical elements on their reserves and with offering the opportunity for reconciliation. Philip Lee of the *Telegraph Journal* observed:

Most frightening of all is the fact that at least some of the anger and tension in our coastal communities is motivated by nothing other than racism. This racism was expressed in its most despicable form when a Nova Scotia fisherman told a CBC report that the fishing crisis could have been avoided if we had "extincted" the Mi'kmaq people in the way the Europeans destroyed the Beotuck people of Newfoundland. In the face of this kind of abhorrent rhetoric, it is remarkable that so many native leaders, including Ben Sylliboy, the grand chief of the Mi'kmaq nation, are still willing to negotiate a peaceful settlement to the crisis. Many non-Natives could take a lesson in conciliation from Mr. Sylliboy.[79]

The start of the Nova Scotia lobster fishery brought renewed fears and tensions. Aboriginal leaders made it clear that they expected a fair share of the fishery. Chief Lawrence Paul worried about the prospects for integrating Mi'kmaq fishers into the industry: "The government and the non-native industry wants all native boats to fish in the same season, but at this point no room has been made for the native fishermen." The Mi'kmaq expected more, he said: "Our position ... is we're going out to fish. The non-Native fisherman may complain, but we're there because we have a right. They're there because they have a privilege, granted through a licence. Rights win over privileges every time." Denny Morrow of the Atlantic Fishing Alliance disagreed profoundly: "I've read the [*Marshall*] decision and it gives no special priority to a native commercial fishery over any other Canadian industry. I agree that there's no room in this industry for more [fishing boats]."[80]

The controversy continued across the region and across the country. Vandals at Burnt Church faced their first day in court. On 13 October 1999 the police charged more than two dozen men in the Miramichi provincial court. Together they faced charges ranging from mischief, obstructing a peace officer, and breaking and entering to having lobster traps aboard a vessel out of season. When the trials started on 18 October, friends and supporters of the accused non-Aboriginal defendants filled the Miramichi courtroom to overflowing.

Commercial fishers showed up in large numbers to offer their support to the men accused of vandalizing Aboriginal lobster traps and wreaking havoc around Burnt Church. A few First Nations people arrived to watch the proceedings, only to find that there was no room left in the courtroom.[81]

The handling of the affair raised questions, and Canadians remained uncertain about the future of the fishing industry on the east coast. The Standing Committee on Fisheries and Oceans of the House of Commons launched an investigation into the *Marshall* decision and the resulting conflicts in late October, promising to report back to Parliament by December. Members saw their mandate, not as preparing a critique of the *Marshall* decision, but as examining ways of implementing the ruling that met both Aboriginal and non-Aboriginal needs. The committee even called historian Stephen Patterson as a witness, providing him with the opportunity he had sought to clarify aspects of the Supreme Court judgment. Patterson's point was simple: the treaties meant that the Mi'kmaq agreed they would, after signing the treaty, be treated as British subjects. As he reported to the committee: "The contextual evidence shows that the native and government officials actually discussed this issue of law and the application of law and they were of one mind on the subject. The natives agreed that we are going to live under your laws and the British kept stressing that is what this is all about."[82] He also argued that the Court, in finding in favour of Marshall, had relied quite heavily on the evidence and wording relating to a treaty with the Maliseet, not the Mi'kmaq. He told the committee: "I am arguing here for the integrity of history, and for the integrity of historical method."[83]

Committee members also toured the Maritimes, meeting with Aboriginal and non-Aboriginal fishers and developing plans for the proper management of the fishery. They received a quick dose of Maritime fury. Fishers blasted the federal government's handling of the affair. "The whole thing was blowing up in front of our eyes and we could not get those messages across," Michael Belliveau of the Maritime Fishermen's Union declared. "Whoever was calling the shots was either woefully ignorant or was willing to use the native-commercial fishermen confrontation as a small price to pay for some larger political objectives."[84] Non-status and off-reserve First Nations complained that governments refused to meet with them and ignored their demands for inclusion in the expansion of Aboriginal treaty rights. Mi'kmaq leaders used the visit to outline their demands, telling committee members during their Halifax stop that they expected 30 to 40 per cent of the fishery.[85] They told of the heightened expectations in their communities, and the difficulties leaders encountered when trying to control fishing activity among a population experiencing unemployment rates of 85 per cent or higher. Commercial fishers expressed their worries about the conservation of stocks and the potential dislocation of non-Aboriginal fishers from an industry that had sustained their communities for generations. The messages had been circulating in the region for months, and the committee members left with clear messages of Maritime appeals for equity, fairness, and a peaceful resolution.[86]

The Standing Committee on Fisheries and Oceans called federal officials to account for the handling of the situation and for reviewing options and problems. The committee report, released in December 1999, sought a balance between Aboriginal and non-Aboriginal fishing rights. It urged the government to develop a voluntary buy-back program, whereby non-Aboriginal fishers would have their licences purchased by the Department of Fisheries and Oceans and allocated to individual bands. Reform Party members on the committee critiqued this aspect of the report, noting that the scale of the buy-back could well destroy the economy in some non-Native communities.[87] The committee also recommended extensive training for First Nations people wishing to enter the fishery and advocated the adoption of a single set of rules for all fishers on the east coast. The recommendations in the committee report coincided with federal government objectives and framed the approach taken over the winter of 1999–2000 to resolve the situation. First Nations were less enamoured of what they described as a "divide and conquer" tactic, which focused on negotiations with individual bands rather than regional solutions. This approach has been the general federal government policy since the tenure of Ron Irwin as minister of Indian affairs and northern development. As Chief Lawrence Paul of the Atlantic Policy Congress of First Nations Chiefs complained, "Nobody for various reasons wants to impact the Atlantic fishery to accommodate our people and our treaty right to be in the fishery."[88]

Maritimers, like other Canadians, find themselves immersed in a debate about contemporary responsibility for historical events and processes. More than one commentator has chastised governments and the courts for reopening discussions about a treaty that is over two hundred years old. Although some quickly agree that Canada's record for dealing fairly and honourably with First Nations is thin and a blemish in the national history books, a good many others argue that the current generation has no responsibility for the behaviour of their ancestors. The question of collective guilt remains largely unresolved; for every person who applauds the courts for reminding the nation of its legal obligations to First Nations, another contends that decades of government "generosity" to Aboriginal people in the form of income-tax-free status, free housing, and educational grants have more than absolved Canada of continuing obligations.

In central and western Canada, growing immigrant populations, with no historical connection to First Nations issues, might well demonstrate far less concern for these matters in the years to come. This situation is difficult to anticipate. Many immigrant groups in Canada are seeking attention to the historical injustices faced by their parents and grandparents – a situation that may make them more sympathetic to Aboriginal concerns. At the same time, the cultural diversity of the immigrant communities in the country, together with the fact that none of them will ever attract the kind of legal and financial attention given to First Nations people, creates a potential breach between them. While they might share anger and sorrow with the manner in which Aboriginal people were treated historically, these immigrant communities are unlikely to shoulder a strong sense of guilt and responsibility for actions that typically predated their arrival in Canada. Some First Nations leaders, particularly in northern and western Canadian, believe that the growing political power of immigrant communities will result in a lessening of concern about Aboriginal issues. The Maritimes has very small immigrant communities, in comparison.

It is not difficult to find examples of non-Aboriginal anger over First Nations rights and, increasingly, Aboriginal people generally. The 24 September issue of the Halifax *Chronicle-Herald*, for example, included a series of letters that reflected the growing frustration. George Swim of Cape Sable Island wrote, "I am tired of hearing about native people and their rights to exploit the natural resources of our country." Darmouth's John Pinchin said that if the Mi'kmaq wanted to hunt and fish, "they should use the same methods that were available during that time period." Andy Born with 3 Thumbs, an off-reserve Aboriginal, criticized the handling of the situation: "As members of a band, my family saw nothing of the food fishery or any of the monies. In essence, the band chief and council, with the aid of the government, kept my family in a state of poverty." David Beresford-Green of Fall River demonstrated his frustration with the situation: "If the natives now claim their fishing was not limited to the immediate coastline, what is to stop them from claiming that, in the past, they went fishing far offshore and intend to do so again? It seems there is now nothing to stop them. Watch out, Japan!" B.C. Bishop of Dartmouth wrote, "With all the uproar over native rights, I'm left wondering what my rights are as a homeowner and taxpayer.

I thought that people were created equal; but according to the government, some are more equal than others."[89]

Much of this frustration can be traced to the legal contests, which threaten to upset the balance in the Maritimes in several profound ways. As in the rest of the country, there appears to be growing unease about the legal extension of Aboriginal rights. The issues under discussion range widely – the right to self-government, corruption on First Nations reserves, the number and variety of government programs for First Nations, total federal spending on Aboriginal people, and official recognition of Aboriginal harvesting rights. While national polls continue to reveal that a majority of Canadians wish for a quick and definitive resolution to the Aboriginal rights question, an undercurrent of hostility festers. Part of this opposition is racially based (although personal observation over the past three years suggests that racism is much less an issue in the Maritimes than in British Columbia or the Prairie provinces). A larger part – the vein that the Canadian Alliance/Reform has attempted to tap nationally – focused on what is described as the fundamental inequity of special status for First Nations people. It appears that attitudes towards First Nations may be hardening in the Maritimes. The *Marshall* decision, along with the dangers exposed, has frightened some Maritimers and angered others. The anti-Aboriginal sentiment that has long been close to the surface in Canada has burst through on occasion and remains an importance force across the region.

Non-Aboriginal anxiety about the *Marshall* decision and First Nations rights generally can be traced in large measure to uncertainty about the Maritime economy. For years, Maritimers seeking opportunity have been forced to leave the region. The once boisterous nineteenth-century economy built on shipbuilding, trade, and forestry was ravaged, Maritimers argue, by the inequities of Confederation and the economic injustice imbedded in the National Policy. This policy, introduced by John A. Macdonald's Conservative Party government, established tariff barriers, railway subsidies, and an aggressive campaign to attract immigrants. It had the practical effect of strengthening the economy in central Canada and, over several decades, stripping the vitality out of the East, which also suffered from the rapid decline in the wooden shipbuilding sector. Over the past forty years, the Maritime provinces have come to rely heavily on federal government transfers, establishing a fiscal dependency that irks regional residents but has, to date, defied all proposed solutions. In the past decade, led by New Brunswick premier Frank McKenna, the region sought to transform itself, relying on "new" economies – telecommunications, information technology, e-commerce, and tourism. Although there have been some successes, particularly in New Brunswick's information technology sector and Prince Edward Island tourism, the region continues to lag behind the rest of Canada. Painful provincial debates about the economic future of the Acadia peninsula in New Brunswick and the status of the steel mills and coal mines on Cape Breton Island remind Maritimers of the tenuous balance between government subsidies and widespread unemployment. Added to this difficult mix are the lingering effects of the moratorium on cod fishing and general uncertainty about the state of the ocean fishery. The region is fatigued by economic distress and by the long wait for good news.

In this context, the *Marshall* decision was anything but positive. The threat to the fishery was immediate and obvious. The bitter, even violent, reaction by lobster fishers to the judgment provided the first sign of the intensity of local emotions – as a scathing rebuke of the fishers' leadership following a violent confrontation at Burnt Church attests:

> DFO officials didn't smash thousands of dollars worth of Native lobster traps in Miramichi Bay. They didn't force their way into three fish-processing plants, terrorizing employees and destroying whatever equipment they could lay their hands on. And they didn't beat windows out of the reserve school at Burnt Church and vandalize the principal's office. All these crimes – and crimes they most certainly are – can and should be laid directly at the door of a few dozen irresponsible fishermen – and their leaders. The Maritime Fishermen's Union, which represents many of the lobstermen who took part in Sunday's rampage, has a decidedly genteel interpretation of what happened. In a press release, the MFU's executive say they regret that licensed fishermen were "forced to disable lobster traps" and that Ottawa's inaction "drove fishermen into the position of having to defend their own livelihoods." If this is the quality of leadership available to licensed fishermen, it's no wonder some of the rank and file are going astray. Destruction of private property, physical intimidation and violence – thuggery, by any other name – are not defensive acts, nor do they have any place in political debate. But these tactics have been tacitly condoned by community and industry leaders for years. They simply wash their hands of responsibility when violence occurs.[90]

Why so much anger? The fishing communities of Nova Scotia, New Brunswick, and Prince Edward Island are economically vulnerable places. In the summer of 1999, before the *Marshall* decision came down, lobster catches had been very low in parts of the Maritimes, particularly off northern New Brunswick, raising fears about the long-term viability of the industry.[91] Uncertainty about prices and markets combined with a profound lack of confidence in the Department of Fisheries and Oceans, the federal agency responsible for managing ocean resources, to create ongoing anxiety. Most of the fishers in these towns and villages trace their involvement in the ocean economy back several generations. These are people with firm roots in their communities and industry, only occasionally with skills that can be marketed locally or regionally, and with a deep cultural commitment to the fishery. For some, the relatively recent strength of the lobster sector has been a bright light in an otherwise gloomy world, and now that strength appears to be threatened.

So it was, as well, with the loggers. During the Thomas Peter Paul episode, loggers throughout New Brunswick (and, to a much lesser extent, Nova Scotia) worried constantly about the future of their sector. Carefully managed forest plots were being cut hastily by First Nations loggers. Reforestation efforts on these harvested segments were non-existent. The First Nations talked of extending their logging activities, and bitter confrontations between Aboriginal and non-Aboriginal loggers erupted across New Brunswick. Government action and the Court of Appeal decision on the *Thomas Peter Paul* case capped the confrontation, but did not erase the memories of harsh words and angry assertions. The launching of the *Joshua Bernard* case, followed by the *Marshall* decision, simply brought these matters back onto the table with a vengeance. Once again, a vulnerable, resource-based industry sector – in this case, forestry – found its future prosperity threatened by the assertion of First Nations rights. Loggers and small logging companies worried that their right to earn a living would be sacrificed by governments and the larger companies in order to secure a deal with the First Nations. Non-Aboriginal communities based on logging – themselves far from prosperous and economically stable owing to shifts in the forest industry – worried that the allocation of cutting rights to First Nations would undercut their businesses in favour of nearby Aboriginal companies and workers. Few saw much benefit coming out of the prospect for continued confrontation over harvesting rights.

A good portion of the regional frustration can be attributed to the continued difficulties of the region as a whole. This part of Canada has been without a major boom; the recent prosperity of Montreal, southern Ontario, Alberta, and, until recently, British Columbia has not been enjoyed by most Maritimers. Improvements have been incremental, typically oversold (the economic effects of Frank McKenna's information technology initiatives), and often offset by devastating closures. The collective impact of burning disappointments has taken its toll: the continued pressure of having to cope with limited government budgets, disdain from the investment sector, the migration of hundreds of skilled workers and university and college graduates each year, the steady decline of once-proud urban centres (particularly Saint John), and the gathering evidence of a region that is falling well behind the rest of the country. As if to punctuate this sentiment, the Denny's restaurant chain from Maine came to New Brunswick in the spring of 2000 to recruit workers for short-order cooking jobs south of the border. The realization that eastern Canada is a source of cheap labour for one of the least prosperous northern states in the United States is demoralizing in the extreme. Although the story is far from being all negative, and regional resilience and determination remain remarkably strong, the Maritimes can not cope with many more body blows.

The First Nations did not intend it as such, but the *Marshall* decision and the Aboriginal rights controversy dealt just such a blow. It adds uncertainty where the region needs stability. It threatens already vulnerable fishing and logging sectors. It has the potential to undercut the viability of economically fragile communities. It gives provincial governments yet another challenge when they already have a table full of difficult problems. The Aboriginal rights issue is openended at a time when the Maritimes could use some closure on major conflicts. The debate is by no means one-sided. Considerable support remains for First Nations rights – more in the major cities than in the logging and fishing communities – and governments have not erected major barriers to Aboriginal aspirations. In the midst of the angry words, there have been numerous offers of reconciliation and cooperation. But the Maritimes, on occasion, exudes fatigue and approaches the discussion over First Nations legal rights like a battered and bruised boxer, not yet sure if another round is possible.

The challenge for governments is to balance the political obligations to the community at large with the legal requirements of Aboriginal rights rulings. It is a challenge that the federal government fumbled profoundly in the fall of 1999 – though it recovered some ground over the subsequent winter – and that the provincial authorities managed with notable skill. When Brad Green, Aboriginal affairs minister for New Brunswick, realized that the *Marshall* decision might extend beyond the lobster fishery, he started meetings with Aboriginal leaders in mid-October to prevent a repeat of the conflict over logging and hunting. The issues were intense – First Nations believed that the decision applied to logging, and the province did not agree – but the desire to avoid conflicts like the one at Burnt Church was very strong. This insistence led, in some people's eyes, to an overly open-ended approach to Mi'kmaq and Maliseet treaty rights, such as the decision not to impose any restrictions on Aboriginal moose hunting.

The Aboriginal rights issue exposes one of the central difficulties in the Canadian system of government – the division of jurisdiction between federal and provincial governments. The federal government has constitutional and legal responsibility (a fiduciary, or trust-like, duty) for First Nations people, and also manages ocean resources, through the Department of Fisheries and Oceans. Provincial governments handle all other natural resources, including inland waters, land, minerals, and timber resources. Aboriginal rights cases, such as *Thomas Peter Paul*, cut across jurisdictional boundaries. Decisions like the *Marshall* judgment applied specifically to one area – in this instance, ocean resources – but have legal implications that potentially impinge on provincial responsibilities.

In other jurisdictions, most notably British Columbia, federal-provincial tensions routinely interfered with progress on Aboriginal matters. So, too, in the Yukon, where for several years in the late 1970s the territorial government impeded negotiations on a land claims settlement. In the *Thomas Peter Paul* case, a largely provincial matter, New Brunswick and Nova Scotia handled the issue themselves, doing so with considerable skill and managing to avoid much of the bitterness and conflict that could easily have surrounded this issue. Equally important, the *Paul* judgment came from a lower court, ensuring continued uncertainty as the appeals proceeded and giving governments time for action. *Marshall* was different. The Supreme Court judgment was final – well, almost final, and subject to continued clarification over the years – and applied specifically to ocean resources. Although the provinces worried about the extension of these newly clarified rights into other areas, the first and more pressing problem related to the fall lobster fishery. It was a formidable test of the Liberal government of Jean Chrétien.

It is difficult to find observers who believe that the federal government handled the *Marshall* decision well. The Departments of Justice, Fisheries and Oceans, and Indian Affairs and Northern Development appear to have been caught unaware by the judgment. Not one of them seems to have had a contingency plan in place, to be used if the Supreme Court ruled in favour of Donald Marshall Jr. Part of the problem had to do with timing. The judgment came down in late September, with the lobster season under way in some areas and closed in others. It was also at a time when the lobsters were feeding voraciously, making it a very good time to set traps, if maximizing the catch was the goal. Had the judgment been rendered, say, in

January, government departments would have had several months to negotiate with First Nations and fishers and to cope with the fallout from the decision. As fate would have it, the timing of the decision gave them only a few weeks to decide what to do, and there is little evidence that federal agencies had prepared for the eventuality. There is a certain unfairness in this assessment, in that the Supreme Court has been unpredictable through the late 1990s. Even though the pattern of decisions appeared to be running in the First Nations' favour, the scale of the *Marshall* victory was unexpected by many specialists in the field. This said, however, First Nations court cases invariably produce winners and losers, and evidence from elsewhere in the country suggests that there might well have been a strong and bitter Mi'kmaq response had Marshall lost on appeal to the Supreme Court. One would have expected, therefore, that government departments would have been prepared for either eventuality.

The *Marshall* conflict marked the beginning, not the end, of the controversy over east coast fishing rights. A few months after the *Marshall* decision, Dhaliwal was presenting himself as an advocate of treaty and Aboriginal rights. By December 1999 Fisheries Department and Mi'kmaq negotiators were already making significant strides towards an interim deal. The guidelines, approved by the Atlantic Policy Congress, incorporated several key principles: the right to fish was communal, not individual; only Aboriginal people could fish under the licences; non-Canadians were not eligible; and the federal government had the right to regulate the fishery. The federal government was also at work on the cornerstone of its policy – purchasing licences from non-Aboriginal fishermen who were willing to leave the fishery in exchange for a buyout.[92] Over the winter – and away from public scrutiny – the Department of Fisheries and Oceans negotiated with individual First Nations. By April 2000 over 1,300 fishers had either sold their licences or entered into discussions with the government. The availability of these licences created the prospect of considerable "space" in the fishery and afforded the federal government with the opportunity to secure band-by-band fishing deals.

By the same time, six bands had negotiated agreements involving federal purchases of fishing licences and funding for boats, training, and fishing gear. The Oromocto settlement involved a long-term project to map and clean up the Oromocto River watershed, with a view to restocking the system with Atlantic salmon and trout, using a fish farm that the band intends to develop.[93] Another eight bands had reached agreements in principle, leaving twenty First Nations without settlements. Several, including Burnt Church, adamantly opposed the Fisheries Department approach and declared their intention to exercise their *Marshall* right without negotiating with Ottawa. Dhaliwal had a considerable carrot – $160 million in support for First Nations who signed agreements with the federal government – but he took the stick out of his own hand. The minister indicated that bands which did not sign agreements would still be able to fish: "Contrary to myth, there is no set deadline for agreements. Communities with no signed agreements before the fishery starts in their area will receive access under a communal licence and a set of rules." The First Nations, particularly those near the lucrative lobster grounds, disagreed and asserted their determination to adopt their own regulations to govern their fishing activities. Dhaliwal clearly hoped that the signed agreements would quell the anger that was rising again in the region, but non-Aboriginal fishers and certain First Nations did not back down from their early position.[94]

In an excellent illustration of the national ramifications of legal judgments, Fisheries was also prodded by the decision to negotiate fishing agreements with fourteen bands on Vancouver Island, signatories to the nineteenth-century Douglas treaties which guaranteed that the First Nations could "carry on [their] fisheries as formerly." Having learned from the *Marshall* case the dangers of allowing such treaty rights to go before the courts, Dhaliwal opted to negotiate agreements with the bands. Non-Aboriginal fishers on both coasts, nervous about the implications for their fishery, protested the negotiations. Phil Eidsvik of the British Columbia Fisheries Survival Organization said of the discussions: "Every time a decision comes down the least bit in favour of an Aboriginal community, the Departments of Fisheries and Indian Affairs run around the country trying to expand it the biggest possible way they can."[95] If anything, however, the BC negotiations suggest that Dhaliwal learned his lesson from the 1999 *Marshall* decision.

Nault appeared to learn his lesson, too. A meeting was hastily called in Ottawa between him and his provincial colleagues from the Maritimes, including Brad Green, Justice Minister Michael Baker of Nova Scotia, and Attorney General Wes MacAleer of Prince Edward Island. Green and the others wanted the federal government on board with their position that logging rights were not explicitly mentioned in the *Marshall* ruling and therefore were not clearly defined treaty rights. Nault subsequently retreated from the debate and left the matter in the hands of Dhaliwal, who appeared adept and well briefed by comparison. The meeting was "crashed" by Betty Ann Lavallée, president of the New Brunswick Aboriginal Peoples Council, and Lorraine Cook, president of the Native Council of Nova Scotia, both of whom hoped to convince federal officials to include non-status and off-reserve Aboriginal people in the negotiations.[96] When the Supreme Court issued its clarification in November, Nault's quick, even rash, comments came under ridicule again: Reform MP and fisheries critic John Cummins said of the minister: "What Mr. Nault was prepared to do when this decision first came down was to give away the ranch. He suggested that the court acknowledge that there was a right to forests and to mineral resources. He just doesn't want to admit that he made a foolish and irresponsible statement when the Marshall decision was first rendered."[97] Nault defended himself, arguing that he simply preferred negotiated deals with First Nations over constant references to the court: "Instead of having the courts define our relationship as a country with First Nations, we as politicians and leaders should do it and stop letting the courts ... make tough decisions the politicians should be making."[98]

The Supreme Court decision on *Marshall* did not directly involve provincial responsibilities. While subsequent cases and interpretations might well extend the ruling into provincial jurisdiction, the immediate fallout and tensions revolved around federally managed areas. New Brunswick natural resources minister Jeannot Volpe responded to the initial decision with caution: "They mention fish and wildlife, but ... would they come back later and say wood is also part of it? I don't know. We will need federal support to find a solution because it is creating uncertainty in the province. It's hard for us to invest long term when we don't know [whether] the supply will be there."[99] The provincial governments, therefore, maintained a much lower profile on the *Marshall* judgment than they had been required to take on the debate surrounding Thomas Peter Paul. Brad Green noted that the *Marshall* decision meant that the government could not stop Aboriginal people from hunting and fishing, and then selling their catch for a profit. He was conciliatory as well: "We want to sit down with the Aboriginal leadership with the province and discuss exactly what Marshall is going to mean, because it does further clarify a treaty right held by the Aboriginal peoples of New Brunswick. I'm not expecting chaos. I'm not expecting a crisis. The Aboriginal peoples of New Brunswick are responsible; I think they are obviously pleased with the decision that was rendered last week, and as well they should be."[100] He continued: "It will facilitate our understanding as a government of the rights of Aboriginal people. It should make it easier to sit down and discuss with them how those rights can be exercised with the least number of restrictions."[101] Green suggested in October 1999 that the Mi'kmaq and Maliseet would be restricted in exercising their Aboriginal right to harvest to their traditional territories (eastern and western New Brunswick, respectively).

He also clearly stated that the province did not accept that the treaty right extended to logging. His argument met with a sharp rebuke from Len Tomah, who said simply, "Nobody draws a line for me when I hunt, trap, fish or harvest."[102] Green, however, promised a different approach than in the past – and different from that adopted by the federal government: "Government has to shift its focus on how it deals with Aboriginal issues. The traditional approach has been to avoid dealing with an issue until a problem arise, then try to correct the problem. Instead, we should be devoting our time and energy to developing a strong, ongoing relationship. We should be coming together not only to solve problems, but because it's important to talk."[103]

The provincial governments resented the inaction by the federal government, for the absence of a strong and consistent national response inflamed conditions along the coast. Similarly, there had been an immediate and angry reaction to Nault's unilateral declaration that the *Marshall* decision applied to other natural resources, thus drawing the provincial governments into the fray. Prince Edward Island, Nova Scotia, and New Brunswick followed the *Marshall* controversy closely, realizing that the potential extension into other sectors promised further unrest and turmoil in the region.

Perhaps the most surprising element in the public furore over the *Marshall* case was the absence of Jean Chrétien. The controversy over lobster fishing was among the most divisive and bitter during the prime minister's tenure in office. The situation begged for a calming hand, for a sign that the federal and provincial governments had matters well under control. The provinces handled their side of the situation well, avoiding sharp statements and rigid positions and working to build cooperation. But the prime minister was nowhere to be seen. No issue in the Maritimes over the past five years has required such direct and senior intervention, and the prime minister did not stray east from Ottawa to address the problem. Just as remarkable is the fact that the region appears to have forgiven him for his inaction, for the political fallout seems to have been small.

The *Marshall* controversy is far from resolved. Passmaquoddy Indians from Maine watched the court case with interest and, early on, declared their desire to capitalize on the judgment. Off-reserve and non-status Indians had been arguing for years that they should be included in any discussions concerning Aboriginal fishing rights. While governments dealt with them politely, they rarely received much attention. In the aftermath of the *Marshall* decision, Betty Ann Lavallée approached Bernard Lord, recently elected New Brunswick premier, declaring the intent of the Aboriginal Peoples Council to act unilaterally if the government did not negotiate with it. As she noted sharply, "If the province does not respond by Thanksgiving then, believe me, we're going to redefine Thanksgiving for them."[104]

The greatest challenge for governments in the conflicts of September–November 1999 lay in the on-site management of hostilities. Communities along the coast were rife with tension. First Nations and non-Aboriginal populations that had lived together with considerable comfort for years found themselves eyeing each other with suspicion and fury. Fishers demanded that the Department of Fisheries and Oceans enforce all the regulations, including keeping unlicensed Aboriginal boats off the sea. First Nations demanded that the same officials protect their clearly authorized treaty rights and ensure them access to the lobster fishery. As the groups squared off against each other on the wharves and in meetings, as nasty words spit back and forth over the heads of police separating the groups, as buildings were burned, traps destroyed, and boats and vehicles damaged, appeals for protection and punishment filled the air. Tensions ran higher than most Canadian realized. As happened on the west coast during similar conflicts over Aboriginal harvesting rights, rumours circulated about fishers carrying guns with them onto the water. In late March 2000, as Aboriginal and non-Aboriginal fishers prepared to return for the spring lobster fishery, at least one non-First Nations fisher warned of the coming "civil war" over Mi'kmaq fishing rights.

No one was killed. Violence was largely limited to property damage. Vicious words circulated, most coming from the non-Aboriginal side, and racial epithets stung like darts. But boats (with a few exceptions) were not rammed in the fishing grounds, as officials feared. Group violence did not break out, although it was a near miss on several occasions. The prospect was real, and it is a credit to the Fisheries officials and the RCMP that nothing more serious transpired. Both groups have their critics – and the criticism tends to come from Aboriginal people, who wanted more action, as well as from non–First Nations people, who felt that their interests were not adequately protected. All acts of property damage were investigated and numerous charges laid. By the spring of 2000 the various cases had worked their way through the court system, with most pleading guilty and receiving relatively minor punishments and admonitions from the court to avoid further conflict. The response from authorities was far from perfect, and First Nations people were justified in feeling a little unsafe in the early days of the conflict. But as time passed, and surprisingly given the complexity and intensity of the issue, authorities managed to push their way between the competing sides and hold them at arm's length from each other. To be fair, leaders on both the First Nations and non-Aboriginal side begged their respective constituencies to remain calm – and, at several critical junctures, meetings organized to bring the two sides together helped to dampen anger and animosity. It is hard to look back on the events of the fall of 1999 and consider the official actions a major success, for the failure to anticipate difficulties exacerbated the difficulties. But from a weak starting position, the Department of Fisheries and Oceans staff and the RCMP officers managed a volatile situation with tact and professionalism, punished offenders, and effectively brought the conflict under control.

Anger flashed through the Maritimes following the *Marshall* judgment–and the residue remains. First Nations will not soon forget the words and actions of non-Aboriginal opponents. The memory of these events will linger for generations and will serve as a block to future attempts at cultural reconciliation. Aboriginal peoples in the region discovered things about their neighbours that they might have guessed, but did not know. Now, there was no escaping the memory of the words, curses, and burning anger in the coastal communities. Non-Aboriginal people, accustomed to the First Nations being quiet and conciliatory, found a determination they were not used to seeing and felt the strength of Aboriginal resolve. Discovering, too, how long the Mi'kmaq people had resented non-Aboriginal domination of the fishery cast a new light on historical relationships along the coast.

As time passed, as the federal government waffled, as leaders on both sides postured, pontificated, and demanded, and as First Nations and non-Aboriginal peoples wondered about the future, it became clear that this was a crisis in desperate need of a solution. Signs of willingness to be conciliatory were abundant on both sides. For every strident word and aggressive push, there was an apology and a helping hand. Non-Aboriginal fishers, realizing that the balance had shifted, sought ways to help Aboriginal people seeking to enter the industry. Some saw federal intervention as a way of allowing them to step out of an uncertain economy with a measure of financial security. Federal offers to buy licences to be turned over to First Nations generally found ready sellers.

It is easy to find fault with the handling of the fallout from the *Marshall* decision. The Supreme Court decision was ambiguous and required a hasty clarification. The federal government's immediate response was slow, overly cautious, unoriginal, and one-sided; the failure of the prime minister or other senior cabinet ministers to come to the region immediately contributed to the intensity and uncertainty of the regional debate. Officials charged with maintaining peace and order on the coast did not do a great job at first, although they kept a lid on emotions and actions as the controversy unfolded. It is equally important to identify the positive efforts that emerged through the controversy. First Nations leaders and elders did an excellent job of keeping the younger and more hot-headed elements in their communities under control. Non-Aboriginal organizations, likewise, produced a few radicals and some unfortunate statements and allegations, but they also offered true leaders who offered conciliation and unofficial consensus-building efforts between cultural groups. After stumbling in the early weeks, Herb Dhaliwal and the Department of Fisheries and Oceans turned their attention to quiet, behind-the-scenes negotiations with individual bands and licence-holders, seeking to resolve the medium-term problem outside the glare of media attention.

What underlies the regional controversy over the *Marshall* decision, however, is an important and unusual determination to seek viable and sustainable agreements. When similar conflicts erupted in central Canada, British Columbia, and the Canadian North (to say nothing of Australia, New Zealand, the United States, and other countries), much valuable time was wasted on recriminations and antagonism. The secret to the comparative success of the Maritimes – and the key to the region's excellent opportunity to establish a new model for Aboriginal–non–First Nations relations – was exposed in New Brunswick's handling of the *Thomas Peter Paul* case. New Brunswick moved beyond the letter of the law and sought, instead, a solution that could gain the support of bands, companies, and governments. The province endeavoured to address the long-term problem of Aboriginal economic marginalization and the need for work, rather than obsess over the nuances of legal judgments and courtroom terminology. Only time will tell if the logging agreements form the basis for a truly different and sustainable relationship. What is clear is that the Maritime approach to First Nations affairs – which, admittedly, had to be jump-started by Aboriginal successes in the courtroom – is more conciliatory, creative, and community-based than it is elsewhere in the country.

The fallout from the *Marshall* decision, once the headlines, angry words, and striking images of conflict and potential violence are accounted for, reveals many of the same elements. Mi'kmaq and Maliseet leaders remain more conciliatory and cooperative than is the norm across Canada. In turn, provincial governments appear to be genuinely committed to new resource-sharing arrangements that have real potential to add to the economic sustainability of First Nations communities. Fishers and their organizations, like the loggers and the logging companies in the wake of the *Thomas Peter Paul* decision, are angry, uncertain, and nervous – but they are also willing to work with First Nations to develop new partnerships and relationships. Across the region, commentators and the general public wonder when the open-ended approach to Aboriginal and treaty rights will end, and worry about the impact of court decisions and agreements on the public as a whole. But there is little of the groundswell of outright opposition to Aboriginal rights that one sees in British Columbia, and little of the ingrained bitterness that lingers over relations in Ontario and Quebec. Non-Aboriginal Maritimers worry about the future, although the debate over Aboriginal rights is but one on a long list of concerns that animates discussion. They are also determined, it seems, to find a regional solution to the problem, one that suits the Maritimes and that respects the legal rights and economic aspirations of First Nations.

There are reasons for optimism, and the belief that First Nations and non-Aboriginal people can work together to find mutually beneficial solutions is not misguided. Two developments in the region, along the Restigouche and Grand Cascapedia rivers, illustrate how these groups have put aside their suspicions and, in some cases, their legacies of difficult relations and have found ways to cooperate. In the former instance, the Listiguj First Nation and local residents overcame a legacy of bitter confrontations over resource rights and, in December 1998, struck an agreement to develop a watershed management team. What had once been a regional hot-spot of Aboriginal confrontation now offered a model for conciliation and cooperation, involving Lisiguj, the Restigouche Riparian Association (fishing camp operators), and the Atlantic Salmon Federation. First Nations people were hired as wardens, before the *Marshall* decision, and a model of Aboriginal and non-Aboriginal coexistence in the fishery had been worked out.

Much earlier, in 1982, the Gesgapegiag Mi'kmaq First Nation and other resource users along the Grand Cascapedia formed the Société de Gestion du Saumon de la Rivière Grande Cascapedia with the intent of co-managing the resource. As Bernard Jerome, one-time band chief, observed of the deal: "We managed to get employment out of it, community development, and at the same time we are exercising our Native rights. We continue to fish with nets, but with a strict quota to make sure that conservation is always being maintained, because without us doing our part in conservation it would be very difficult for the Cascapedia River to handle the pressure. I'm not giving anything up. I'm just using my right in a more contemporary style as opposed to a traditional style."[105] The response, positive and negative, to the *Marshall* decision did not create a new system of Aboriginal–non-Aboriginal relations in the Maritimes. The region was, instead, able to look to a history of conciliation and cooperation that, even in the blistering heat of the *Marshall* controversy, provided reasons for optimism.

Canadians have looked at the *Marshall* decision and the subsequent controversy from a national perspective and have chosen to interpret the event in the light of blockades in British Columbia, controversies in Alberta, bitter conflicts in Quebec, and violent standoffs in Ontario. These elements are at play in the Maritimes, and the prospect of substantial violence was very real through the fall of 1999 and remained in evidence through the spring of 2000. In the fast-moving, emotion-filled world of Aboriginal rights debates, there are no assurances. But behind the scenes, aided by a federal government anxious to re-establish credibility with all sides after the fiasco of September–October 1999, the Aboriginal and non-Aboriginal people of the Maritimes appeared determined to build on their history, not the national one, and to develop solutions that suit their circumstances, not necessarily the specific dictates of the Supreme Court. The challenge is a difficult one and the stakes are very high. The continuing conflict over fishing rights at Burnt Church threatens to reignite the controversy. What is more, the full meaning of the *Marshall* decision is yet unknown, thus making it impossible to anticipate the end of the debate over First Nations rights in the Maritimes.

At its root, however, the legal and political tussles reflect the underlying relationships between Aboriginal and non-Aboriginal people. Susan Levi, a councillor at Big Cove, wondered at the end of September 1999 if people realized that the First Nations were determined to stand their ground. Still, she argued, there was reason for hope: "We, as the First Nations government, had to beg for access to the natural resources in order to provide employment for our people so they can provide for their families and to bring back their pride and self-esteem. We, as First Nations people, realize the Europeans are here to stay. Not once have we tried to change you. We have learned to understand your ways and accepted your way of life. The day you learn to understand our way of life and try not to change us and accept that we are here to stay is probably also the day the three governments can work together and make Canada a proud and beautiful country."[106] Aboriginal people saw hope and opportunity in the *Marshall* decision. Most non-Aboriginal Maritimers and Canadians preferred to see only the crisis.

Some, too, saw further crisis in the offing. Another major court challenge, involving Aboriginal logger Joshua Bernard, was awaiting a provincial court decision. The spring lobster season approached and, although some bands were nearing agreements with the federal government, a few, like Burnt Church, refused to come to a settlement. Questions lingered about the full extent of the *Marshall* decision, and uncertainty remained the cornerstone of Aboriginal affairs in the Maritimes. "Wait until you see the spring". Alex Denny of the Mi'kmaq Grand Council warned in February 2000, "I think it will break loose again. Every solitary one of us will end up in jail and that will include the Grand Council because I'm going out."[107] Dhaliwal, by now a familiar figure in the region, delivered a major speech on east coast fishing to the Atlantic Provinces Economic Council in Halifax on 24 March 2000. As part of a broad, state-of-the-industry address, the minister restated his plan to buy up fishing licences and recruit non-Aboriginal fishers to train First Nations people. He made it clear that the Aboriginal fishery would not represent a net addition to the pressure on the ocean stocks. He assured listeners that Mi'kmaq would have to observe regular seasons and regulations. He announced, without specifics, progress on negotiating band-by-band agreements and indicated that groups that came on side would receive additional money for training and for enhancement of local fisheries and equipment (implicitly indicating that those who stayed away from the table would be denied such funding). Those who refused to sign an agreement would be granted a communal licence and would be required to observe regulations. "In short," he noted, "we are putting the pieces in place for a successful, orderly, conservation-oriented Aboriginal fishery, without major disruption to the commercial fishery ... I am confident we will be on the way to a successful and responsible Aboriginal fishery. But in order to do that, we need generous, reasonable attitudes, the attitudes that made this country great and world-respected in the first place. This will require the support of all the communities coming together."[108]

As if to remind Maritimers that winter, as much as good politics and negotiations, had stopped the crisis of the fall of 1999, Burnt Church again produced signs that the tensions of the past were still around. The offer by the Maritime Fishermen's Union to replace the damaged traps from the previous October was rejected because of conditions attached to the offer. Christian Peacemaker Teams, fearing a return of violence and racially loaded confrontations, arrived with plans to position themselves on the wharf in an endeavour to bring some calm to the region. And the Burnt Church First Nation refused to abide by federal regulations and announced the preparation of a band-drafted set of fishing regulations. The contest over licences and conservation strategies remained contained to Burnt Church and did not expand throughout the region. In most communities, the agreement with the federal government held, and the prospects for peace seemed reasonable.

The *Marshall* decision, stripped to its most basic elements, was about providing Mi'kmaq people with the ability to fish commercially and to earn some money from the resources in their traditional homelands. Calvin Barnaby from Burnt Church said: "Everybody brought their spirits up. There's food on the table for the kids. They're putting clothes on their backs. They were buying their kids school supplies. There was pride."[109] Against the backdrop of Supreme Court decisions and high-pressure negotiations, these words of optimism and encouragement seem somewhat basic. Such sentiments, however, represent the real purpose – and impact – of the Mi'kmaq struggle for the recognition of treaty and Aboriginal rights.

CHAPTER SEVEN

Postlude to Marshall: *Joshua Bernard, Lobster Licences, and the Refinement of Mi'kmaq Rights*

The legacy of the *Thomas Peter Paul* and *Donald Marshall* cases continued on, just as negotiations and debate also continued. As Canadians have learned over the past twenty years, Aboriginal gains have been incremental and the legal struggles virtually continuous. A court defeat is routinely succeeded by a slightly different challenge. A victory for the First Nations is generally followed by government attempts to narrow the scope of the decision and Aboriginal efforts to extend the judgment into other areas. Hundreds of cases, mostly debates over specific details but some raising sweeping questions of First Nations rights, are presently before the courts. There are hundreds more waiting in the wings. More by political default than deliberate Aboriginal intent, the court system has become the central forum for the resolution and definition of the formal relationships between indigenous and non-indigenous Canadians. This lineup promises that the controversy over *Paul* and particularly *Marshall* will not be the end of the debate, but simply a major milepost along a very uncertain path. Across Canada, First Nations men (very few women, except on Aboriginal women's rights) continue to burst into regional and national prominence by dint of their arrest and trial on matters relating to Aboriginal rights. Within their communities and across the nation, they become, often reluctantly, media personalities and heroes, standard-bearers for the cause of indigenous aspirations. Because of the centrality of Aboriginal and treaty rights cases for First Nations economic hopes, their trials become media circuses, guaranteed to attract attention regardless of the outcome.

With the names of Thomas Peter Paul and Donald Marshall Jr freshly entrenched in the Maritime consciousness, another young man emerged to join them in the limelight: Joshua Bernard. In mid-June 1998, much to the surprise of the people involved, the nineteen year old was charged under the Crown Lands and Forest Act. The Eel Ground man had had his loaded vehicle seized in May and did not expect to be formally charged. When he showed up in court with his father, Albert, and his brothers, he anticipated a discussion about the seized equipment. Instead, he was charged. Albert Bernard was angry, arguing that he had obeyed the law, had cut trees only when the *Thomas Peter Paul* decision was still in effect, and was merely cleaning up his site, as directed to do by the provincial government. As Bernard said, "We're law-abiding citizens, over the years we have not gone on Crown land and we've never disobeyed the law."[1]

Albert Bernard, whose equipment was returned the following week while his son's case worked its way through the courts, and his sons presented a useful test case. They were not among the more radical element, for they stopped cutting when the *Paul* decision was overturned. The family sold its car, borrowed money to get into the logging business, and appears to have followed the prevailing rules, in as much as they could be ascertained.[2] Albert appealed to have his son's case dropped, but that was not to happen. Instead, First Nations and government lawyers targeted Joshua Bernard's charge as the trial that would address, much better than the *Thomas Peter Paul* situation, the legitimacy of Aboriginal rights and treaty claims to the forestry resources of New Brunswick. As Betty Ann Lavallée, president of the New Brunswick Aboriginal Peoples Council noted when Thomas Peter Paul faced his sentencing hearing: "It's been a good learning curve for us. I would guarantee that any court case that goes in the next time, let there be no doubt that the proper documentation is going to be in there."[3] Later, she said: "This time when it goes into court, we'll be armed to the teeth. This has the potential to blow the issue wide open again. It's going to be a hot time in the province after that."[4]

The *Joshua Bernard* case began in November 1998, with Bruce Wildsmith, the lawyer who defended Donald Marshall, appearing on Bernard's behalf. Unlike the brief *Thomas Peter Paul* case, the *Bernard* trial had all the elements of a classic Aboriginal rights test case, with the defendant and the Crown alike lining up a bevy of expert witnesses, many of the same people who appeared on the *Marshall* case, to present evidence. As Wildsmith stated well before the trial started: "We'll be going back to the issue that they were here first before the Europeans arrived. They used the land, harvested the resources, survived off it and despite conflicts between the European power and a series of treaties made that impacted on Nova Scotia and New Brunswick, the land was never ceded."[5] Put differently, Wildsmith intended to substantiate the *Bernard* case in way that had not been done for *Thomas Peter Paul*.

The court case, presented to Judge Dennis Lordon, was fairly straightforward. Joshua Bernard was driving a truck carrying twenty-two spruce logs, allegedly cut from Crown land.[5] Though without a licence and with no permit for the wood – and despite his work as an auxiliary police officer with the RCMP – Bernard claimed he did not know he was doing anything wrong. Albert Bernard testified about his relationship to Major Jean Baptiste Cope, Joshua's ancestor, who had signed the treaty with the British and who, according to Albert, "hunted, fished and lumbered from Newfoundland to the Gaspe." When Joshua Bernard took the stand, he stated "From my understanding, I was doing no wrong. I thought that I was allowed ... Me and my brothers, when the time came down, we sold some stuff, cars and we bought the truck."[7] Expert witnesses, including John Reid, a history professor from Saint Mary's University, and William Wicken, a historian from Ontario's York University, testified in support of the Mi'kmaq claims, as did Steven Augustine, a Mi'kmaq hereditary chief and ethnohistorian with the Canadian Museum of Civilization. Augustine informed the court about Mi'kmaq oral tradition, land and resource use, and spirituality, highlighting the Mi'kmaq connection to their traditional territories.[8] For the defence, the Crown called Dr Stephen Patterson, of *Marshall* fame, and Dr Andrew Baskerville, a professional forester.

The *Marshall* decision, coincidentally, came down in the middle of Joshua Bernard's trial, providing valuable new arguments to the defence team. The Supreme Court decision was both timely and crucial. As Wildsmith observed: "It's just the way the system works. The highest court in the land is the Supreme Court and when they speak everybody's supposed to listen. When the New Brunswick Court of Appeal speaks, everybody below them is supposed to listen. When the Court of Queen's Bench speaks, the provincial courts are supposed to listen. We're at the entry level here with a provincial court judge. He will have to make his mind up and then we'll see what happens from there."[9]

As Wildsmith said outside the trial courtroom: "Part of our argument here today relates to trading rights, and the Supreme Court of Canada has given us an authoritative interpretation of those trading rights. This is extremely significant because the treaty question is a major point in this case. We'll put it to his honour, and his honour will have to decide whether logs are the same as eels." Referring to the *Marshall* decision as a "great shot in the arm and a major milestone in the history of the Micmac people," Wildsmith reminded observers that "it's only as good as what governments and courts make it."[10] A portion of the trial also focused on Patterson's testimony that the eighteenth-century context of the treaty did not bestow continuing commercial rights on First Nations in the region. The

Crown obviously hoped that Patterson's arguments would find more favour than they had before the Supreme Court of Canada. The trial concluded in January 2000.

Lordon delivered his verdict on 13 April 2000. The defendant had admitted a "prima facie case: he was at the time and place alleged in possession of timber that had been cut by other Indians from Crown lands without authorization from the Crown. The spruce logs in question were in the course of being transported by the Defendant for sale to Anderson's Mill in Miramichi City." This decision, which came after consideration of the twenty-seven volumes of documentary evidence, is an excellent example of the mixture of historical analysis and jurisprudence associated with First Nations treaty cases. After a lengthy review of the historical circumstances surrounding the eighteenth-century treaties, Lordon declared: "The evidence convinces me that there was not traditional trade in logs and that trade in wood products produced by the Mi'kmaq such as baskets, snowshoes, and canoes was secondary to fur trade and was occasional and incidental." Moreover, "there is no evidence before me that the harvesting of logs was in any way part of the distinctive culture of the Miramichi Mi'kmaq at the time of contact." He then addressed the defence arguments about treaty rights, Aboriginal rights, Aboriginal title, First Nations occupation of the lands involved, and the Royal Proclamation of 1763. Having reviewed the arguments brought forward, and having rejected each in turn, he found Joshua Bernard "guilty as charged."[11] The First Nations immediately declared their intention to appeal, and there were no protests or outbursts after the decision came down. Mi'kmaq and Maliseet expected that the case, regardless of how it came out, would be appealed, and they had steeled themselves for the long haul. The trial before Lordon was simply stage one in a process that will eventually stretch all the way to the Supreme Court in Ottawa. This time, unlike September 1999 when the *Marshall* decision came down, everyone in the Maritimes will be watching.

As the *Bernard* case works its way through the appeal process, the issue of New Brunswick Aboriginal logging rights will once again land on the desks of the Supreme Court of Canada. When it does, the First Nations will face a different court. Chief Justice Antonio Lamer has stepped aside, and has been replaced by Justice Beverley McLachlin. The new Chief Justice wrote a dissenting opinion on the *Marshall* case, arguing for a narrow interpretation of eighteenth-century treaty rights. As she stated: "Based on the wording of the treaties and an extensive review of the historical evidence, the trial judge [who decided against *Marshall*] concluded that the only trade right conferred by the treaties was a 'right to bring' goods to truckhouses that terminated with the demise of the exclusive trading and truckhouse regime. This led to the conclusion that no Crown breach was established ... The record amply supports this conclusion." Being Chief Justice does not give Judge McLachlin extraordinary powers and in no way ensures that the Court's ruling on an eventual *Bernard* appeal will follow the logic of her dissent on *Marshall*. What the new appointment highlights is the uncertainty of the legal process, depending as it does on the actions, interpretations, assumptions, predispositions, and legal perspectives of a diverse and ever-changing group of judges.

Nova Scotia Mi'kmaq, backing their own logging case before the courts, followed the *Bernard* judgment with interest and immediately declared their determination to press forward. The Nova Scotia trial involved 30 Mi'kmaq loggers, with interests covering a large portion of the province, unlike Bernard's more narrowly focused case. Bernd Christmas, a legal adviser to the Union of Nova Scotia Indians, said that the New Brunswick decision was unlikely to affect their trial.[12] The determination of the Nova Scotia Mi'kmaq to proceed with their case only underscored the open-ended nature of the legal issues created by the Marshall decision. Not only were there numerous matters specific to the Supreme Court judgement that required clarification, Mi'kmaq and Maliseet people were anxious to discover how far their treaty rights extended. Even as the Joshua Bernard's legal team prepared for an appeal, at least one other major logging case was working its way into the courts.

As the first round of the *Bernard* case concluded, the saga of the *Marshall* decision continued. Through the winter of 1999–2000, Department of Fisheries and Oceans officials met with band chiefs and councillors and attempted to put fishing agreements in place. There was particular nervousness about Burnt Church, the focal point for much of the conflict in the fall of 1999 and home to the most assertive First Nation in the region. Uncertainty remained about how far the *Marshall* decision extended, with New Brunswick enduring debates about moose hunting[13] and Nova Scotia witnessing the seizure of two First Nations crab fishing boats in mid-February 2000. Chief Lawrence Paul accused Fisheries of "acting like the gestapo" and continued: "All they're doing is sowing more seeds of anger. I don't think Natives are going to be pushed and charged and harassed without a confrontation."[14] Alex Dedam of Burnt Church said, "We're talking access, but we're just getting tokenism from DFO at the moment."[15] The real story of the winter of 1999–2000 was not the occasional outburst and conflict, but the numerous closed-door meetings held throughout the region by federal officials attempting to reach negotiated settlements before the start of the spring lobster season. An observer described the arrangements in one area, overlooked by those more interested in conflict than reconciliation: "Mi'kmaq bands in various parts of the Maritimes quietly cut deals with local fishermen on protocols for their entry into the lobster fishery. The deals came quickest in areas like Pictou County, NS, where members of the Maritime Fishermen's Union had already been working with would-be Mi'kmaq fishermen, and a relationship of trust and communication had preceded the court ruling. The media mostly ignored these agreements."[16]

Slowly, and with little fanfare, agreements were reached – but not with Burnt Church. Early in April the band declared its intention to ignore federal fishing regulations and to impose its own regulatory regime on band members. Kathy Lambert of Burnt Church put the community's frustrations in context: "There are bad feelings. The non-native fishermen are worried about their livelihood. But how about our livelihood? Eighty-five per cent of the people here are unemployed. It's a good feeling when you can go and work and earn a few bucks. I mean, we're not in there to get rich. A lot of natives just want to make a few bucks."[17] The federal government avoided this scenario with other bands by offering a variety of economic development and training packages to convince the bands to sign on. Burnt Church rejected the proposals and even secured support from Christian Peacemakers (Mennonite and Quaker), who came to the reserve in early April to show their solidarity with the Mi'kmaq.[18] Janet Shoemaker declared that their intent was to serve as witnesses, to listen to the First Nations, and to represent the Aboriginal case to the public and to government. As she observed, "We try to think of creative ways to put pressure on people in power who are oppressing."[19]

Burnt Church remained the major anomaly into the summer of 2000. Pressed by First Nations, area residents, Maritime fishers, and the Standing Committee on Fisheries and Oceans,[20] Fisheries Minister Herb Dhaliwal, head negotiator James MacKenzie, and the Department of Fisheries and Oceans worked through the winter and early spring to finalize agreements before the start of the 2000 lobster fishery. While many First Nations people throughout the region resented the federal government's offers and the negotiated settlements, most communities signed on. Some First Nations leaders were upset with the community-based approach. Alex Denny, head of the Mi'kmaq Grand Council, stated: "I'm worried sick because the negotiators are attacking band by band. It's divide and conquer ... Once they sign these agreements, they're held by where it hurts."[21] Dhaliwal's approach of quiet negotiations had, for a time at least, bought relative peace and calm along the east coast. The bitter words and animosities of the fall of 1999 did not resurface the following spring. Even at Burnt Church, where Mi'kmaq fishers and Fisheries officials played a game of lobster trap "tag," there was more posturing than confrontation. Both sides were determined to make a point. For Burnt Church, it was the basic argument that First Nations had, under the *Marshall* decision, the right to fish for commercial purposes and to regulate their harvest. The federal government, also citing the *Marshall* decision and clarification, asserted that it had an obligation and a duty to enforce the fisheries regulations.

The Burnt Church dispute continued to attract the time and attention of the Department of Fisheries and Oceans. In April 2000 community members declared their intention to regulate their own fishery, even though they anticipated the federal rejection of their assertion of authority.[22] Even though a settlement appeared to have been reached near the end of April,[23] the leadership ultimately refused to negotiate a final settlement. Nevertheless, Dhaliwal allocated a substantial fishery to the community – the equivalent of seventeen commercial licences, or more than 5,100 lobster traps, and over $300,000 in crab quotas that, according to the minister, had not been taken up. On the broader issue of Aboriginal control of fisheries regulation, Dhaliwal was quite clear: "It appears that some, though not all, parties at Burnt Church want to regulate and control the fishery, independently of the Government of Canada. One cannot assert only the part of a Supreme Court decision that one agrees with, and reject the rest. The fish resources are the common property of Canada; and the Supreme Court affirmed my authority and responsibility to regulate for conservation and other purposes." Dhaliwal reiterated his determination to enforce federal regulations, while remaining open to further dialogue with the Burnt Church First Nation. He was willing to accept Burnt Chruch's lobster tags, provided an appropriate regulatory agreement could be reached with the community.[24] Band members continued to fish, declaring, "We feel it's our inherent right and we're not going to let anyone stop us."[25] With regard to their determination to manage the resource, Burnt Church leader James Ward declared: "To accept their rules is the acceptance of oppression. It would be a clear infringement of our treaty rights."[26] For their part, Fisheries officers removed unlicensed traps, and the contest continued into the summer.[27]

Other communities, including Big Cove, signed agreements with the federal government. The deal with Big Cove was valued at $6.5 million. The agreement, which Chief Robert Levi said he signed in preference to having one imposed on him, added twelve licences to the existing sixteen held by the band, included a crab licence, and provided funds to build twenty-two additional fishing vessels, more than doubling the band's fishing fleet. The 2,400 band members also received money for fishing gear, training, and local infrastructure, designed to ensure that the band was able to capitalize on commercial fishing opportunities.[28] For Big Cove and many other communities, the *Marshall* decision had had a direct and immediate impact. If the agreements fell far short of what the Mi'kmaq wanted or assumed was theirs by treaty right, the settlements nonetheless brought substantial commercial benefits.

Non-Aboriginal vigilance and suspicion continued, capped by suggestions that First Nations were mixing the commercial and food fisheries, to the detriment of fishing stocks. Non-Aboriginal fishers formed the Atlantic Fishing Industry Alliance, based in Yarmouth, to better represent their interests with the federal government. Denny Morrow, Alliance spokesperson, highlighted their concerns: "We're not comfortable with bureaucrats ... deciding how much access the native community gets under the treaty right to the lobster fishery or the snow crab fishery or any [other]." Further, he indicated the industry's anger at the "abuse that we've seen take place in the food fishery over the last 10 years."[29] The Aboriginal right to fish for subsistence purposes, as per the *Sparrow* decision, took precedence over all other resource uses except conservation, and non–First Nations fishers worried that Aboriginal harvesters were mixing the two enterprises. The Department of Fisheries and Oceans had responded to the changed circumstances by negotiating reduced food fishery allocations. Lennox Island First Nation, for example, saw its food fishery quota drop by three-quarters (from 80,000 pounds to 20,0000) and, at Big Cove, the allocation declined from 120,000 pounds to 50,000 pounds. Indian Brook formerly ran 475 traps for the food fishery, a number reduced to thirty-five. Other First Nations communities similarly negotiated reductions in their food fishery.[30]

While concerns circulated and worries grew, some non-Aboriginal Maritimers expressed their continued support for the First Nations approach. A coalition of twenty-eight social activist organizations, including such diverse groups as the Aboriginal Rights Coalition Atlantic, Bay of Fundy Inshore Fishermen's Association, Black Business Development Agency, Christian Peacemaker teams, Eel Ground Community Development Centre, First Nations Environmental Network, Fredericton Oxfam, Fundy Environmental Action Group, Kikahan Committee of Tobique, People against Nuclear Energy, Raging Grannies of Fredericton, Sacred Mountain Society of Eskasoni, Sierra Club of

Canada, Eastern Atlantic Group, Tantramar Environmental Alliance, and Terre-à-Terre (Down-to-Earth), petitioned the federal government to cooperate with the Burnt Church band. They noted that

> Mi'kmaq people have been fishing the Miramichi Bay from time immemorial. Currently, they seek to continue to manage that ecosystem in a sustainable manner and, at the same time, provide for their families from that resource. Despite a recent Supreme Court decision affirming their Treaty Rights to make a moderate living from fishing, they are threatened by constant Department of Fisheries and Oceans (DFO) interference and harassment in their fishery. On the bay, tensions and divisions between the Mi'kmaq, Acadian and English communities and lack of leadership from the Government of Canada and DFO in building a co-operative solution could lead to a breakdown of the situation and violence, such as was experienced in the area last fall.[31]

The resolution called on the government to recognize the Burnt Church tags and to work with the band to develop a sustainable, cooperative management system. James Ward, a resident of Burnt Church, said of the resolution: "It's outstanding. The people of Burnt Church really appreciate their support. It's great to see social groups willing to support us; groups like this that have a more social conscience."[32]

In June 2000 Minister Dhaliwal provided a update on the state of negotiations with First Nations. He pointed out – underscoring the dramatic transition associated with the *Marshall* decision – that over one hundred Aboriginal vessels had legally become part of the east coast fishing fleet, authorized to harvest crab, lobster, and other ocean species. Voluntary licence "retirements" from commercial fishermen (people paid to surrender their licences) opened space in the fishery for Aboriginal communities. In total, close to 150 "licence packages," representing a total of 550 licences, had been secured. The arrangements worked out with the First Nations went beyond fishing licences and quotas. They included commitments to fund training, improvements to local fishing infrastructure, and other economic incentives. While the deals seemed basic, in comparison with the euphoric assumptions that followed the September 1999 Supreme Court decision, they represented a vast expansion of First Nations economic and fishing support from the pre-*Marshall* era.

In his summary, Dhaliwal noted that twenty-four First Nations communities had signed agreements. Even though there were questions whether the *Marshall* decision applied in Quebec, settlements were reached with the Gesgapegiag, Gespeg, and Malécite de Viger First Nations. On Prince Edward Island, both Abegweit and Lennox Island signed. In Nova Scotia, agreements were concluded with

Eskasoni, Horton, Millbrook, Pictou Landing, Wagmatcook, and Waycobah. New Brunswick First Nations communities at Big Cove, Buctouche, Eel River Bar, Fort Folly, Indian Island, Kingsclear, Oromocto, Pabineau, Red Bank, and Saint Mary's signed on. Three more had reached Agreements in Principle. Another three communities – Woodstock, Madawaska, and Eel Ground in New Brunswick – negotiated settlements under the Aboriginal Fisheries Strategy, which allowed for the harvesting of fish for food, social, and ceremonial purposes. Equally important – and much less remarked upon – non-status and off-reserve First Nations, represented by the Native Council of Prince Edward Island, the New Brunswick Aboriginal Peoples Council, and the Native Council of Nova Scotia, negotiated arrangements under the Aboriginal Fisheries Strategy. These agreements did not extend to commercial fishing rights. By the summer of 2000 a total of 207 commercial licences involving ninety-one vessels had been allocated to First Nations (including lobster, 71, tuna, 9, shrimp, 4, snow crab, 8, scallop, 3, sea urhcin, 3, herring, 13, mackerel, 6, groundfish, 8, swordfish, 5, gasperau, 8, oyster, 13, eel, 23, sea cucumber, 1, smelt, 12, clams, 10, quahaug, 1, squid, 4, and rock crab, 4).[33]

In an address to First Nations and non-Aboriginal fishers at Caraquet, New Brunswick, on 7 June 2000, Dhaliwal offered a positive appraisal of his government's efforts:

Last fall a Supreme Court decision gave Aboriginal people in this region new access to the commercial fishery. That decision caused surprise. It caused confusion. It could have caused a lot of trouble. But it didn't, because people have worked together. Most First Nations have taken a highly responsible attitude; and I salute leaders such as Chief Second Peter Barlow [from Indian Island]. They have shown patience. They have shown co–operation. And they have shown a concern for fishery conservation.

Let me add that co–operation has come from the commercial industry as well. Yes, there were one or two regrettable incidents last fall. And yes, one or two First Nations themselves still remain suspicious. But most people have realized, we can all work together. Most First Nations have signed interim fishing agreements. These agreements put fishing on an orderly basis, and they provide boats, licences, and other assistance towards a successful fishery.

Today boats from Indian Island and Big Cove are fishing peacefully from this wharf. Non–Aboriginal fishermen are working side by side with them. It's the same story all over the Maritimes and Gaspé. People have realized there is no real threat to the commercial fishery. We are making room for First Nations through voluntary licence retirements. And in some cases where First Nations lack recent experience in the fishery, commercial fishermen are helping to train them.

The Aboriginal fleet remains relatively small, maybe a couple of hundred boats by the end of the year. But that small fleet represents a big opportunity. A typical boat can give work to two, three, or even more people, plus shore employment. On a small reserve, this can make a major difference.[34]

That Dhaliwal could reduce the tensions in the fall of 1999 to "one or two regrettable incidents" was the wordsmithing of a politician suffering from an overdose of optimism. Conditions had not been set right quite as quickly or definitively as he suggested. At the same time, he was right to highlight the substantial change from eight months earlier, when violence and confrontation threatened to engulf the east coast fishery.

The contest and controversy over Aboriginal rights is deceptive. In the fall of 1999 the prospect of continuing conflict seemed all but inevitable. A few months later, in the summer of 2000, the confrontations had died down and the anger and frustrations had seemingly been replaced in most areas by cooperation and accommodation. Many key issues have not been resolved, and the agreements negotiated between 1999 and 2000 are interim in nature. Negotiations will continue long into the future. Passamaquoddy people, who once occupied territory that became Canada but now live in Maine, asserted their rights to fish in the Bay of Fundy in late April and early May, with between twenty-five and thirty fishers collecting clams, lobster, and fish off Deer Island and challenging Canadian officials to stop them. Fisheries communications director André-Marc Lanteigne said of the report: "The Marshall decision confirms that the treaty right is a community-based right and they have no community in Canada. So if there is fishing in Canadian waters, either it is authorized through a court order that they may have on the transboundary stock or they're fishing illegally and we'll have to check into that."[35] In the first days of July 2000, one of the Mi'kmaq communities conducted an assessment of the potential for lobster harvests in its area. It declared that, if the report was positive, it would start a summer commercial lobster fishery, well in advance of the regular commercial season. Non-Aboriginal fishers and government officials seethed and expressed their frustration. And so the cycle seems to be beginning again.

Complex legal and political debates are not easily resolved, and the Maritime fishing dispute remains highly contentious. As the final revisions were being made to this book, tensions flared once again. By the summer of 2000, twenty-nine communities in the region had negotiated interim agreements with the Department of Fisheries and Oceans and were participating, in a legal and licensed fashion, in the commercial lobster fishery. Two communities, Burnt Church in New Brunswick and Indian Brook First Nation in Nova Scotia, refused to sign.[36] Indian Brook, rubbing salt in DFO's wounds, used a fishing boat purchased for the band by the department to continue its commercial fishery in the closed season. The department responded by seizing several boats and charging a number of Indian Brook fishers. According to the captain of the *I'lnusibuk*, one of the boats taken by the DFO: " They rushed in with all their riot gear. They boarded with I would say 20 DFO officers. It wasn't necessary. One man could've came on and I would have let them seize the boat. They're trying to intimidate us to keep us off the bay that way."[37] Reg Maloney, chief of Indian Brook, said of the government's action: "We have the right but they have the might. They can do anything they wish."[38]

Burnt Church, site of the fall 1999 confrontations, moved close to the boiling point again in August 2000. The government offered the community a sizable package as an interim agreement. According to Dhaliwal, the federal offer included five lobster boats, a new wharf worth $2.2 million, $250,000 for new buildings associated with the fishery, and money to replace damaged traps and for maintenance and training. In return, Burnt Church would be required to abide by government fisheries regulations and would have to limit off-season fishing to a small food and ceremonial catch.[39] While other bands agreed, Burnt Church refused. It fished through the commercial season and announced its intention to keep fishing for lobster once the official season had closed.

The Mi'kmaq band refused to accept DFO's regulations and argued that, under the *Marshall* decision, it had the right to establish its own fisheries rules. Rejecting the government's offer of forty lobster pots for food and ceremonial purpose, the community called for a vote on the implementation of the band's scheme, which permitted four licensed pots for every member of the band. According to James Ward, a Burnt Church man who played a key role in drafting the management strategy, government harassment had gone too far. Indicating that he planned to put the Mi'kmaq case to the United Nations Human Rights Commission, Ward said, "We think it is the best case of an abuse of human rights."[40] The leadership put its plan before the community on 9 August 2000 and received a resounding endorsement, with 308 members voting in favour and only 28 opposed. The potential of 6,000 lobster pots in the water off-season enraged local non-Aboriginal fishers and stiffened the resolve of the Fisheries department, which faced the prospect of all the other agreements in the region unravelling if it agreed to the Burnt Church demand.

Aboriginal comments during the highly public debate indicated that a significant gap had emerged between the DFO and Burnt Church understandings of the *Marshall* decision. The government acted on the based of the Supreme Court clarification, which made it clear that First Nations had to abide by government-imposed regulations and conservation measures. Burnt Church argued that *Marshall* acknowledged their right to fish for commercial purposes and put no such constraints on the membership. Further, many of the Burnt Church people quoted in the press referred to their "inherent right" to fish – a radically different concept from the treaty-based right that had actually be confirmed by the Supreme Court. Their defiance was striking. Douglas Dedham, a young Mi'kmaq fisher, said, "On the boat or in the court, I'm willing to take a bullet or a charge."[41] Run-ins escalated on the water, including several near swampings of small Mi'kmaq lobster boats. Largely because of DFO's substantial presence, and because the lessons of the previous year had been learned, non-Aboriginal fishers stood well back from the growing conflict.

    Late in the evening of 13 August, DFO moved in aggressively. Fisheries vessels, guided by powerful spotlights, moved across Miramichi Bay, picking up as many as 700 to 1,000 lobster traps left out the previous day by Burnt Church fishers. The community was enraged. Young men spoke openly of inviting Warrior societies to assist their struggle. Band members threw up a roadblock on the main road and lit a massive bonfire. The RCMP responded in kind, setting up roadblocks on either side of the Mi'kmaq blockade and checking vehicles heading onto the reserve. Non-Aboriginal fishers urged the government to hold to its position, while other First Nations offered words of encouragement to Burnt Church. When band leaders talked of replacing the captured traps – an expense that would further deplete the limited resources of the Burnt Church community – they received promises of assistance from other First Nations groups. An atmosphere of defiance continued.

    Conflict escalated in the following days. Angry Mi'kmaq fishers threw fish guts at Fisheries officers. Both sides accused the other of provoking confrontations on the water, resulting in several near-miss collisions and minor boat rammings. Several Mi'kmaq fishers were sprayed with pepper spray. And Mi'kmaq observers claimed – over DFO denials – that firearms had been drawn and used to intimidate the protesters. James Ward, one of the more out-spoken members of the Burnt Church band, said: "This is going to get worse ... This will not be tolerated by our people."[42] The department sought to have a group of Mi'kmaq men, charged with obstructing fisheries offices, barred from Miramichi Bay. Justice Denis Lordon denied the government's request. Mohawk supporters from Quebec announced their decision to travel to Burnt Church in an act of solidarity. The Listuguj First Nation from Quebec dispatched a dozen Rangers, the band's fisheries officers, and three boats to assist the Mi'kmaq protest.[43]

The standoff continued. Accusations flew in all directions, and First Nations supporters began to arrive in larger numbers. Kahnawake First Nation (Mohawk) in Quebec sent five councillors and supplies to Burnt Church, determined to show its support for the community.[44] It was a reminder – hardly needed – of the Oka conflict that held the nation riveted a decade earlier. Then, on 16 August, following a tense day on the Miramichi Bay, Burnt Church and the Department of Fisheries and Oceans announced that they had reopened a dialogue and had, even more, agreed on a "truce."[45] The Mi'kmaq made it clear that they were not engaging in negotiations – their position had not shifted – but they did want to find a way to lessen the conflict on the water and bring an end to the roadblock.

Although most First Nations leaders remained relatively quiet, Reg Maloney, chief of the Shubenacadie Band Council, stated that many Mi'kmaq supported the people of Burnt Church. As he wrote, "DFO's response is that they honour the Marshall decision but only if it is exercised during the regular open season. The Shubenacadie band says that DFO must first justify the imposition of the regular seasons limits before the holders of the Treaty right are interfered with and that, until such justification is provided, the fishing will continue. DFO says that their justification is based on conservation concerns, primarily that the trap yield is 10 times greater during the closed season than it is during the open season. The Shubenacadie band's response is that even if it were true that the yield is 10 times greater, the amount of traps (800) sought to be eventually used by the band is less than one-tenth of the allowable catch during open season in that area (St. Mary's Bay). Furthermore, the Shubenacadie band has only been using approximately 150 traps thus far – a figure far below any legitimate conservation concern."[46] For Maloney, the folks at Burnt Church, and many other First Nations people, the Department of Fisheries and Oceans position on Mi'kmaq fishing was simply wrong.

Burnt Church had probably pushed the envelope further than the federal government could tolerate. The department and the federal government could not back down without throwing all other agreements open for renegotiation and without infuriating non-Aboriginal fishers and communities. As the *Globe and Mail* editorialized, "While the Burnt Church natives may have gone to sea to catch lobsters, they may well return having committed strategic hara-kari."[47] While the *Telegraph-Journal* called for a second court assessment of the rights of Mi'kmaq fishers, the *National Post* compared the developing conflict to the Oka standoff in 1990, described the interim agreements with twenty-nine First Nations communities as "gifts," and chastised the federal government for its willingness to compromise on Aboriginal rights. As one editorial argued: "A government committed to the rule of law and to conserving the fisheries would treat these rogue bands as it would any other law-breaking gang. But Canada now has the most supine Indian Affairs Ministry in its history, and a militant new Grand Chief of the Assembly of First Nations. The showdown is set to escalate, and it is lamentably clear who is going to blink first."[48] Grand Chief Matthew Coon Come, indicating his support for the Burnt Church people, demanded that the federal government pull back: "This is a small population .... being continually harassed as if they are going to deplete the entire ocean."[49] The Grand Chief visited the reserve on 16 August and pledged the support of his national organization to the Burnt Church cause:

When individual peoples, such as Burnt Church, take necessary and courageous steps to raise the standards for all, I will be there with them. And when they point out to Canadians that fairness and equity are essential if there is ultimately to be social peace and justice in this country, I will be there to stand with them. And their national organization will bring their message of human rights and social dignity right across Canada and to the world.

I say to the minister: Call off your troops ... I believe that all Canadians want fair and equitable solutions that will enable our people to get off welfare, get to work, raise our families and build vibrant communities. For this to happen, we must regain access to and jurisdiction over lands, water and resources, for more than our people to just scrape by with the bare "necessities" of life – food, shelter if we are lucky, clothing and a few amenities.

This is the cry from the heart of Burnt Church."[50]

A final postscript. The appointment of former Ontario premier Bob Rae as a mediator for the Burnt Church controversy brought short-lived optimism. By 20 September, however, Rae had booked out of the discussions, fearing that the Mi'kmaq, commercial fishers and federal government were too far apart. The bitter struggle continued and the prospect for an escalating conflict seemed only too real.

Why, given the generally positive developments of 1999–2000 for First Nations people, are the residents of Burnt Church and Indian Brook continuing to press for more and asserting nationally and internationally their "right" to fish commercially? While the immediate answer is to be found in the leadership, internal dynamics, and history of specific communities (Burnt Church has long been a touchpoint on Aboriginal fishing issues), the larger explanation can be found on a drive through any of the Mi'kmaq settlements in the region. These are poor villages, with staggeringly high rates of unemployment, few local prospects, and many signs of social and cultural trauma. They know that their demands, presented as a major escalation in the fishery, represent only a tiny percentage – Mi'kmaq leaders say around 1 per cent of the area total – of the local harvest (see Appendix B). These are communities that have had few reasons for optimism in the past, that have argued for decades that they had a right to a share – they never demanded the entire industry – of the east coast fishery. In such settings, it is predictable that some members and bands will reach for it all and will be angered by the politics of compromise and negotiation.

This is, it seems, an appropriate point to end the narrative about the *Marshall* case and the subsequent fallout. The conflict is not over, as Indian Brook and Burnt Church clearly demonstrate. The fall fishery will likely see additional conflicts, and debate about the meaning and scope of the *Marshall* decision will continue well into the future. Almost a year after the Supreme Court decision, uncertainty continues to dog the east coast fishery. Among First Nations, there is a mix of optimism and intransigence. The optimism comes from the fact that they now have a substantial toe-hold in the commercial fishery. Who would have thought, in August 1999, that, within a year, Mi'kmaq fishers would be a formidable economic force and would be quickly building both the capacity and the ability to take a permanent and substantial place in the fishing industry? The intransigence originates in the well-founded Aboriginal belief that they have waited much too long for a recognition of their treaty rights.

Much remains to be done. At least one Aboriginal leader has spoken of the need for compensation for the First Nations for being blocked from the commercial fishery for so many years – a prospect that is sure to anger many non-Aboriginal people in the region and across the country. Fisheries agreements will have to be renegotiated. As André-Marc Lanteigne noted: "To truly define what Marshall is, it will take years. These agreements, they are a first step, they are interim and expire in March. When we go to renegotiate them, the new plans may look completely different."[51] More lobster licences held by non-Aboriginals will be purchased for First Nations use. More Aboriginal men and women will become proficient in the industry and will take their place as long-term fishers. And slowly, ever so slowly, First Nations communities will begin to see the social and economic benefits that come from achieving some small measure of financial stability.

First Nations insist that the matter is far from settled. While Burnt Church attracted the greatest attention in the summer of 2000, other communities also wished for far greater control over the commercial fishery. Many First Nations believed that the *Marshall* decision applied more generally, and was not restricted to fishing and hunting. They hoped to extend the treaty right to cover mining and other resource sectors. The *Bernard* case, a victory for the Crown in April 2000, was being appealed and will, in time, reach the Supreme Court of Canada. A victory for the First Nations would reopen the issues raised by the *Thomas Peter Paul* case and would do for the forest industry what *Marshall* did for the fishery. A loss would no doubt contribute to an outburst of First Nations anger and a strong internal debate about future court challenges. Many other issues – the applicability of the *Marshall* decision to First Nations from Quebec and Maine, long-term agreements on food and commercial fisheries, growing First Nations expectations about other resource sectors, management issues related to big-game hunting, First Nations demands for regulatory authority – remain only partially answered. Supreme Court decisions like that on the *Marshall* case generally represent a beginning, not an end, of the legal, political, and administrative work surrounding matters of Aboriginal and treaty rights.

Because Canadians appear genuinely to abhor violence and confrontation, there will be a desire to purge the collective memory of the angry words and aggressive acts of 1999. The images of conflict that filled television screens during the fall of 1999 will soon be forgotten and, in time, the name of Donald Marshall Jr will become synonymous more with Aboriginal fishing rights (as it should) than with the nearly tragic clashes along the east coast of Canada. But the *Marshall* controversy – and the *Thomas Peter Paul* contretemps from 1997 and 1998 – must be remembered and explored for insights into Aboriginal expectations, barriers to settlements, and the potency and limits of Aboriginal and treaty rights in the Maritimes. To ignore the lessons from these conflicts is to lose the opportunity to anticipate difficulties and, even better, to develop solutions in advance of future confrontations. Canada's record in the past in this regard is not strong: the experiences of British Columbia, the Yukon, and other Canadian and international jurisdictions did not figure prominently in Maritime discussions about Thomas Peter Paul and Donald Marshall Jr. One hopes that the Maritime region in particular, and the country in general, will seek insight and even inspiration in the bitter, divisive, and revealing conflicts over Aboriginal and treaty rights that engulfed the Maritimes in the last three years of the twentieth century.

CHAPTER EIGHT

What Does It Mean? The Marshall *Decision, East Coast Fisheries, and Aboriginal Rights*

The passage of time has muddied, not clarified, east coast waters. The *Marshall* decision remains a matter of widespread debate in the region, as the public discussion revealed during the spring 2000 lobster season and as observers noted after the April 2000 provincial court decision in the *Joshua Bernard* case. The full implications of the *Marshall* judgment will not be known for many years, as First Nations, provincial governments, non-Aboriginal residents, the federal government, and the courts continue to wrestle with the legal, political, and practical consequences of the Supreme Court ruling. Observers of the trajectory of Aboriginal rights in Canada have learned to be sceptical of those who offer definitive answers to the complex questions surrounding Aboriginal and treaty rights in Canada. Cynics assume that the Aboriginal rights "industry" will propel the debates forward for decades, enriching lawyers, empowering politicians, and making heroes out of another generation of Aboriginal people like Thomas Peter Paul, Donald Marshall Jr, and Joshua Bernard.

First Nations, Maritime governments, the private sector, and the federal government face problems and opportunities in the coming months and years. There will be plenty of both, for there is little that is clean and simple in the resolution of two-hundred-year-old treaty rights and Aboriginal legal entitlements. British Columbia and the Canadian North have wrestled with the uncertainty, occasionally celebrated major victories, and gritted their teeth at the persistence and seeming intractability of the issues. As First Nations have discovered across the country, determining Aboriginal and treaty rights is rather like peeling an onion. There is always another layer, and the texture and taste are unknowable until they are exposed. No list of potential difficulties and options can be exhaustive, and the working out of tensions and conflicts depends in large measure on the quality, integrity, and perseverance of the political leadership involved in the issues. With this caveat, however, it is useful to consider some of the bumps, twists, turns, and road stops that the Maritimes and Canada might well encounter along the road that was extended by the *Marshall* decision.

While attention focuses largely on First Nations–non-Aboriginal conflict, it is vital to realize that major struggles are underway within First Nations communities. The battle over the voting rights of off-reserve band members, resolved in the Supreme Court's 1999 decision on the Corbiere case,[1] will force a significant realignment of band politics. So, too, will the continuing struggle between non-status Indians and Metis for a share of the benefits from Aboriginal rights victories and federal and provincial government programs. Internal tensions tend to escalate in line with legal gains.

The only certainty about the *Marshall* decision is that it has created enormous uncertainty for the Maritimes. The Supreme Court judgment, designed to address one specific legal quandary, has, as is so often the case, created a variety of additional problems and challenges. It will take years – decades, perhaps – for the legal issues to be clarified and resolved and for workable solutions to be developed. The racial tensions and hotbeds created by the *Marshall* decision will likely linger even longer. Before identifying potential solutions, it is useful first to consider some of the problems and issues that will have to be faced in the coming years.

Over the past one hundred years, governments, charitable organizations, and First Nations have identified a series of "solutions" to what is often described as the "Indian problem." The problem is clear: Aboriginal marginalization, cultural and social difficulties, and economic distress. The would-be solutions have ranged from assimilation to Christianization, from residential schools to government subsidies, from segregation and separation to complete integration. All have been judged by history to have been failures, as has the paternalistic ethos that led to their establishment. Over the past fifteen years, Aboriginal self-government has been presented as the critical missing element in the effort to rebuild and invigorate First Nations societies. A great deal of hope surrounds the transfer of power and money from the federal government to bands.

For the Maritimes, the *Marshall* decision is being presented as something of a panacea, the crucial opportunity to set right generations of discrimination and non-Aboriginal interference in First Nations affairs. The judgment will help in some ways, providing economic advantages that simply did not exist before September 1999. But it also carries considerable difficulties, particularly the escalation of hostilities between non-indigenous and First Nations people in the Maritimes. While the *Marshall* decision gives the Mi'kmaq and Maliseet new opportunities, it lacks the authority, clarity, and all-party support necessary to truly represent a foundation for a completely new relationship.

The *Marshall* judgment, seen on a continuum that stretches from *White and Bob* to *Delgamuutw*, has reinforced the Aboriginal position on their legal rights and convinced many that future court cases will result in greater First Nations power. For many Mi'kmaq and Maliseet people, *Marshall* is a key, but small, step along the path to eventual Aboriginal empowerment. First Nations advocates of sovereignty see *Marshall* as a relatively minor success – it recognizes limited treaty rights to commercial harvesting rights, not an inherent indigenous right to commercial resources – and intend to push for much greater authority. While non-Aboriginals recoil in dismay over the implications of the *Marshall* decision, it is vital to recognize that more assertive First Nations demand and expect more power and even greater recognition of their Aboriginal rights. Heightened expectations rise very quickly. Only a few months after the *Thomas Peter Paul* decision by Judge Turnbull, Aboriginal leaders were demanding compensation for Sable Island natural gas, a conflict that took months to resolve, and were insisting that the Fredericton-Moncton highway, initially planned as a toll road, would require payment to First Nations communities.[2]

The *Marshall* decision specifically addressed the harvesting of eels. By implication, it has been assumed that it relates to lobster, crab, and other ocean resources. The *Joshua Bernard* and/or the Nova Scotia Mi'kmaq cases will demonstrate in time whether the Supreme Court decision applies to commercial logging. Nova Scotia Mi'kmaq hoped that the *Marshall* decision would convince the government to drop the charges against thirty-one Mi'kmaq loggers charged with violations of provincial forestry regulations. Chief Lawrence Paul of the Assembly of Nova Scotia Mi'kmaq Chiefs asserted: "Right now the province is giving us no choice but to fight this matter in the courts. Premier Hamm and his government still seem to be of the opinion that these treaties are fairy tales. They don't want to recognize anything until the courts force them."[3] The trial commenced in July 1999, stopped and started again through the fall, ending in the summer of 2000. A decision has not yet been reached.[4] Many First Nations leaders and some government officials assume that *Marshall* will apply more widely – to minerals, tourist sites, and land. Negotiations may result in the implicit acceptance that the *Marshall* decision applies quite widely. Failing a compromise agreement, First Nations will almost certainly press for an extension of their treaty right to use all resources for commercial purposes. Each attempt to extend Aboriginal rights, to say nothing of legal or political decisions to enlarge First

Nations authority, will be greeted with howls of protest from non-Aboriginal peoples and will generate uncertainty in the region.

The New Brunswick moose harvest is a good case in point. The *Marshall* decision made it clear that Aboriginal people could hunt and fish and, as a treaty right, sell the products of their harvesting for commercial profit. While attention has focused on lobsters and logs, a substantial change has occurred in the forests. According to provincial Natural Resources Department officials, unlicensed Mi'kmaq and Maliseet hunters shot over 1,000 moose during the 1999–2000 season – almost half the allowed provincial harvest of 2,000 animals. A single man from Tobique, New Brunswick, claimed to have killed twenty-four moose by himself. Aboriginal hunters shot more moose than they needed for food and sold them, often from the back of pickup trucks along major highways. According to Richard DeBow of the New Brunswick Wildlife Federation, there were no accurate figures for the Aboriginal moose hunt and "the rumours are that you can now buy a moose up on a reserve for $400." Don McAskill, a non-Aboriginal hunting camp operator, directed his anger at the Supreme Court: "We have a few people in Ottawa who need to be taken around the back of the barn and educated about the real world. They're all village idiots as far as I'm concerned."[5]

The province operates a tightly controlled moose harvest that routinely attracts around 60,000 applications for the 4,500 permits awarded annually. Marshall changed the dynamic entirely. The government of New Brunswick publicly stated its intention not to charge Aboriginal people with hunting moose illegally, even if they were exercising their treaty right (selling for profit) rather than the Aboriginal right (harvesting for food and community use). The province indicated a desire to meet with First Nations leaders to attempt to establish band-by-band quotas. As Natural Resources Minister Jeannot Volpe observed: " I don't want to force anything on them. [Native hunters] don't want it to be imposed. I want to work with them. They want to work with us. We're all working for the same objective."[6] Whatever is agreed, it is clear that the number of moose available for non-Aboriginal hunters will decline, perhaps precipitously. Furthermore, government officials and conservation organizations are deeply concerned about the potential for overharvesting and long-term depletion of the resource – a charge Aboriginal people reject as being disrespectful of First Nations self-government and environmental ethics.

In a sad twist on the *Marshall* rights issue, Nova Scotia encountered a serious problem with its moose harvest as well. Apparently, extensive hunting was being done under the guise of Aboriginal harvesting.

A representative of the Nova Scotia Department of Natural Resources reported that non-Aboriginal poachers would take along an Aboriginal person who had the right to harvest moose. If they were stopped, the Aboriginal person would be assigned responsibility for the moose carcass. T. Nevitte, an official with the department in Kentville, said: "There is criminal involvement there, for certain. There's a web of people involved in it. On many, many occasions hunters are seen outside of the licensed hunt, where you have two or three people in a vehicle, one being a Native, and a couple of moose in the back, and the claim is they belong to him or her. You begin to suspect [something] when those people end up there again and again, the same faces, the same vehicles."[7]

As early as mid-October 1999, while conflict still raged over lobster, Mi'kmaq leaders began to demand that government and industry take their new rights, broadly defined, more seriously. Chief Benjamin Paul of the Union of New Brunswick Indians appeared before the National Energy Board to demand a share of royalties on natural gas transported on the new Sable Island pipeline.[8] The Mi'kmaq eventually took this matter to court and lost in their attempts to delay construction. At the same time, a handful of Aboriginal loggers ventured into the woods, believing that the *Marshall* decision applied to timber harvests as well, only to be stopped by provincial forest officials who thought otherwise. Chief Robert Levi of Big Cove – who first called the regional and national media – took a group of loggers onto Irving Ltd land and defied the government to arrest him. Although a dozen reporters showed up, provincial officials were noticeably absent.[9] Levi did not achieve his main goal (a truckload of timber was seized shortly thereafter), but he once again served notice that the First Nations leaders intended to assert – and test – a broad definition of their treaty rights under the *Marshall* decision. As Levi argued in early November 1999: "Right now, we're cutting under Marshall and we feel we're not breaking any laws. If anyone tries to steal our equipment, they'll be met with opposition. We have to protect our equipment."[10] The New Brunswick government of Bernard Lord rejected Levi's demand that the logging deals, negotiated under the 5 per cent ceiling during the controversy surrounding the *Thomas Peter Paul* decision, be expanded. Levi and Big Cove eventually reached a deal with the government of New Brunswick in the middle of November. It was only an interim deal; the final resolution lay in the offing. This debate – whether the *Marshall* decision extended to commercial logging rights for First Nations – would ultimately be resolved in the courts.

There are other issues to consider. The *Marshall* case has already consumed a great deal of time and caused hundreds of thousands of dollars, to be expended by First Nations, governments, and non-Aboriginal groups. The future holds the promise of much more litigation, as all participants seek clarification and vindication. While the issues are before the courts, uncertainty and confusion will reign, costs will escalate, and a great deal of time and effort will be required. Court cases can sap vitality from participants, for they absorb human and financial resources that could be used elsewhere. Moreover, as the *Marshall* case demonstrates, legal judgments are rarely final and more often spark an ongoing cycle of expensive court challenges. Maritimers will, almost certainly, learn to watch court cases with much greater attention than in the past.

Victory for one often represents a loss for others. Any resource authority gained by the Mi'kmaq and Maliseet will, invariably, mean declining authority for non-Aboriginals. Given a finite resource, there is no other option. Non-Aboriginal resource users will see their livelihood threatened. There may be compensation insulating individuals from personal financial dislocations, but the broader society will, invariably, pay a price. Shifting resource incomes from non-Aboriginal to First Nations people will strengthen one economy at the cost of another. These dislocations will not be greeted with enthusiasm, and protests are virtually inevitable. If the transfer of resource income is relatively low, the bitterness and anger will be dissipated over time. Sentiment runs strongly through the Maritimes that one group – non-Aboriginal resource users – will pay the greatest price for the *Marshall* decision. They fear that, even with private compensation, the local industries and the communities will decline substantially. If this occurs, and such change is likely, outrage will fester and, given the right circumstances, erupt in vigorous protests.

Some of the costs associated with these conflicts are more difficult to quantify. Since the *Thomas Peter Paul* decision, overt expression of anti-Aboriginal sentiments has escalated. No doubt much of the anti–First Nations feeling lies unspoken among the Maritimes population. Just as certainly, the uncertainty generated by the *Paul* and *Marshall* decisions enflamed racially based emotions. Nasty words, spoken in dockside confrontations, public meetings, and media commentaries, flew around like poisonous darts.[11] First Nations people who wondered how they were viewed by non-Aboriginal people wondered no more. As a woman from Freeport, Nova Scotia, wrote with sadness: "People who were once allies have now become enemies due to one agreeing with native rights. Those who support native rights are ostracized and treated like dirt in their own communities. Threats have even been uttered and these are coming from the non-natives; the natives want peace. What do violence and vandalism prove? They only create problems that eventually will escalate. The natives have put up with this kind of attitude of destruction for centuries."[12] As uncertainty lingers, and as First Nations victories continue (if they do), it is safe to assume that racial tensions will escalate. Conversely, if First Nations court cases are not successful, radicalism and confrontational First Nations tactics will expand. The Maritimes avoided a meltdown in 1999, when the potential for violence was very real. The prospects for continued tensions are strong and will continue the realignment of First Nations–non-Aboriginal relations in the Maritimes.

Consider the words of Nova Scotian writer Charles Moore, whose thoughts were widely shared in the region in 1999–2000:

You simply can't create several classes of citizens living side by side in the same society without causing festering resentment – if not outright hostility that too easily explodes into violence. The "cultural mosaic" notion is a romantic crock dreamed up by leftist ideologues that, like most leftist theories, hasn't a prayer of working in the real world. The u.s. style "melting pot" cultural blueprint may not be perfect, but it surely beats the stuffing out of programmatic multiculturalism when it comes to nation-building and creating a functional society. We need a national debate on whether we want Canada to be a polyglot of special interest groups elbowing for court-mandated social advantage, or a real nation.[13]

For many Maritimers, the *Marshall* decision offered a future of racial conflict, not harmony.

To complicate matters, First Nations are far from confident that the letter and intent of the *Marshall* decision will be honoured. The concept of "government lawlessness" in the management of indigenous affairs is deeply entrenched in history. That First Nations people have rights, even if clearly delineated by the courts, is no assurance that these rights will be enjoyed in full. Governments have a variety of mechanisms available to them that can limit the exercise of First Nations legal authority. Negotiations can drag on for months, if not years. Governments can reduce budgets for First Nations organizations, shift key personnel responsible for First Nations files, delay decisions on relatively straightforward legal matters, or use a variety of legal or administrative measures to undercut First Nations freedom and options. The response of the federal government since the September 1999 *Marshall* decision is a good illustration of the effectiveness of these measures – and a warning to First Nations that governments have a variety of extra-legal (but not illegal) tools available to them. In other words, securing a power "in law" is no assurance that the First Nations will be able to exercise these same rights "in practice."

Gaining access to resources in the early twenty-first century is also something of a phyrric victory. Aboriginal treaty rights have been secured in declining economic sectors. The regional logging industry has been far from prosperous in recent years, and the resources for ocean and river harvesting have been uncertain at best. Given the eagerness with which First Nations people intended, post-*Marshall*, to capitalize on their rights, the potential for increased pressure on resources is very real. The rapid expansion of First Nations logging in 1997–98 under the Turnbull decision of the *Thomas Peter Paul* case raised concerns about uncontrolled resource use. First Nations, not surprisingly, bitterly reject the suggestion that they will over-harvest resources. The Supreme Court has clearly stated that Aboriginal harvesting rights cannot overrule government efforts to conserve natural resources. Experience elsewhere in Canada, particularly in the West Coast fishery, suggests that the juxtaposition of a declining/threatened resource and expanding Aboriginal rights to these resources can create difficulties. In British Columbia the lengthy decline of salmon resources, for example, resulted in a great deal of finger-pointing at First Nations and strong protests against continued First Nations harvesting. A similar structure – declining fish and logging resources coming after the expansion of First Nations rights – in the Maritimes would likely heighten tensions within the resource communities.

Even as the victories in the courts have added up, however, First Nations people find themselves facing a considerable ideological opposition. First Nations have, since the early 1970s, found the courts very much to their liking. Although the cost and effort to secure a Supreme Court judgment are considerable, the benefits have been clear. There would be no land claims process without *Calder*, no guaranteed Aboriginal harvesting without *Sparrow*, no expanded assumption of federal responsibility without *Guerin*. Just as certainly, these legal victories created the political atmosphere that made the inclusion of Aboriginal and treaty rights in the constitution possible, resulted in the development of self-government initiatives, and convinced the federal government to greatly enhance programming and funding for First Nations people.

But not everyone is happy with the new direction, and a formidable challenge has emerged to the concept of Aboriginal rights. In British Columbia the charge has been led by media personality and talk-show host Rafe Mair and, more substantially, by former constitutional adviser Melvin Smith. The ideological leader of the campaign against the expansion and entrenchment of Aboriginal rights is Thomas Flanagan, a University of Calgary political scientist and frequent commentator. Flanagan, one-time research director for the Reform Party, argues that Canada has gone too far. The uncritical consensus that he describes as building around the idea that First Nations are, indeed, "nations" has resulted in a steady transfer of power into Aboriginal hands. And, as Flanagan points out in his strongly argued book *First Nations? Second Thoughts*,[14] the concept is founded on the belief that early habitation of North America automatically bestows special status, up to and including the often-asserted position that these were and are "sovereign nations." This process, he argues, has made a handful of Aboriginal activists rich and powerful and has brought neither peace nor economic opportunity to First Nations reserves. While the leadership benefits, Flanagan argues, rank-and-file Aboriginal people continue to live in poverty and face a very uncertain future. Critics, Flanagan included, point to nasty confrontations, well-documented abuses of power, and political conflicts at the band level to back up the argument that continuing down the path of Aboriginal empowerment will not address the fundamental needs of First Nations people.

The emergence of a strong and well-informed critique of the Aboriginal legal, treaty, and constitutional rights agenda in Canada represents a potentially vital change. The willingness of governments to negotiate accords, to respond quickly to court decisions, and to support self-government rests on the assumptions that this initiative is supported by First Nations, is in the nation's best interests, and has widespread backing among non-Aboriginal Canadians. The case advanced by Flanagan, Smith, and others offers an alternative view, one that might well gather strength in the coming years. Political parties, including the Canadian Alliance on the federal scene, the Liberal Party in British Columbia, and various provincial conservative parties, will use this academic critique to support their opposition to expanding First Nations' rights. In the Maritimes, the controversy, conflicts, and difficulties associated with the extension of Aboriginal rights following the Turnbull decision on the *Thomas Peter Paul* case and the Supreme Court judgment on *Marshall* have raised questions in some quarters about the legitimacy of Aboriginal legal aspirations. Nationally, the situation has worried resource users, politicians, and the business community, who see *Marshall* as yet another illustration of the open-ended nature of Aboriginal and treaty rights.

Politicians, rather than challenging opponents of Aboriginal rights, have generally shied away from the issue. The Maritimes, the

Mi'kmaq, and the Maliseet were not well served by federal authorities in 1999–2000. Provincial governments, particularly in New Brunswick, acted more quickly and more creatively. Despite the overwhelming impression that Aboriginal rights rest on court decisions, government decisions might well be equally important. With strong leadership and a clear agenda, governments can protect First Nations interests while developing a compromise of regional benefit and relevance. Federal leadership on Aboriginal issues generally, or First Nations concerns in the Maritimes specifically, has been very limited. A much stronger, more assertive, federal presence is essential. Further, the federal government will have to be seen simultaneously to be protecting and ensuring the long-term stability of non-Aboriginal communities and resources users. This is a formidable requirement, and government actions in recent years have given little reason for optimism.

Political problems, however, are not limited to federal and provincial leaders. In 1999–2000, public attention focused on First Nations' growing legal rights and their authority vis-à-vis other Maritimers. In the background, another struggle continued, receiving very little public attention, inside and between First Nations. The extension of legal rights adds to the potential for internal tensions and difficulties. As First Nations negotiated resource agreements over timber and lobster, critics within communities launched bitter attacks on their leaders. Similarly, and again British Columbia provides a good example of potential difficulties, agreements involving one First Nation can and do impinge on the rights of other Aboriginal groups. Inter-Aboriginal rivalry generally gets little coverage, even though it continues to grow in importance and intensity. As indigenous rights expand – and as the value of the decisions grow – so do the internal struggles. The mismanagement of logging rights by some New Brunswick reserves, battles over allocation of lobster quotas, and other struggles will undoubtedly focus Aboriginal attention on internal politics and will likely result in bad publicity and a few nasty confrontations in the coming years. Non-Aboriginal critics will seize on disharmony to argue that the First Nations position is not clear and that vaunted assumptions about the integrity and sustainability of self-governing First Nations bands are in doubt. More seriously, these criticisms and conflicts have the potential to weaken First Nations consensus and to create divisions at precisely the time communities are facing critical decisions of long-term importance. The Nisga'a, for example, experienced growing internal conflict early in 2000 as their treaty was ratified by Parliament. Some communities will be able to weather these bitter divisions; others will have great difficulty negotiating agreements with governments and industry when they face conflicts within and between their communities.

The *Marshall* decision addresses a crucial but narrow question of Aboriginal entitlement. It does not (and could not, given the legal parameters within which the Supreme Court operates) address the broad and complex issues facing the Mi'kmaq and Maliseet, such as First Nations' urgent need for solutions to the challenges they face. The *Marshall* decision, some assert, is the solution their communities so urgently need. The anxiety in First Nations populations is palpable, and so is the desire to find good news among the litany of difficulty and sad tales. However, the challenges facing First Nations in the region are extensive, and one court decision – even one as generally favourable as *Marshall* – cannot undue two hundred years of marginalization and disempowerment.

The *Marshall* decision, in its broadest and most optimistic interpretation, represents a small but crucial advance towards economic justice, but the opening is not large. Not all communities and not all First Nations people will benefit equally, and those who gain some financial opportunity will hardly find a windfall. Few First Nations people will become comfortable, let alone rich, from *Marshall*-mandated rights. The "moderate" income expectations are, after all, clearly spelled out. The decision will not solve all the Mi'kmaq and Maliseet economic ills and will not bring quick prosperity to First Nations communities in the Maritimes. Nor will social and cultural difficulties be set right in short order.

By passing judgment on the *Marshall* case, the Supreme Court has unwittingly narrowed the focus of public, regional, and internal debate about Mi'kmaq and Maliseet social, economic, and political issues. Public interest in First Nations matters, never wide, has sharpened its focus onto the specific concerns of legal and treaty rights. The prospect exists that intense interest in treaty and legal rights will lessen public concerns about other less tangible and less immediate issues. Equally, the scale and potential implications of the *Marshall* decision clearly encourage First Nations leaders and communities to focus their efforts and resources on court challenges and legal rights, potentially to the detriment of important and valuable opportunities in other areas. This is not to argue, from the First Nations perspective, that the *Marshall* decision is a negative force; rather, it is to suggest that the court victory might well divert attention from crucial areas requiring attention and redress.

So, what does the *Marshall* decision finally mean? Simple, definitive answers have little likelihood of accuracy when dealing with the complex legal, political, and cultural issues revolving around First

Nations treaty and Aboriginal rights debates. First Nations people deserve, for reasons of natural and moral justice, an opportunity to participate fully in Canadian society, on terms that are compatible with cultural values and community needs. The *Marshall* decision provides one small but important brick in the slowly expanding wall of Aboriginal legal entitlements and recognized treaty rights. But *Marshall*, as the events of 1999–2000 demonstrated, created as many problems as it solved, exposed cracks and tensions that were previously unknown, and stirred regional anger in ways that few would have predicted. In raising a series of issues and questions about the future of First Nations treaty rights in the Maritimes and in contemplating options available to federal, provincial, and First Nations politicians and to the communities in the region, it should be obvious that the issues are cloudy, the answers murky, and the solutions elusive. Identifying the challenges is not all that difficult; finding workable resolutions is the real problem. If resolving such differences was easy, it surely would have been done a long time ago.

Permit me to conclude with a fairly precise indication of how I see these issues proceeding in the coming years. So much national attention focused on the *Marshall* case that the crucial lessons of the *Thomas Peter Paul* case, largely ignored across the country, have generally been lost. The provincial response in New Brunswick to *Paul*, while far from perfect in Aboriginal eyes, was strong, consistent, and sustainable. Despite protests from industrial and non–First Nations observers, the government stuck to its determination to share the harvestable timber in the province with Aboriginal communities. And if some of the communities fumbled the opportunity, most made relatively good use of the assured access to the timber resources. What is more, there is every indication that New Brunswick First Nations will do even better as they develop greater expertise as loggers and businesspeople. *Marshall* received the attention, but the New Brunswick reaction to *Paul* provides the best example in the region of a constructive, long-term, and reasonable solution that addresses both Aboriginal aspirations and non-Aboriginal and industry-wide expectations.

If there is a further lesson in the Maritime experience, it is that there are clear limits to the value of legally determined solutions. The Supreme Court recognizes these bounds. On a regular basis, it has appealed to First Nations and governments to negotiate solutions to outstanding Aboriginal rights cases. And still, from coast to coast, First Nations people continue to put their faith in legal contests, celebrating the victories as vindication and hope and responding to losses by heading back to the lower courts to try again. Non-Aboriginal

Canadians must realize that this reliance on the legal system – though costly, slow, and all-consuming for the participating groups – illustrates the degree of frustration and distrust that First Nations feel towards the political process. Aboriginal people generally have little faith in the politicians' ability and willingness to address their needs and have come to believe that recourse to the courts is the only way to force official action. *Marshall* demonstrates the legitimacy of this view. There are dozens more First Nations people fishing in Atlantic waters than a few years ago as a direct result of the Supreme Court decision. But the costs, in legal bills, lost time and opportunity, and tensions with non-Aboriginal neighbours, are also considerable. First Nations will continue down the path of litigation until such time as they are presented with a viable alternative. The New Brunswick government's response to *Thomas Peter Paul* is, in this regard, pivotal, for it demonstrates that solutions can be found without the direction of the Supreme Court of Canada.

Even with the Supreme Court's clarification of *Marshall* late in 1999, a great deal remains unresolved. Both sides have the option of returning to the courts to seek a resolution to these issues. The costs, in human and financial terms, of such an approach are considerable. The potential for conflict and renewed tensions is equally substantial. Imagine the impact of another ten *Marshall*-type decisions over the next decade – a mere one per year – with the First Nations winning and losing an equal number. The Maritimes could be living on an emotional roller-coaster, with each side spending its time in anxious uncertainty. The lack of clarity on question of regional resource use could, as in the West and North, lead companies to withhold investment and to slow economic activity. British Columbians have lived with this economic uncertainty for a generation now. It is difficult to be precise about the actual cost of withheld investments, for some decisions that were attributed to unresolved land claims and treaty might well have been made for other reasons. Across the province, however, resource developers have repeatedly argued that they cannot and will not proceed with major investments until Aboriginal title and rights questions are resolved and until some measure of certainty has been provided. One small example will illustrate the point. In late June 2000 press reports documented how a proposed massive ski hill project in British Columbia, to be developed by Nancy Greene Raine and her husband, had collapsed because of the inability of the federal and provincial governments to conclude a treaty with the St'at'imc First Nation. As one reporter succinctly observed, "The standoff has underscored the potential development paralysis posed by stalled treaty talks between the B.C. government and Native groups."[15] Similar stories have appeared many times over the past decade and, as it has been in British Columbia and elsewhere, so it might be in the Maritimes. Uncertainty carries a substantial cost, one the fragile Maritime economy can ill afford. Nothing can stop activists on either side from recourse to the courts. It is likely that legal contests will continue to figure prominently in future relations between First Nations and other Maritimers.

The national legal bill in Canada continues to mount. There are hundreds of Aboriginal rights cases working their way through the courts. In the Maritimes, almost every week brings an announcement of another charge against a Mi'kmaq or Maliseet person for ignoring federal or provincial resource regulations. Who knows which one of these cases will result in a short-lived and tumultuous decision like *Thomas Peter Paul* or one of lasting authority like *Marshall*. These battles are crucial, and one can hardly criticize the First Nations for sticking to this path. After all, it was only the Supreme Court victories that resulted in the official recognition of Aboriginal inherent rights to harvest resources and that renewed the authority of pre-1970 treaties. It is incumbent on non-Aboriginal governments and peoples to present a viable option, one that does not rely on the winner-take-all approach of the court, and that does not perpetuate a system that routinely placed First Nations and non-Aboriginal Canadians on opposite sides of the courtroom.

The Maritimes provides an alternative, one based on a higher level of cooperation, conciliation, and local solutions. The region is not perfect, as the violence and anger after the *Marshall* decision attest. But there are good and productive models at work here, based on close contact at the community level, cooperation on the part of industry, and a willingness by provincial governments to seek reasonable solutions that are acceptable across the ethnic divide. The federal government's role on *Marshall*, like its actions in British Columbia on treaties over the past decade, reveals that it is more part of the problem than the solution. Overly sensitive to political opponents – and the Canadian Alliance challenge to Aboriginal rights presents a serious threat in this quarter – and far too cautious in responding and in making decisions, the federal government appears to be more comfortable with litigation than with conciliation, and seems to prefer short-term solutions more than long-term remedies. Any lasting solution to the challenges faced, and presented, by First Nations will have to involve broad participation and enjoy a large measure of community buy-in. If First Nations are not behind their leaders, then settlements will ultimately mean very little. Similarly, if the non-Aboriginal population resists, complains, and protests, it has the political, economic, and social clout to smother otherwise significant First Nations gains. Legal contests involve combatants; negotiated settlements ultimately involve partnerships.

The irony is that the First Nations – which have every reason to be angry, distant, and even combative – are probably more prepared for meaningful collaboration than are most non-Aboriginal Canadians and Maritimers. Each group has its hot-heads and more radical elements: there are sovereigntists and protesters on the Aboriginal side, and racists and people stridently opposed to any "special" status for First Nations (these two groups are not the same) on the non-Aboriginal side. But First Nations are more aware than non-Aboriginal people of the need to cooperate and collaborate. Their history reminds them of the greater numbers and political authority of the dominant society, and they see the benefits from working with government and industry. Non-Aboriginal groups, for the most part, are reluctant to head down this fairly obvious path and seem more comfortable with the continued reliance of the uncertainty of the court process. Now that the heat surrounding *Marshall* is flaring again, perhaps Maritimers and other Canadians will contemplate a future dominated by many *Marshall*-type contests. First Nations will win some and lose others. But there is an element of loss in all these cases, as there is for all Canadians. Surely an alternative to continued legal contests, with their attendant uncertainty and animosity, is preferable.

There are options. One possibility is to pursue the model established in New Brunswick after the *Thomas Peter Paul* decision. Setting aside the question of whether or not Mi'kmaq and Maliseet people have a commercial right to harvest timber – the answer at this point is that they do not, but the *Bernard* case might well change that ruling – the government of New Brunswick continued with its plan to allocate a portion of the annual allowable cut to First Nations. It continues to interpret the *Marshall* decision with considerable openness and flexibility, such as in moose hunting, and it appears to be willing to consider other initiatives. Most importantly, this approach to First Nations affairs survived the change in government and does not appear to have become unduly politicized. Nova Scotia is proceeding along similar lines, and relations between government and Mi'kmaq communities in Prince Edward Island appear to be positive as well. In short, it is possible to identify a series of small but significant steps which bring Aboriginal people to the table and which allow them to leave the discussions with dignity and hope. Still, New Brunswick only came to the table when Thomas Peter Paul won his court case (later overturned) and First Nations loggers headed into the forest. Without the legal "trigger," it is unlikely that anything would have been done.

The conflict over the legal cases of Thomas Peter Paul and, to a lesser extent, Donald Marshall Jr demonstrated one of the particular strengths of the Maritimes. All parties – First Nations, provincial governments, community groups, and companies – have been consistently respectful of legal obligations and rights. But they have also not been constrained by legal commitments. Recognizing the volatility of the Aboriginal rights issue, all groups sought promises that went outside specific legal requirements. First Nations met with fishing groups in Nova Scotia and worked our resource-sharing arrangements. After initial opposition to First Nations logging, local firms such as J.D. Irving Ltd began to work with individual First Nations to purchase logs and coordinate cutting. The government of New Brunswick, seeking a solution that would calm tensions, negotiated logging agreements with First Nations which went beyond legal obligations.

The future of the First Nations in the Maritimes rests more on an extension of these relationships than on further court victories. Once companies and governments came to the table, they found most First Nations leaders to be reasonable, cooperative, and interested in long-term, mutually agreeable solutions. A sustainable solution to First Nations legal rights will require a continuation of the good will that has been evident on both sides, but is not assured into the future. If the Maritimes moved down this path, the general public will see few dramatic changes and even fewer clashes. Cooperative, local solutions will gradually integrate First Nations resource use into the regional economy without large-scale arguments or open conflict.

Some Canadians wish that the issue would simply go away, and many have made it clear that they wished that the constitutionally protected status of First Nations people could be removed. This vision of political and legal reform is simply a pipe-dream; it will not happen, even if it was the solution to the complicated Aboriginal situation facing the country. Among the few strong cards in the First Nations hand are constitutionally protected rights and the specific provisions and support provided by the Indian Act, other government programs, and recent legal decisions. There is no reason why Aboriginal people would, or even should, give away the only major instruments of power at their disposal. As a consequence, we face a future in which First Nations will continue to seek recourse through the courts and will attempt to build a strong wall of Aboriginal rights to protect and provide for themselves. Just as the *Calder, Sparrow,*

Marshall, and other decisions of the past thirty years have forced dramatic changes in government positions and First Nations legal status, the country can anticipate more of the same, as the many Aboriginal and treaty rights cases continue to wind their way through the Canadian judicial system.

But where is the bold step? The efforts made in New Brunswick and the Maritimes are tiny, incremental initiatives, taken in large measure in response to specific legal decisions or challenges. And while they will help, they do little to address the larger and more complex issues facing First Nations and restricting relations between Aboriginal and non-Aboriginal populations in the Maritimes. Meanwhile, to a degree that most non–First Nations people do not recognize, frustration and anger build among the indigenous people, who wonder how long the bitter legacy of the past will remain as a dominant feature of their current existence. Hostility is particularly evident among the young – especially young men who struggle to find a role for themselves within their community and the broader society – and far too much of the anger is taken out internally, through suicide or other self-destructive behaviour. There is much shame in our past, but there is an even greater shame in being unwilling to address historical problems and to recognize the contemporary legacy of past injustices.

The Maritimes has several clear choices, including sticking with the status quo and all of the attendant uncertainty. The region faces many years of additional treaty challenges, as well as an inevitable legal contest over the question of unresolved land title in the region. Mi'kmaq and Maliseet often argue that the eighteenth-century treaties were for peace and cooperation and did not involve land surrenders. If the courts agreed with this argument, the *Marshall* decision would simply slide into irrelevance alongside such a judgment. Provincial and federal governments can continue to deal with the issues on a case-by-case, band-by-band, fashion, hoping that divisions between and within First Nations will keep protests under control, thereby postponing any need to deal with the really large issues. None of these approaches seems likely to enjoy much success; rather, they could well cost lots of money, and might result in a series of *Marshall*-type decisions that could truly rock the region. Should the *Josuha Bernard* case end in victory at the Supreme Court, for example, Mi'kmaq and Maliseet people would have their claim to a treaty right to cut trees for commercial benefit recognized by the courts.

The *Marshall* decision rests on judicial interpretation of the nuances of the Peace and Friendship Treaty that is over two hundred years old. The Dummer's and Mascarene's treaties anticipated virtually none of the realities facing the Maritimes in the twenty-first century. In the absence of a new agreement between Mi'kmaq, Maliseet, and non-Aboriginal Canadians, these treaties will remain the primary legal framework for this relationship. The Supreme Court judgment makes it clear that the treaty lives, however ossified and irrelevant, and has economic and political powers that few anticipated. Further court challenges could easily extend that power, thus infuriating non–First Nations Maritimers. Conversely, court contests could severely limit Aboriginal rights, thereby destroying Mi'kmaq and Maliseet aspirations and eviscerating their optimism about the future. How can either of these alternatives, plus the uncertainty and conflict that would attend continued litigation, be seen as viable and preferable?

Virtually all observers of First Nations affairs realize the challenges facing the Mi'kmaq and Maliseet and worry about these communities' abilities to address these problems. In 1994 Roger Augustine led a Micmac-Maliseet task force on comprehensive land claims, an effort that achieved no substantial results. The federal government clearly felt little reason to move, a situation that the *Thomas Peter Paul* and *Marshall* decisions may well have changed.

The option of preparing a new treaty with First Nations is rarely discussed, but it holds consider potential – and some risk. There is an urgent need to rethink and restructure First Nations affairs in the Maritimes. The current structure, which combines revitalized eighteenth-century treaties, the Indian Act, the Department of Indian Affairs, reserves, Aboriginal self-government, constitutional guarantees, economic and social difficulties, and cultural issues, holds little promise for significant improvements. All observers who follow Aboriginal affairs know that new approaches are urgently needed and that reconciliation between indigenous and non-Aboriginal people is key to any lasting solution. Is it unreasonable to consider negotiating a new treaty, one that recognizes existing Aboriginal rights, responds to First Nations aspirations, and builds a new relationship with non-indigenous people? Treaty negotiations have been in process across Canada and in many other countries, particularly since the 1970s. Where they have been handled properly – the Yukon and New Zealand stand out – they have provided a foundation for a dramatic improvements in relations between indigenous and non-indigenous groups and in economic and social conditions for the Native peoples. Where they have not been considered with dispatch and determination, as in British Columbia and Australia, the process has angered Aboriginal and non-Aboriginal people alike.

Treaty-making is difficult, time-consuming, and costly. It also presents participants with a chance to get things right, and to set policies and agreements that reflect contemporary realities. Treaties are, now as in the past, compromises. Despite the loud rhetoric to the contrary, the Nisga'a in British Columbia did not take the federal and provincial governments to the proverbial cleaners. They surrendered a great deal of ground to secure an agreement, creating considerable division within their communities in the process. The Nisga'a treaty-making process required enormous courage on the part of all participants, and opposition was heated, angry, and persistent. Critics have not given up, but have launched court challenges of their own against the accord. Treaty-making, at the same time, gives all parties a chance to look afresh at the issues at hand and to search for solutions that respect the needs and aspirations of all parties to the agreement. What resulted in the Nisga'a case was a compromise, a reasonable balance between Aboriginal aspirations and the initial positions of the provincial and federal governments.

The Maritimes present Canada with a unique and valuable opportunity – and with a clear indication of what lies ahead if a dramatic step is not taken. Without a treaty process in place – and this assumes that the First Nations would agree to such an initiative – the region can anticipate more cases like *Thomas Peter Paul* and *Marshall*. There will be winners and losers in each instance and, gradually, the population will invariably come to realize that all Maritimers lose, regardless of the outcome. There is an alternative. The initiative clearly rests with non-Aboriginal governments, for the *Marshall* decision has empowered and reinvigorated the First Nations in the Maritimes. Properly handled, an approach from provincial governments in the Maritimes and the government of Canada could well be greeted favourably by First Nations communities. Negotiations will take a long time and will prove to be difficult. Not all First Nations would likely proceed down the path at the same speed and with the same determination to settle.

Following on the experience in other jurisdictions, however, the treaty-making process can help address the major problems facing Aboriginal and non-Aboriginal communities. The mutual learning that comes from open dialogue can be truly impressive and can help heal long-standing disputes and bridge deep cultural gaps. Treaty-making brings Aboriginal and non-Aboriginal people together and can begin the long overdue process of reconciliation. The road to a final settlement is inevitably bumpy, made more so by the Canadian pattern of replacing provincial and federal governments, and thereby restarting discussions with new political masters. In the end, however, all parties have an opportunity to place their concerns and wishes on the table and to seek solutions that provide First Nations and other Canadians with a solid template for future relations.

There are no magic solutions to the problems created in First Nations–newcomer relations over the past four centuries in the Maritimes. No court decision, treaty negotiation, government program, self-government accord, or gesture of friendship will undo the marginalization, discrimination, and dispossession from land and resources that occurred over the generations. It is perfectly understandable that First Nations have sought recourse through the courts, which have proven since the 1970s to be the most reliable and even the fastest means of getting the attention of Canadian governments. Still, an Aboriginal victory in the courts means only that the government is found to have acted inappropriately in the eyes of Canadian and British law. Court cases do not address the broader issues of moral and ethical culpability, of either First Nations traditional law or broader moral questions about appropriate ownership. If Maritimers and other Canadians decide to ask First Nations to move onto a different path, they had better come to the table with something new, innovative, reasonable, and optimistic. Failing this, they can look forward to many more years of uncertainty and difficulty.

Only the passage of time will tell if the country has opted for a reasonable and successful course of action. Sadly, there is little reason for optimism. Anger and frustration are growing among the First Nations, and so is non-Aboriginal resistance to the assertion of indigenous rights and claims. The short-term outlook of provincial and federal governments, and the short-term perspective of business and industry, militate against the long-term planning and commitments that are required. As the *Marshall* situation demonstrated, First Nations legal gains are almost always greeted by a hostile response. Although matters tend to quiet down over time, the effect of bitter words and nasty actions linger for years thereafter. Canada has rarely been noted for bold steps, even though such action is clearly required on the Aboriginal file. Our pattern of muddling through, postponing decisions, and relying on the courts for direction will likely continue, with the Aboriginal people in the country paying the largest share of the price for our national inability to address historical challenges.

The Supreme Court decision on the appeal of *Marshall* sent shock waves across the country and surprised and dismayed many people in the Maritimes. If it was a wake-up call, however, the region and the country appear to have hit the snooze button on their alarm clocks. Almost a year later, the issues raised by *Marshall* have been segmented, narrowed, and bureaucratized. At one level, this is a sign of the success of our political and administrative systems; the conflicts of 1999 were, save for escalating conflict at Burnt Church, replaced by cooperative arrangements in 2000. But *Marshall* was not just about lobster or even fishing rights. It was about recognizing the legitimacy of eighteenth-century treaties and rebuilding trust relationships between First Nations and other Canadians. Fishing licences have been allocated, and Aboriginal people have more freedom to hunt and sell the products of their harvests. But the Maritimes remain far removed from the idea of a living treaty and have done little to rebuild the bridges to Aboriginal communities. The lessons of the *Marshall* controversy are quickly being forgotten, to be rediscovered the next time the Supreme Court rules on a major Aboriginal rights case. And then, as in 1999, there will be expressions of outrage, worry, and frustration, followed by short-term, palliative steps to solve the immediate political problems. It is time to stop forcing First Nations to shoulder the burden for a regional and national history of injustice. And it really is time to stop postponing negotiations designed to forge new, more positive relationships between First Nations and other Canadians. The Maritimes would be a great place to start this process.

Appendices

APPENDIX A

Maritime First Nations Communities: Population

First Nations Communities of the Maritimes

Maritime First Nation Communities, Population, 1998

Province	Reserve	Off Reserve
NEW BRUNSWICK		
Big Cove	1,930	437
Buctouche	68	21
Burnt Church	1,111	203
Eel Ground	473	310
Eel River Bar	299	242
Fort Folly	31	66
Indian Island	88	59
Kingsclear	554	194
Madawaska	101	123
Oromocto	204	233
Pabineau	101	104
Red Bank	363	125
Saint Mary's	683	457
Tobique	1,310	414
Woodstock	231	504
NOVA SCOTIA		
Acadia	177	720
Afton	312	145
Annapolis	80	119
Bear River	95	161
Chapel Island	418	97
Eskasoni	2,792	510
Horton	95	174
Membertou	696	229
Millbrook	631	509
Pictou Landing	355	140
Shubenacadie	1,124	855
Wagmatcook	543	55
Waycobah	631	67
PRINCE EDWARD ISLAND		
Abegweit Band	172	122
Lennox Island	333	361

Source: Indian Register Population by Sex and Residence, 1998

Maritime First Nations Population by Place of Residence, 1999

Province	Population	On Reserve (Own Band)	On Reserve (Other Band)	Total	On Crown Land	Off Reserve
Nova Scotia	11,748	7,759	190	7,949	15	3,784
New Brunswick	11,039	7,416	131	7,547	–	3,492
Prince Edward Island	989	479	26	505	1	483

Source: Indian Register Population by Sex and Type of Group, Responsibility Centre, and Region, 1999

APPENDIX B

Lobster Quotas and Mi'kmaq Fishing Rights

Making sense of the east coast lobster fishery and of the potential impact of Mi'kmaq commercial harvesting on the industry is extremely difficult. Aboriginal leaders say, with confidence, that their planned harvests represent only a tiny increase in the total commercial catch. They wonder aloud about the motivations behind the non-First Nations protest. Non-Aboriginal fishers, for their part, claim that a rapidly expanding First Nations fishery will both damage a fragile resource and upset carefully managed markets, causing considerable economic dislocation in the process. Government officials have remained relatively quiet on this score, preferring to echo the sentiments of Herb Dhaliwal, the minister of fisheries and oceans, to the effect that there is a conservation and management system in place. According to the minister, First Nations fishers are required by the Supreme Court decision on *Marshall* to abide by federal regulations.

The situation is further clouded by other factors. First, there are accusations, most notably by commentator Parker Barse Donham, of widespread illegal fishing by non-Aboriginal fishers, particularly off Nova Scotia. According to Donham, illegal fishing substantially outstrips the planned Aboriginal harvest. Second, non-Aboriginal fishers have, in years past, complained about federally imposed quotas and have argued that the fishery could sustain a larger harvest. They now appear to be arguing the reverse, a contradiction noticed by more than a few First Nations leaders. Third, there is a widespread regional distrust of the Department of Fisheries and Oceans and its conservation measures. This distrust has it roots in the controversy surrounding the depletion of the east coast cod fishery, a dispute that threw into doubt government claims that it has a scientific foundation for its conservation strategies. Finally, there is the inevitable debate among scientists themselves (often, but not exclusively, a division between government scientists and those working for universities, industry, or environmental groups). For example, estimates for current lobster exploitation rates in the Southern Gulf range from 63 to 83 per cent, and for the crucial Southwest Nova Scotia field, from 51 to 64 per cent. Fisheries science is far from exact, and planning a complex regional and commercial fishery, when research budgets have been far from generous, is a difficult assignment.[1]

The net effect, to put it simply, is that there is considerable guesswork and a great deal of debate about the size, scale, and sustainability of the east coast lobster fishery. The industry is not new, for a significant regional fishery began in the 1850s, with the inevitable peaks and valleys thereafter. According to estimates, Atlantic fishers landed over 45,000 tonnes of lobster in 1898, an amount not exceeded until the early 1990s. At the low point in the 1920s and 1930s, the annual harvest was around 12,000 tonnes. The Southern Gulf of St Lawrence was always the most accessible and reliable fishing ground, but it, too, saw the harvests decline substantially and remain low between 1915 and 1975. The smaller harvests – as late as the mid-1970s, annual harvests in the Maritimes were less than 15,000 tonnes – were due to overfishing and limited commercial markets. Buoyed by high prices and surging demand in the 1980s, the lobster harvest peaked in 1991 with the catch registered at close to 50,000 tonnes, according to Fisheries sources. The harvest has been declining since that time.

The lobster fishery is a sizable industry, producing over $160 million in product in the Southern Gulf of St Lawrence in 1998, and close to $150 million in lobster sales in the Southwest Nova Scotia region. These two areas alone accounted for almost three- quarters of the total Maritime and Gulf Region lobster fishery. By way of comparison, the value of the Bay of Fundy fishery was only $27 million, with Cape Breton pulling in another $13.5 million in 1998. On a regional basis, particularly in light of the generally weak state of the Maritime economy, the lobster industry is a critical sector. In the smaller communities along the coast, the lobster harvest is economically vital.

The growth in lobster prices and demand, which began in the 1970s, attracted many fishers into the industry. In the 1970s lobster licences were readily secured and not overly valuable. With improvements in the markets, they have become very valuable – and saleable – items. The lobster industry has been, for the most part, a small boat fishery, which means that a minimal amount of specialized gear is required to enter it. This characteristic is one of the attractions of the Miramichi Bay fishery, where it is possible to fish commercially using small boats and without extensive ocean experience. The mid-shore fishery has been expanding as fishers seek new and richer lobster grounds. By 1997–98 there were more than 6,000 licensed lobster fishers in the region, including over 3,250 in the Southern Gulf and almost 1,100 on the Eastern Shore of Nova Scotia. There were close to 1,000 in Southwest Nova Scotia, over 5,000 on East Cape Breton, fewer than 400 in the Bay of Fundy, 325 off Magdalen, and 222 in the Gaspé region. These fishers placed well over 1.5 million traps in the water in 1997–98 (broken down regionally and rounded as follows: Southern Gulf – 950,000, SW Nova Scotia – 390,000, Eastern Shore of Nova Scotia – 265,000, East Cape Breton – 155,000, Bay of Fundy – 125,000, Magdalen – 98,000, and Gaspé – 56,000).

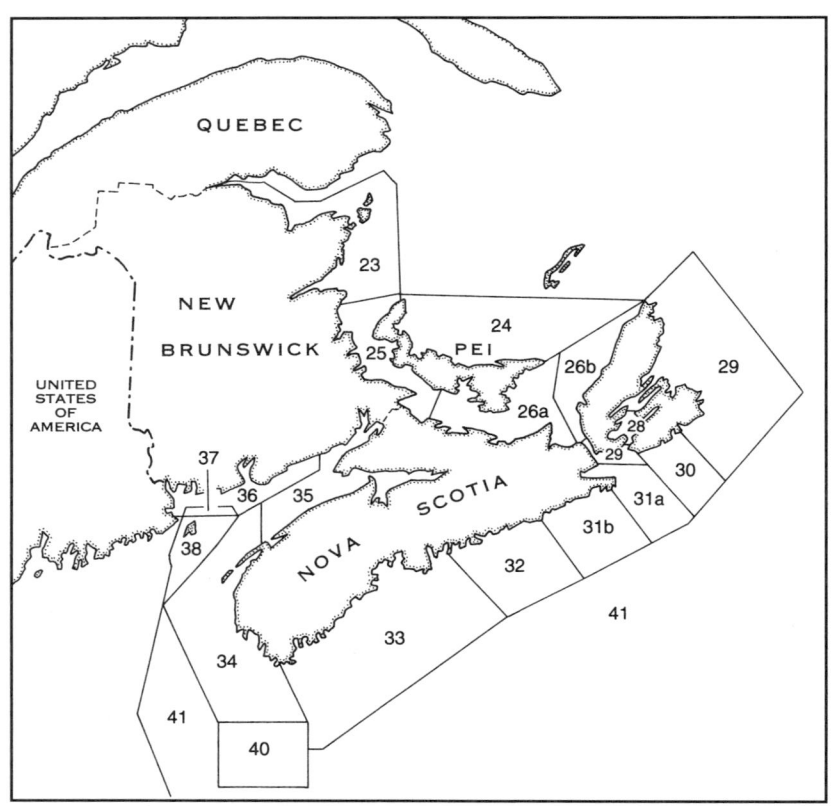

Lobster Districts and Open Seasons in the Maritime Provinces

District	Season
23, 24, 26(a, b)	30 April–30 June
25	9 August–11 October
27	15 May–15 July
28	9 May–9 July
29	10 May–10 July
30	19 May–20 July
31a	29 April–30 June
31b, 32	19 April–20 June
33, 34	last Monday in November to 31 May
35	last day of February–31 July
	14 October–31 December
36, 37	31 March–29 June
	second Tuesday in November–14 January
38	second Tuesday in November–29 June

- District 40: Closed to inshore-offshore fishing.
- District 41: Area open all year.
- This information is subject to change without notice. Please consult your local DFO Fishery officer for further information.

Source: Fisheries and Oceans Canada Web page.

These figures help put the Burnt Church position in some context. The Mi'kmaq community established a local limit of four traps per person in the community. With a reserve population of approximately 1,200 people, this figure represented a total of approximately 5,000 traps. In 1997–98, according to DFO figures, fishers used over 950,000 traps in the Southern Gulf region – by far the most active lobster fishing area in the Maritimes. The Burnt Church fishery, as planned by the Mi'kmaq community, represented a total of .5 per cent of the total lobster traps in the Southern Gulf fisheries district. In Lobster Fishing Area 23, there are almost 750 licence holders, each authorized to use up to 375 traps. This number translates into over 280,000 traps. The Burnt Church strategy would represent less than 2 per cent of that total. Given what the *Marshall* decision said about a "moderate income" and assurances of the Mi'kmaq right to fish commercially, the Burnt Church demand does not appear dramatically out of line.

The Atlantic Policy Congress of First Nations Chiefs often reacted with bitterness to accusations of Aboriginal over-fishing and to the suggestion that First Nations commercial rights would destroy local resources. According to APC statistics for Nova Scotia, only 217 First Nations fishermen were active in the industry, with an average of fifty-four traps per person. This number totalled fewer than 12,000 traps. The commercial non-Aboriginal fishery in the province, the chiefs pointed out, involved 3,070 licensed fishers using close to 300 traps each, for a total of over 920,000 traps. It was hard to argue, particularly with only ten of thirty-seven First Nations bands in the Maritimes fishing lobster, that they posed an immediate threat to the industry.[2]

There is another critical issue at play. The debate is not simply about the number of traps permitted for Mi'kmaq use – a contentious enough issue. The Mi'kmaq also assert their right to extend the lobster season and to regulate their harvesting activities. In lobster fishing zone 23 (Miramichi Bay), the official season runs from 8 May to 9 July (see table 1). By fishing through the summer of 2000 – an option not available to non-Aboriginal commercial fishers – Burnt Church threatened to upset the balance in the industry. The seasons are established for several purposes, including conservation and market management, ensuring that all the region's fishers do not sell their annual harvest at the same time. Burnt Church is determined to extend the season, meaning that each of its traps will likely harvest more lobster than a restricted season non-Aboriginal commercial trap and that the community will be selling lobster when other fishers are unable to do so. Industry representatives are worried that unregulated harvesting and marketing of lobster could have a negative impact on what has become a crucial economic sector.

The east coast lobster fishery is very carefully regulated. In the Southern Gulf of St Lawrence, for example, there are five management regions, two different open seasons, four different minimum carapace sizes, and four different trap limits per licence. The rules are complicated and are monitored

Table 1
Lobster Management Regime, Southern Gulf of St Lawrence, 1997

Lobster Fishing Area	Minimum Carapace* Size	Fishing Season	Number of Licence Holders	Maximum Number of Traps per Fisher
LFA 23	66.7 mm	May–June	749	375
LFA 24	63.5 mm	May–June	637	300
LFA 25	66.7 mm	mid-Aug. to mid-Oct.	867	250
LFA 26A	65.1 mm	May–June	767	300
LFA 26B	70.0 mm	May–June	256	300

Source: DFO Science, Stock Status Report C3–12 (1998), Southern Gulf of St Lawrence Lobster, October 1998
* The carapace is the lobster shell.

by the Department of Fisheries and Oceans, although, to be fair to DFO, the resources available for monitoring have not been adequate. The regulations underpin a successful industry, with over 17,000 tonnes caught in the Southern Gulf in 1997–98 and another 11,000 tonnes off Southwest Nova Scotia. Fishers in the industry are very defensive about the sector and are anxious to sustain their harvests and, if possible, to expand the industry.

The commercial licences have proved to be extremely valuable. The estimated landed value per licence in LFA 34 (Southwest Nova Scotia) exceeds $150,000; for LFA 25, it is much lower, at slightly more than $38,000. The area north of Prince Edward Island, LFA 24, produced about $74,000 per licence. For LFA 23, the zone that includes Burnt Church, the estimated landed value per licence was $42,000. The presence of an Aboriginal commercial fishery is seen as a threat to those incomes. Fishers are not overly worried about a negotiated solution, in which space for First Nations commercial fishers is created by buying out existing licence holders at fair market value. They are extremely nervous about Burnt Church-like assertions of Aboriginal commercial rights that add uncertainty and threaten to upset the regulatory balance in the area.

Although the statistics of the lobster fishery suggest that non-Aboriginal and government reaction to the Burnt Church and Indian Brook demands is overblown, other issues cloud an already complicated matter. The *Marshall* decision is rife with uncertainty. No one really knows how many First Nations people will become commercial fishers, what percentage of the harvest they will take five, ten, and fifteen years down the road, or how the federal government is going to create space for Aboriginal people in an already fully subscribed fishery. When you add in persistent questions about the sustainability of the lobster harvest – and such thoughts are inevitable given the fate of the east coast cod fishery – the anxiety of local fishers makes more sense. It is vital, in this context, to understand something of the Aboriginal view of their harvesting rights and their ability to regulate the First Nations commercial harvest in the future.

While the Burnt Church controversy provides a public airing of certain differences relating to Aboriginal fishing, the Atlantic Policy Congress of First Nations Chiefs offers a glimpse of what might lie ahead. In a crucial document entitled *The Mi'kmaq/Maliseet/Passamaquoddy Integrated Natural Resources Management Policy,* the APC outlined its expectations arising out of the *Marshall* decision:

The objective of this policy is natural resource management pursuant to the inherent right of self-determination and the treaty relationship between the Mi'kmaq, Maliseet and Passamaquoddy and the Crown and the implementation of the treaties in the context of natural resources. This policy is intended to form the basis of what will ultimately become Mi'kmaq, Maliseet and Passamaquoddy natural resources law.

The Mi'kmaq, Maliseet and Passamaquoddy recognize that any deterioration of natural resources impacts upon their rights. These Nations also recognize the importance of viable and sustainable communities and livelihoods. Accordingly, the Mi'kmaq, Maliseet and Passamaquoddy must be involved with decisions respecting all economic activities that may have an impact on the health and viability of natural resources.

This policy intends to provide a foundation for the preservation and sustainability of lands, waters and resources within the traditional territories of the Mi'kmaq, Maliseet and Passamaquoddy based on their traditional values and treaty responsibilities. It also intends to provide a foundation for the sustainability of Mi'kmaq, Maliseet and Passamaquoddy communities and livelihoods based on their treaty rights without jeopardizing the integrity, diversity and productivity of their native environment.

The Mi'kmaq, Maliseet and Passamaquoddy continue to assert their exclusive authority over conservation of the natural resources and the consequential right to direct access to those resources.

To the Atlantic Policy Congress, the situation is very clear. The First Nations retain their sovereignty, which was reflected in the eighteenth-century treaties with the British government and which the Supreme Court of Canada, through the *Marshall* decision, has formally acknowledged. As the APC declared: "The very essence of a treaty relationship is its nation to nation character. The Mi'kmaq, Maliseet and Passamaquoddy entered into a treaty relationship with the Crown during the 18th century. Implicit within this relationship is the recognition of the equivalent sovereign jurisdiction of the Mi'kmaq, Maliseet and Passamaquoddy nations. Also implicit within this relationship is the position that all jurisdictional areas have been retained by the Mi'kmaq, Maliseet and the Passamaquoddy as self-governing nations." (Some historians would contest the assumptions contained in this statement.) The recognition of "existing Aboriginal and treaty rights" in the Canadian Constitution (section 35) can be combined with the *Marshall* decision and the asserted inherent right to self-government. These powers, the APC argues, as well as the right of self-determination, has given Aboriginal people the right to exercise control over the regional fishery and to exploit natural resources for commercial purposes. To address the technical requirements of resource management, the APC prepared a Mi'kmaq, Maliseet, and Passamaquoddy Fisheries Act (Fishery [General] Regulations – SOR/93–53) and a variety of other regulations, designed to provide structure and formality to the Aboriginal fishery.[3]

The assertions are less radical or potentially disruptive than they appear at first glance. Non-Aboriginal fishermen, for example, demand a "one set of rules" approach for the fishery. To this suggestion, the Atlantic Policy Congress replied: "The Mi'kmaq, Maliseet and Passamaquoddy do not disagree with the principle of one set of rules and regulations but we emphasize that we must have a significant role in the development of those rules within good faith negotiations. Furthermore, we would also emphasize that any regulations Canada chooses to unilaterally put forward must not infringe upon the recognized right and if it does, it must meet the rigorous test of justification laid out by the Supreme Court of Canada in the *Badger* decision."[4] In other words, the Atlantic Policy Congress does not intend for there to be an east coast fishery without substantial Aboriginal input into the regulations and, preferably, First Nations involvement in monitoring and enforcement.

The debate at Burnt Church and Indian Brook, therefore, masks different, more complex issues that actually sit at the heart of the *Marshall* decision controversy. Current First Nations harvesting can, to a lay person's eyes, be easily accommodated within the east coast lobster industry, but is crucial to note that First Nations rights under *Marshall* are not limited to lobster and that Aboriginal fishing for other species may expand in the years to come. There is considerable flexibility, particularly with the opportunity to buy out commercial lobster licences, within the industry to accommodate short to medium-term expansion in the sector. But First Nations make it clear that the fishing industry of the future will not look like the fishing industry of the past. They fully expect to play a direct role in setting harvesting limits, enforcement, resource monitoring, and other regulations. Having been left on the shore for decades, watching a largely non-Aboriginal fishery profit from local resources, First Nations are determined that they will never again be left out of the industry.

The following appendices are available at
www.mcgill.ca/mqup/marshall

C   *Rex* v. *Syliboy*, Nova Scotia County Court, 10 September 1928
D   *Regina* v. *Donald Marshall Jr.*, Nova Scotia Court of Appeal, 26 March 1997
E   *Regina* v. *Peter Paul*, New Brunswick Court of Queen's Bench, 28 October 1997
F   *Regina* v. *Peter Paul*, New Brunswick Court of Appeal, 22 April 1998
G   *Regina* v. *Marshall Jr.*, Supreme Court of Canada, 17 September 1999
H   *Regina* v. *Marshall Jr.*, Supreme Court of Canada Motion for Rehearing and Stay, 17 November 1999

APPENDIX I

Treaty of 1760

Treaty of Peace and Friendship concluded by H.E.C.L. Esq. Govr and Comr. in Chief in and over his Majesty's Province of Nova Scotia or Accadia with Paul Laurent chief of the LaHave tribe of Indians at Halifax in the Province of N.S. or Acadia.

I, Paul Laurent do for myself and the tribe of LaHave Indians of which I am Chief do acknowledge the jurisdiction and Dominion of His Majesty George the Second over the Territories of Nova Scotia or Accadia and we do make submission to His Majesty in the most perfect, ample and solemn manner.

And I do promise for myself and my tribe that I nor they shall not molest any of His Majesty's subjects or their dependents, in their settlements already made or to be hereafter made or in carrying on their Commerce or in any thing whatever within the Province of His said Majesty in any thing whatever within the Province of His said Majesty or elsewhere and if any insult, robbery or outrage shall happen to be committed by any of my tribe satisfaction and restitution shall be made to the person or persons injured.

That neither I nor any of my tribe shall in any manner entice any of his said Majesty's troops or soldiers to desert, nor in any manner assist in conveying them away but on the contrary will do our utmost endeavours to bring them back to the Company, Regiment, Fort or Garrison to which they shall belong.

That if any Quarrel or Misunderstanding shall happen between myself and the English or between them and any of my tribe, neither I, nor they shall take any private satisfaction or Revenge, but we will apply for redress according to the Laws established in His said Majesty's Dominions.

That all English prisoners made by myself or my tribe shall be sett at Liberty and that we will use our utmost endeavours to prevail on the other tribes to do the same, if any prisoners shall happen to be in their hands.

And I do further promise for myself and my tribe that we will not either directly nor indirectly assist any of the enemies of His most sacred Majesty King George the Second, his heirs or Successors, nor hold any manner of Commerce traffick nor intercourse with them, but on the contrary will as much as may be in our power discover and make known to His Majesty's Governor, any all designs which may be formed or contrived against His Majesty's subjects. And I do further engage that we will not traffick, barter or Exchange any Commodities in any manner but with such persons or the managers of such Truck houses as shall be appointed or Established by His Majesty's Governor at Lunenbourg or Elsewhere in Nova Scotia or Accadia.

And for the more effectual security of the due performance of this Treaty and every part thereof I do promise and Engage that a certain number of persons of my tribe which shall not be less in number than two prisoners shall on or before September next reside as Hostages at Lunenburg or at such other place or places in this Province of Nova Scotia or Accadia as shall be appointed for that purpose by His Majesty's Governor of said Province which Hostages shall be exchanged for a like number of my tribe when requested.

And all these foregoing articles and every one of them made with His Excellency C.L., His Majesty's Governor I do promise for myself and on of sd part – behalf of my tribe that we will most strictly keep and observe in the most solemn manner.

In witness whereof I have hereunto putt my mark and seal at Halifax in Nova Scotia this _____ day of March one thousand

Paul Laurent

I do accept and agree to all the articles of the forgoing treaty in Faith and Testimony whereof I have signed these present I have caused my seal to be hereunto affixed this day of March in the 33 year of His Majesty's Reign and in the year of Our lord – 1760

Chas Lawrence

By his Excellency's Command
Richard Bulkeley – Secty

Notes

PREFACE

1 Supreme Court of Canada, *Donald Marshall Jr. v. Canada*, 17 September 1999.
2 New Brunswick Court of Appeal, *Her Majesty the Queen v. Thomas Peter Paul*, 22 April 1998.

CHAPTER ONE

1 "Donald Marshall Jr. is back in court as part of the healing," *Hamilton Spectator*, 29 June 1999.
2 "Marshall ruling opens door on fishery," Moncton *Times & Transcript*, 28 June 1996. See also "Marshall vows to appeal illegal fishing conviction," *Toronto Star*, 28 June 1996.
3 Ibid.
4 "Two-hundred-year-old treaties case could have widespread impact," Fredericton *Daily Gleaner*, 11 February 1997.
5 "Court reserves Micmac fishing case decision," *Times & Transcript*, 6 November 1998.
6 "Supreme Court recognizes Micmac rights," *Hamilton Spectator*, 18 September 1999.
7 "Marshall celebrates landmark victory," Halifax *Chronicle-Herald*, 18 September 1999.
8 "The Marshall decision is a door to liberation," Saint John *Telegraph Journal*, 23 September 1999.
9 "Top court ruling reaffirms native rights," *Daily Gleaner*, 21 September 1999.
10 "Decision treats Mi'kmaq fairly – finally," *Sunday Herald*, 17 October 1999.
11 "Mi'kmaq rights upheld," *Chronicle-Herald*, 18 September 1999.
12 "Natives drop nets," *Daily Gleaner*, 22 September 1999.

13 "Micmacs are quick to set traps," *Telegraph Journal*, 22 September 1999.
14 "Native pushing Ottawa on rights to resources," *London Free Press*, 25 October 1999.
15 "Supreme Court recognizes Micmac rights," *Hamilton Spectator*, 18 September 1999.
16 "Tension Mounts," *Daily Gleaner*, 23 September 1999.
17 "Supreme Court misunderstood testimony, professor says," *Times & Transcript*, 18 September 1999.
18 Ibid.
19 "Court alters ruling," *Daily Gleaner*, 2 October 1999.
20 Motion of Rehearing and Stay, Donald Marshall Jr. v. Her Majesty (respondent) the Queen and The Attorney General for New Brunswick, the West Nova Fishermen's Coalition, the Native Council of Nova Scotia and the Union of New Brunswick Indians (interveners), 17 November 1999, Supreme Court of Canada.
21 "Native loggers, fishermen reined in," *Telegraph Journal*, 18 November 1999.
22 "Supreme admission of incompetence," ibid., 30 November 1999.

CHAPTER TWO

1 The most useful overview of the history of Mi'kmaq peoples in the first three centuries of contact is William Wicken, "Encounters with Tall Sails and Tall Tales: Mi'kmaq Society, 1500–1760" (PhD thesis, McGill University 1994), 2 vols.
2 The best source of Mi'kmaq creation stories is Even Thomas et al., *Introductory Guide to Micmac Words and Phrases* (Rexton: Resonance Communications 1991).
3 Vine Deloria, "Foreword," in David Hurst Thomas, *Skull Wars: Kennewick Man, Archaeology, and the Battle for Native American Identity* (New York: Basic Books 2000), xv–xvi.
4 Stephen Davis, "Early Societies: Sequences of Charge," in P.A. Bucknes and J.G. Reid, eds., *The Atlantic Region to Confederation: A Reader* (Toronto: University of Toronto Press 1994), 3–21.
5 Virginia Miller, "The Micmac: A Maritime Woodland Group," in Bruce Morrison and C. Roderick Wilson, eds., *Native Peoples: The Canadian Experience*, 2nd ed. (Toronto: Oxford 1995), 349–52.
6 There is a debate about the identity of a specific group known as the Maliseet before 1700. See Bruce Bourque, "Ethnicity of the Maritime Peninsula, 1600–1759," *Ethnohistory* 36 (1989): 257–84.
7 Alfred G. Bailey, *The Conflict of European and Eastern Algonkian Cultures, 1504–1700* (Toronto: University of Toronto Press 1969);

L.F.S. Upton, *Micmacs and Colonists* (Vancouver: UBC Press 1979); Wicken, "Tall Sails and Tall Tales"; Daniel Paul, *We Were Not the Savages* (Halifax: Nimbus Publishing 1993).
8 Royal Commission on Aboriginal Peoples, *Report of the Royal Commission on Aboriginal Peoples*, 1: *Looking Forward, Looking Back* (Ottawa 1996), 51.
9 Miller, "The Micmac," 361.
10 Ibid., 365.
11 Wicken, "Tall Sails and Tall Tales," 428.
12 Ibid., chapter 7, covers Mi'kmaq relations with the French and British governments in detail.
13 Ibid., 444.
14 Quoted in Ruth Holmes Whitehead, *The Old Man Told Us: Excerpts from Micmac History, 1500–1950* (Halifax: Nimbus Publishing 1991), 241.
15 L.F.S. Upton, *Micmacs and Colonists*, 140.
16 Roger Nichols, *Indians in the United States and Canada: A Comparative History* (Lincoln: University of Nebraska Press 1998), 196.
17 Paul, *We Were Not the Savages*, 146
18 The proclamation identified the area as "Fronsac Passage and from thence to Nartagonneich, and from Nartagonneich to Piktouk, and from thence to Cape Geane from thence to Emchih, from thence to Ragi Poutouch, from thence to Zedueck, from thence to Cape Prommentia, from thence to Mirimichy, and from thence to Bay des Chaleurs, and the environs of Canso, from thence to Mushkoodabroet, and so along the Coast, as the Claims and Possessions of the said Indians, for the more especial purpose of hunting, fowling and fishing" Upton, *Micmacs and Colonists*, 58–9.
19 Ibid., 59.
20 Ibid., 127.
21 RCAP, *Looking Forward, Looking Back*, 126.
22 Nova Scotia Court of Appeal, CAC 129874, *Marshall v. Queen*, Factum of the Appellant, 1996.
23 Nova Scotia Court of Appeal, CAC 129874, *Marshall v. Queen*, Factum of the Respondant, December 1996.
24 Nova Scotia Court of Appeal, CAC 129874, Selected Historical References (Respondant), 1996.
25 Nova Scotia Court of Appeal, CAC 129874, Selective Summary of the Trial Testimony, Appendix x, 1996, 88–94.
26 Nova Scotia Court of Appeal, CAC 129874, Selective Summary of the Trial Testimony, Appendix x, 1996, 39–43.
27 Quoted in Whitehead, *The Old Man Told Us*, 208.
28 Upton, *Micmacs and Colonists*, 171–2.

29 John Malloy, *A National Crime: The Canadian Government and the Residential School System, 1879 to 1986* (Winnipeg: University of Manitoba Press 1999), 149.
30 Quoted in RCAP, *Looking Forward, Looking Back*, 418.

CHAPTER THREE

1 J. Rick Ponting, *First Nations in Canada: Perspectives on Opportunity, Empowerment, and Self-Determination* (Toronto: McGraw-Hill Ryerson 1997), 72–3.
2 Jim Meek, "Native Sum," *Canadian Business*, 12 November 1999, 76–80.
3 The data are taken from James Frideres, *Aboriginal Peoples in Canada*, 5th ed. (Toronto: Prentice Hall 1998), chapter 5: "Profile of Aboriginal Peoples."
4 Donald Savoie, *Aboriginal Economic Development in New Brunswick* (Moncton: The Canadian Institute for Research on Regional Development 2000), 124.
5 Ibid., 77–96.
6 Frideres, *Aboriginal Peoples in Canada*, 240–1.
7 Ibid., 145.
8 Supreme Court of Canada, *Regina and Batchewana Indian Band* v. *John Corbiere et al.*, 20 May 1999.
9 "Let natives settle standoff dispute at Big Hole Tract among themselves," Saint John *Times Globe*, editorial, 5 July 1995.
10 "End the gill-netting," ibid., 7 July 1995.
11 "Chiefs condemn clear-cutting in Christmas Mountain," Saint John *Telegraph Journal*, 10 September 1996.

CHAPTER FOUR

1 Frantz Fanon, *The Wretched of the Earth* (New York: Grove Weidenfeld 1991).
2 Nova Scotia County Court, *R.* v. *Syliboy*, 10 September 1928.
3 Paul Tennant, *Aboriginal People and Politics* (Vancouver: UBC Press 1990), is the best source on these British Columbia court cases.
4 Ibid., 222.

CHAPTER FIVE

1 "Seeing the forest for the trees," Saint John *Telegraph Journal*, 2 January 1998.
2 James [sákéj] Youngblood Henderson "Impact of Delgamuuku Guidelines in Atlantic Canada" <http://mrc.uccb.ns.ca/impactdelgamuukw.html>.

3 "Natives win rights to Crown land timber," Fredericton *Daily Gleaner*, 28 August 1996.
4 New Brunswick Court of Queen's Bench, *R. v. Peter Paul*, decision by Justice John Turnbull, 28 October 1997, para. 33.
5 "Natives exploit new law of the land," *Telegraph Journal*, 7 February 1998.
6 "Natives harvest Crown-land wood for Quebeckers," ibid., 16 January 1998.
7 "Natives look to cut a land deal," ibid., 9 February 1998.
8 "Appeal unlikely to stop native logging," ibid., 24 February 1998.
9 "Native logger supported," *Daily Gleaner*, 22 April 1998, 3A.
10 "Native fight for cutting rights," ibid., 27 February 1998.
11 "Justice's question Turnbull's research," ibid., 27 February 1998.
12 "Treaties didn't include harvesting – court," ibid., 23 April 1998.
13 "Reeling from ruling," ibid.
14 "Thomas Peter Paul doesn't feel guilty," *Telegraph Journal*, 23 April 1998.
15 "Hope found in the woods," ibid., 27 April 1998.
16 "There is no way they are coming out of the woods," ibid., 4 May 1998.
17 Ibid.
18 "Premier pleads for deal," ibid., 25 April 1998.
19 Ibid.
20 "Native forestry company flees woods," ibid., 30 April 1998.
21 "Nova Scotia plans to offer natives land, avoid crisis," ibid., 24 April 1998.
22 "Land without borders?" *Daily Gleaner*, 20 May 1998.
23 "Chief warns province not to harass native loggers," *Telegraph Journal*, 21 May 1998.
24 "Natives deliver terse message," *Daily Gleaner*, 23 May 1998.
25 "Court's ruling must be honoured by all citizens," ibid., editorial, 24 April 1998.
26 "Studying the law books," *Daily Gleaner*, 24 April 1998.
27 "Allaby ready for top court," ibid., 20 June 1998.
28 The lawyers for Irving argued that the written evidence – treaty documents, correspondence, and analysis – was insufficient to sustain a major court decision based on historical issues. "N.B. defends logging rights," ibid., 19 August 1998.
29 "Court refuses logging appeal," Moncton *Times & Transcript*, 6 November 1998.
30 "Native right to sell fish headed for court test," *Telegraph Journal*, 2 March 1998.
31 "Native will be sentenced in fall," ibid., 16 July 1998.

32 "Prosecutor miffed as sentencing in native logging case delayed," ibid., 21 November 1998.
33 "Judge decides against penalty for Peter Paul," ibid., 25 November 1998.
34 "Natives exploit new law of the land," ibid., 7 February 1998.
35 "Native look to cut a land deal," ibid., 9 February 1998.
36 "Thomas Peter Paul: Newsmaker of the Year," ibid., 26 December 1998.
37 "Natives exploit new law of the land," ibid., 7 February 1998.
38 "Hope found in the woods," ibid., 27 April 1998.
39 "Can't see the forest for the treaties," ibid., editorial, 21 February 1998.
40 "Malecites order province, Irving out," ibid., 20 February 1998.
41 "Natives exploit new law of the land," ibid., 7 February 1998.
42 "Native Activism's new face," ibid., 10 February 1998.
43 Ibid.
44 "Natives reject province's latest offer," ibid., 12 May 1998.
45 "Natives forming united front," ibid., 15 May 1998.
46 "Native forestry company flees the woods," ibid., 30 April 1998.
47 "Harvest dreams: Part two of two," *New Brunswick Reader*, 15 May 1998.
48 "Peace in the forests," *Telegraph Journal*, editorial, 24 April 1998.
49 "Natives must form a united front," ibid., editorial, 15 May 1998.
50 "Native mill still possible," ibid., 2 June 1998.
51 "Portrait of an activist," ibid., 30 September 1998.
52 Ibid.
53 "Five loggers detained; Crown will decide if they will be charged," ibid., 22 May 1998.
54 "Man at centre of logging issue faces new charges," ibid., 27 October 1998.
55 "Peter Paul given year in jail," ibid., 29 January 1999.
56 "Supreme Court refuses to hear logger's appeal," ibid., 6 November 1998.
57 "Thomas Peter Paul goes on trial in July," ibid., 19 January 1999.
58 "100 natives shut down logging operations," ibid., 4 June 1998.
59 "Micmac warriors wise," ibid., editorial, 16 June 1998.
60 "Native will be sentenced in fall," ibid., 16 July 1998.
61 "High court to rule on appeal tomorrow," ibid., 4 November 1998.
62 "Judge challenges claim that case could resolve land-rights issue," ibid., 26 May 1998.
63 "Judge orders return of truck seized by Natural Resources," ibid., 25 June 1998.
64 "Aboriginal council files complaint against government," ibid., 30 September 1998.

65 "N.B. Metis demand traditional rights," *Times & Transcript*, 23 July 1999.
66 "Native loggers offer to settle," *Telegraph Journal*, 26 June 1998.
67 "Logging group considers itself a 'major player,'" ibid., 30 June 1998.
68 "Five loggers detained; Crown will decide if they will be charged," ibid., 22 May 1998.
69 "To the victor go the spoils," ibid., editorial, 14 August 1998.
70 "No turning back," Saint John *Times Globe*, 6 November 1998.
71 "Petition opposes logging deal," *Telegraph Journal*, 15 December 1998.
72 "Big Cove to discuss logging deal," ibid., 17 December 1998.
73 "The system doesn't help Canada's native people," *Daily Gleaner*, 13 November 1998.
74 "Test case is necessary to define forest rights," *Telegraph Journal*, editorial, 6 November 1998.
75 "Aboriginal task force recommendations," *Daily Gleaner*, 29 March 1999.
76 "Court's ruling must be honored by all citizens," ibid., editorial, 24 April 1998.
77 "Native loggers meet to forge new forestry strategy," *Telegraph Journal*, 10 April 1998.
78 "Tyler might spark new logging test case," ibid., 6 June 1998.
79 "Nova Scotia natives stake claim to trees," ibid., 10 December 1998.
80 "Native logging trial could be test case, defence lawyer says," ibid., 28 November 1998.
81 "N.S. Premier wants native logging guidelines," ibid., 6 April 1998.
82 "Nova Scotia plans to offer natives land, avoid crisis," ibid., 24 April 1998.
83 "Big Cove chief will meet with minister to sort out dispute over logging rights," *Times Globe*, 2 November 1999.
84 Francis Simon, letter to the editor, *Telegraph Journal*, 21 July 1999.

CHAPTER SIX

1 "DFO ready to get tough," Saint John *Telegraph Journal*, 25 September 1999.
2 "Fisheries Minister will act if lobster stocks threatened," Saint John *Times Globe*, 23 September 1999.
3 Boycott lobsters, lobster buyers asked," *Telegraph Journal*, 24 September 1999.
4 "Fisheries minister won't be rushed into action in light of Marshall ruling," Moncton *Times & Transcript*, 25 September 1999.
5 "Future of lucrative fishery unknown," Fredericton *Daily Gleaner*, 11 October 1999.

6 "Escaping the fish war," *Telegraph Journal*, 12 October 1999.
7 "A tale of two wharves," ibid., 20 October 1999.
8 "Group says non-native fishermen should be compensated," *Times & Transcript*, 1 October 1999.
9 "New Fisheries Minister is all business," ibid., 15 September 1999.
10 "Natives may fish, hunt but no logging yet: Minister," *Times Globe*, 21 September 1999.
11 "Minister stresses patience," *Daily Gleaner*, 23 September 1999.
12 "DFO unprepared for Marshall court ruling," Halifax *Chronicle-Herald*, 7 December 1999.
13 "Of free-for-alls on the water," *Times Globe*, editorial, 6 October 1999.
14 "Blame poor leadership for violent protests," *Telegraph Journal*, editorial, 5 October 1999.
15 "The times have changed, and so must our laws," *Times & Transcript*, 7 October 1999.
16 "Both sides welcome mediator in lobster war," *Telegraph Journal*, 16 October 1999.
17 "Dhaliwal wades through trouble," *Times & Transcript*, 7 December 1999.
18 "Text of statement by Herb Dhaliwal," ibid., 2 October 1999.
19 "Fishing deal coming," *Daily Gleaner*, 2 October 1999.
20 "Off-reserve natives fight for inclusion," *Telegraph Journal*, 2 October 1999.
21 "Treaty talks," *Daily Gleaner*, 21 October 1999.
22 "Minister allows native fishery," *Times & Transcript*, 2 October 1999.
23 "Non-native fishermen call for compensation," *Telegraph Journal*, 2 October 1999.
24 "Hamm eyes suspending Supreme Court ruling," *Chronicle-Herald*, 1 October 1999.
25 "Suspend treaty ruling, PM urged," ibid., 23 September 1999.
26 "Fisheries Minister warns of crackdown," *Times Globe*, 28 September 1999.
27 *Chronicle-Herald*, 1 October 1999.
28 "Is $45,000 a day a 'moderate living'?" *Daily Gleaner*, 30 September 1999.
29 "Lobster tensions mounting," *Chronicle-Herald*, 22 September 1999.
30 "Native-caught lobster," ibid., 24 September 1999.
31 "DFO ready to get tough," *Telegraph Journal*, 25 September 1999.
32 "Fisherman fear for livelihood as natives fish for lobster," *Times Globe*, 24 September 1999.
33 "Boycott natives, lobster buyers asked," *Telegraph Journal*, 24 September 1999.
34 "Non-natives give DFO deadline," ibid., 28 September 1999.

Notes to pages 136–45

35 "Non-Natives will 'have to share,'" *Chronicle-Herald*, 23 September 1999.
36 "Native fishermen ignore DFO request," ibid., 27 September 1999.
37 "Chief to nation: keep fighting," *Chronicle-Herald*, 30 September 1999.
38 "Marshall pleads for calm," *Telegraph Journal*, 29 September 1999; "Solomon needed," *Chronicle-Herald*, 2 October 1999.
39 "Non-natives take protest to MP," *Telegraph Journal*, 30 September 1999.
40 "Chiefs agree on task force," ibid., 30 September 1999.
41 "Mi'kmaq celebrate 'overdue justice,'" *Chronicle-Herald*, 2 October 1999.
42 "Mi'kmaq to mark new era," ibid., 1 October 1999.
43 "Natives' lobster traps destroyed," *Telegraph Journal*, 4 October 1999.
44 "Fishery dispute erupts in anger," *Times Globe*, 4 October 1999.
45 "Dhaliwal hints he may impose rules," *Telegraph Journal*, 6 October 1999.
46 "Fuel to the Fire," *Times Globe*, 6 October 1999.
47 "Chiefs united over ban," *Daily Gleaner*, 7 October 1999.
48 "A tale of two wharves," *Telegraph Journal*, 20 October 1999, submitted by Janice Harvey, marine conservation director, Conservation Council of New Brunswick, and David Coon, policy director and ecological fisheries director, Conservation Council of New Brunswick.
49 "Native fishermen return to the water day after violence," *Times & Transcript*, 5 October 1999.
50 "Dhaliwal hints he may impose rules," *Telegraph Journal*, 6 October 1999.
51 "Minister vows to end fishery," *Times & Transcript*, 5 October 1999.
52 "Fuel to the fire," *Times Globe*, 6 October 1999.
53 "Fisheries tensions flare," *Chronicle-Herald*, 18 October 1999.
54 "Frustrated lobstermen put to sea in protest," ibid., 16 October 1999.
55 "Showdown averted," *Sunday Herald*, 17 October 1999.
56 Parker Barse Donham, "Lobster Wars," *Canadian Dimension* 34, 1 (February 2000): 26–8.
57 "Natives not in rush to embrace moratorium," *Times Globe*, 7 October 1999.
58 "Minister will try to resolve dispute," *Telegraph Journal*, 5 October 1999.
59 "Natives not in rush to embrace moratorium," ibid., 7 October 1999.
60 "Fishing moratorium rejected by natives," ibid., 8 October 1999.
61 "Life has changed fundamentally in Burnt Church," ibid., 12 October 1999.
62 "Natives not in rush to embrace moratorium," *Daily Gleaner*, 7 October 1999, "Chiefs agree to shutdown," *Chronicle-Herald*, 7 October 1999.
63 "Natives vow to keep fishing," *Daily Gleaner*, 8 October 1999.
64 "Chiefs united over bad," ibid., 7 October 1999.
65 "Mi'kmaq should renounce Canadian citizenship," ibid., 11 October 1999.

66 "Most from Big Cove will stop fishing," *Telegraph Journal*, 9 October 1999.
67 See "Voice of the People," *Sydney Herald*, 8 October 1999.
68 "Chief back season opening," *Chronicle-Herald*, 9 October 1999.
69 "Most from Big Cove will stop fishing," *Telegraph Journal*, 9 October 1999.
70 "Natives have right to profile from all natural resources," *Times & Transcript*, 15 October 1999.
71 "Butt out, federal minister advised," *Telegraph Journal*, 20 October 1999.
72 "Burnt Church angered by limits," ibid., 12 October 1999.
73 "Fishery debate boils over again," *Times Globe*, 14 October 1999.
74 "Burnt Church First Nation blasts Dhaliwal," *Telegraph Journal*, 15 October 1999.
75 "Negotiator in lobster crisis to visit N.S. tomorrow," ibid., 18 October 1999.
76 "Chief wants RCMP to act," *Daily Gleaner*, 25 October 1999.
77 "Chiefs reject lobster moratorium," *Times & Transcript*, 14 October 1999.
78 "Fishery to open," *Daily Gleaner*, 11 October 1999.
79 "Natives are right to keep fishing," *Telegraph Journal*, 11 October 1999.
80 "End of moratorium could mean more strife," *Chronicle-Herald*, 8 November 1999.
81 "Fishermen and friends packed court to hear charges," *Telegraph Journal*, 19 October 1999.
82 "Natives agreed to live by the laws of the Crown," ibid., 29 October 1999.
83 "Top court lacked background in Marshall ruling," *Times & Transcript*, 17 November 1999.
84 "Land management plan has broad implications," *Daily Gleaner*, 1 December 1999.
85 "Native fishing committee gets earful," ibid., 26 November 1999.
86 "Negotiate or litigate, say Mi'kmaq leaders," *Telegraph Journal*, 27 November 1999.
87 "Licence buy-back urged," *Daily Gleaner*, 17 December 1999.
88 "Chiefs pan committee's report on native fishery," *Chronicle-Herald*, 10 February 2000.
89 "Voice of the People," ibid., 24 September 1999.
90 "Blame poor leadership for violent protests," ibid., editorial, 5 October 1999.
91 "Lobster fishermen hurting," *Daily Gleaner*, 30 August 1999.
92 "Native fishing interim deal is approved," ibid., 4 December 1999.
93 "Oromocto agrees to native fishing rights," *Times Globe*, 7 April 2000.
94 "Minister says bands can fish without federal agreements," *Telegraph Journal*, 8 April 2000, A3.

95 "Dhaliwal offers fishing deals to B.C. natives to avoid litigation," *National Post*, 8 April 2000, A7.
96 "Region united on native rights," *Daily Gleaner*, 22 October 1999. See also "Conflirting Opinions," *Chronicle Herald*, 1 October 1999.
97 "Natives lose ground," *Daily Gleaner*, 18 November 1999.
98 "Natives don't own forests," *Times & Transcript*, 18 November 1999.
99 "Natives win right to hunt and fish," *Telegraph Journal*, 18 September 1999.
100 "Province won't concede logging rights to natives," ibid., 21 September 1999.
101 "Eel-fishing rights decision used in Crown native logging case," *Times & Transcript*, 21 September 1999.
102 "Clarify native rights with a reference case," *Telegraph Journal*, editorial, 11 October 1999.
103 "Where Dhaliwal bungled, Green must learn," *Times Globe*, 15 October 1999.
104 "Off-reserve natives toughen stance," *Daily Gleaner*, 23 September 1999.
105 "Conservation is a challenge we must face together," *Telegraph Journal*, 23 September 1999.
106 "Despite court decisions, natives are still criticized," ibid., 28 September 1999.
107 "Tensions high between fishermen, Mi'kmaq," ibid., 2 February 2000.
108 Speaking Notes for the Honourable Herb Dhaliwal, minister of fisheries and oceans Canada, 24 March 2000.
109 "Natives net brighter future as door opens to fisheries," *Chronicle-Herald*, 22 December 2000.

CHAPTER SEVEN

1 "Eel ground logger surprised by charge," Saint John *Telegraph Journal*, 17 June 1998.
2 "Judge orders province to return seized truck," ibid., 23 June 1998.
3 "Supreme Court refuses to hear logger's appeal," ibid., 6 November 1998.
4 "Indians take logging fight to court," *Toronto Star*, 19 April 1999.
5 "Lawyer to call experts to argue natives have right to cut trees," *Telegraph Journal*, 21 July 1998.
6 "Ranger identifies accused as driver of logging truck," ibid., 23 January 1999.
7 "Trial of second 'native test case' resumes," ibid., 20 April 1999.
8 "Native's trial begins over illegal wood cutting," ibid., 14 September 1999.
9 "Lawyer hoping ruling will make a difference," Fredericton *Daily Gleaner*, 21 September 1999.

10 "Province won't concede logging rights to natives," *Telegraph Journal*, 21 September 1999.
11 New Brunswick Provincial Court, *R. v. Bernard*, NBJ No. 138, Case No. 12130113, 13 April 2000.
12 "Native loggers push case despite conviction," Halifax *Chronicle-Herald*, 14 April 2000.
13 "N.B. out to control natives armed with court decision," ibid., 20 January 2000.
14 "Seizure of native boats revives East Coast fishing dispute," *National Post*, 15 February 2000.
15 "Native fishen deal proves illusive," *Chronicle-Herald*, 19 May 2000.
16 Parker Barse Donham, "Lobster Wars," *Canadian Dimension* 34, 1 (February 2000): 26–8.
17 "Lobster season will test native, non-native relations," *Chronicle-Herald*, 8 June 2000.
18 "Deficit natives test Ottawa's limits on fishery," ibid., 8 May 2000.
19 "Burnt Church natives vow to regulate their own lobster fishery," Saint John *Times Globe*, 5 April 2000.
20 "Government response to the Standing Committee on Fisheries and Oceans: The Marshall Decision and Beyond – Implications for Management of the Atlantic Fisheries, April 2000. Department of Fisheries and Oceans Web site <http://www.ncr.dfo.ca/COMMUNIC/Reports/marshall/gr–marshall_e.htm>.
21 "Mi'kmaq warns feds of potential violence," *Chronicle-Herald*, 2 February 2000.
22 "Burnt Church natives vow to regulate their own lobster fishery," *Times Globe*, 5 April 2000.
23 "Band coucil reviews DFO's offer on fishing," ibid., 25 April 2000.
24 "Update on fisheries affected by the Supreme Court's Marshall decision," 26 May 2000. DFO Web site <http://www.ncr.dfo.ca/COMMUNIC/Statem/2000/marshall–may26e.htm>.
25 "Native fishermen test Ottawa's resolve in lobster fishery," *Times Globe*, 8 May 2000.
26 "Let natives manage lobster fishery, groups urge," ibid., 18 May 2000.
27 "Native women defy ruling on lobster fishing," *National Post*, 8 May 2000.
28 "Big Cove signs $17 million lobster deal with Ottawa," *Times Globe*, 1 May 2000.
29 "Fishing alliance states position," *Chronicle-Herald*, 7 April 2000.
30 "Update on fisheries affected by the Supreme Court's Marshall decision," 26 May 2000. DFO Web site <http://www.ncr.dfo.ca/COMMUNIC/Statem/2000/marshall–may26e.htm>.
31 "Resolution for Rights: Cooperation or Conflict," petition presented to Hon. Herb Dhaliwal, Minister of Fisheries and Oceans, 17 May 2000 <http://www.web.net/nben/ffa/oo/fishe.htm>.

32 "Let natives manage lobster fishery, groups urge," *Times Globe*, 18 May 2000.
33 This summary comes from "Update on fisheries affected by the Supreme Court's Marshall decision, 22 June 2000." DFO Web site: <http://www.ncr.dfo.ca/Communic/statem/2000/marshall-june22e.htm>.
34 Statement by Herb Dhaliwal, Minister of Fisheries and Oceans, Caraquet, New Brunswick, 7 June 2000. DFO Web site <http://www.ncr.dfo.ca/COMMUNIC/Statem/2000/marshall–june7e.htm>.
35 "Maine natives fishing in Fundy," *Times Globe*, 2 May 2000.
36 "Atlantic native fish deals on Web," *Times & Transcript*, 10 August 2000.
37 "Natives defiant after Ottawa seizes fishing boats," *National Post*, 7 August 2000.
38 "N.S. Mi'kmaq flout lobster laws using boat Ottawa bought for them," ibid., 3 August 2000. See also "Hopes fade for fishing deal in N.B.," *Chronicle-Herald*, 8 June 2000.
39 "Burnt Church votes to defy DFO and set more lobster traps," *Times Globe*, 10 August 2000.
40 "Tensions expected to rise over native fishing," ibid., 8 August 2000.
41 "Burnt Church hits the water," *Telegraph Journal*, 12 August 2000.
42 "Mi'kmaqs plan to dely federal agents," *Globe and Mail*, 15 August 2000.
43 "Attempt fails to ban native men from Miramichi Bay," *National Post*, 15 August 2000; "Natives blockage highway," *Time Globe*, 14 August 2000.
44 "Burnt Church getting help from Oka native," *Times Globe*, 15 August 2000.
45 "Natives say they'll 'dialogue' but not negotiate with Ottawa," *Telegraph Journal*, 16 August 2000.
46 "Native fishery no threat to stocks," Chronicle-Herald, 10 August 2000.
47 "Aboriginal fishermen: The politics of hara-kari," *Globe and Mail*, 12 August 2000.
48 "Ottawa's lobster trap," *National Post*, 14 August 2000.
49 "Mikmaqs plan to defy federal agents," *Globe and Mail*, 15 August 2000.
50 "Call of your troops," ibid., 18 August 2000.
51 "You're just angry we won," *Telegraph Journal*, 12 August 2000.

CHAPTER EIGHT

1 Supreme Court of Canada, *Canada and Batchewana Indian Band* v. *John Corbiere et al.*, 20 May 1999.
2 "Natives look to cut a land deal," Saint John *Telegraph Journal*, 9 February 1998.

3 Mi'kmaq loggers to stay off Crown land," Halifax *Chronicle-Herald*, 8 November 1999.
4 "Loggers' trial hits Halifax," ibid., 18 April 2000.
5 "N.B. moose under assault by aboriginal hunters: officials," *National Post*, 20 January 2000.
6 "Minister won't force moose rules on natives," Saint John *Times Globe*, 10 April 2000.
7 "Nova Scotia eyes moose poachers," *Telegraph Journal*, 12 December 1999.
8 "Natives want gas money," *Times Globe*, 13 October 1999.
9 "Mi'kmaq cut, sell logs from Crown land," *Telegraph Journal*, 26 October 1999.
10 "Collison course," Fredericton *Daily Gleaner*, 5 November 1999.
11 For a good cross-sector of Nova Scotia opinion, running slightly against Aboriginal rights, see "Voice of the People," *Sunday Herald*, 24 October 1999.
12 "Loggers' trial hits Halifax," ibid., 18 April 2000.
13 "Is $45,000 a day a 'moderate living'?" *Daily Gleaner*, 30 September 1999.
14 Thomas Flanagan, *First Nations? Second Thoughts* (Montreal: McGill-Queen's University Press 2000).
15 "Treaty battle snuffs out B.C. dreams," *Globe and Mail*, 29 June 2000.

APPENDIX B

1 The technical information provided in this appendix was taken, in the main, from a powerpoint presentation prepared for Department of Fisheries and Oceans staff working on the *Marshall* issue. I would like to thank Ken Jones, chief, Resource Management – Atlantic, Fisheries Management, Department of Fisheries and Oceans, for making this information available. Mr Jones pointed out that the information was compiled in December 1999 and that some trap limits and other details had changed for the 2000 season.
2 Atlantic Policy Congress of First Nations Chiefs Web site <http://www.apcfnc.ca/marshall.htm>, special Web page devoted to the *Marshall* decision.
3 Ibid. See MMP Regs. MMP Fisheries Act.
4 Atlantic Policy Congress response to the Report on the Marshall Decision by the House of Commons Standing Committee on Fisheries and Oceans <http://www.apcfnc.ca/pscf_response1.htm>.

Index

Abegweit fisheries agreement, 177
Abenaki Confederacy, 31, 32–3
Abenaki Treaty, 1693, 97
Aboriginal Fisheries Strategy, 129
Aboriginal history, xii–xv
Aboriginal people and the courts, 202–4
Aboriginal Peoples Council, 134, 161
Aboriginal Rights Coalition Atlantic,176
Aboriginal rights: court cases, 4; in Canada, 72–93; in the courts, xvi; international context, 73–4; non-Aboriginal support for in the Maritimes, 156; political implications, 195
Acadia, 31
Acadia First Nation, 142
Acadians, deportation of, 33, 38
Act to Regulate the Management and Dispersal of the Indian Reserves in This Province, 1844, 44
Afton River, 89
Alberta Report, xii
Allaby, Cleveland, 95, 105–6, 103–4, 116
Allen, Rod, 132
alliances, military and political, 29, 31
American Indian Movement, 48–9, 74
anti-Aboriginal sentiments and court decisions, 191
Arsenault, Frederic, provincial court judge: and *Thomas Peter Paul* case, 96, 104, 106
Assembly of First Nations, xii, 77, 183
Assembly of Nova Scotia Mi'kmaq Chiefs, 139, 188
Atlantic Fishing Industry Alliance, 149, 176
Atlantic Policy Congress of First Nations, 14, 133, 138, 151, 158, 212ff

Atlantic Provinces Economic Council, 167
Atlantic Salmon Federation, 165
Augustine, Gary, 116
Augustine, Millie, 134, 145
Augustine, Noah, 57, 60, 100, 101, 102, 107, 109, 110, 114–15, 116, 119; murder charges against, 115
Augustine, Roger, 68–9, 110, 112, 203
Augustine, Steven, and *Bernard* trial, 171
Avenor, 107, 113

Baie des Chaleurs, 137
Bailey, Alfred G.: and *The Conflict of European and Eastern Algonkian Cultures*, 26
Baker, Michael: Nova Scotia minister of justice, 159
Barlow, Second Peter, 98, 110, 178
Barnaby, Calvin, 168
Baskerville, Dr Andrew: and *Bernard* trial, 171
Bay of Fundy: Aboriginal use of, 24
Bay of Fundy Fisheries Council, 130
Bay of Fundy Fishermen's Association, 136
Bay of Fundy Inshore Fishermen's Association, 176
Bear, Arthur, 99
Bear, Henry, 18, 69
Belcher, Lieutenant-Governor Jonathan, 39
Belliveau, Mike, 128, 132, 133, 134, 138; and Standing Committee on Fisheries and Oceans, 150
Beothuk of Newfoundland, 29
Beresford-Green, David, 152

Berger, Thomas, 77, 84
Bernard, Albert, 170; testimony at Joshua Bernard's trial, 171
Bernard, Chief Allison, 52
Bernard, Joshua: court ruling, 172; and Mi'kmaq logging rights case, 104, 155, 166–7, 169–73, 185, 186, 200
Big Cove, 13, 60, 98, 100, 101–2, 108, 111, 113, 116, 166; fisheries agreement, 178; food fishery at, 176; and lobster agreement, 175; logging agreement with provincial government, 121
Big Hole Tract: fishing controversy over, 69–70
Bill C-31 (1985), 60, 64–5
Binnie, Justice Ian, 10, 15–16
Bishop, B.C., 152
Black Business Development Agency, 176
Black Power movement (USA), 74
Born with 3 Thumbs, A., 152
Bornish Highlands ecological reserve: Aboriginal logging in, 124
Breau, Zoel, 135
British Columbia: and Aboriginal rights, 111–12; ski hill project, 198
British Columbia Fisheries Survival Organization, 159
Brooks, Randy, 108
Buctouche fisheries agreement, 178
Burnt Church, vii, 13, 117, 128, 129, 137, 139,143; accusations of racism at, 144; actions of the Department of Fisheries and Oceans, 181; assertion of right to regulate the lobster fishery, 175, 212–14; charges related to vandalism at, 149–50; commercial fishing charges, 105; community regulation of the fishery, 180; community support for position on fishing, 180; conflict with federal government over lobster rights, 174–5; confrontation at, 154; demands for lobster rights, 173; federal offer of a lobster agreement with, 158; federal offer re: lobster fishing rights, 180; limited lobster fishery, 146; Listuguj First Nation, 182; lobster fishery, 136, 138, 167; lobster fishing protest, 180–3; meetings to resolve the lobster crisis, 146; negotiations with the Department of Fisheries and Oceans, 182; non-Aboriginal protests, 141; non-Aboriginal vandalism at, 140; reaction of Herb Dhaliwal to, 147; refusal to sign an agreement on lobster fishery, 180

Calder case, 76, 84–6, 92, 106, 126, 193; federal government's response to, 85–6
Calder, Frank, 85
Campbellton, 56
Canadian Alliance Party, 65, 153, 194, 199
Canadian Press, x
Caraquet, 178
Carmier, Camille, 140
Cassidy, Kevin, 136
CBC Newsworld and lobster protests, 140
centralization: attempt with Mi'kmaq, 47
Charlottetown accord: defeat of, 78
Charter of Rights and Freedoms, 6, 64
Che Guevara, 74
Chrétien, Jean: as minister of Indian affairs and northern development, 76, 85; as prime minister, 135; and criticism of federal government's role, 141–2; and handling of the *Marshall* decision, 161
Christian Peacemakers, 167, 176
Christianity and indigenous peoples, 29–30, 45
Christmas, Alex, 47
Christmas, Bernd, 13, 52–3, 130, 173
Christmas Mountain: logging dispute over, 69
Clement, Stewart, 113
collective right, Mi'kmaq and Maliseet, to fish, 12
commercial licences, Aboriginal, 178
community size, First Nations, 51
Confederacy of Mainland Mi'kmaq, 4
Conne River, Newfoundland, 130
Constitution, Canadian: Aboriginal rights and the, 64, 76–9; section 35, 77–8, 79, 87, 88–9, 91, 92
Constitution Act, 1982, 6, 77
contact: Mi'kmaq, Maliseet, and newcomer, 28–50

Cook, Lorraine, 159
Coon, David, 9
Coon Come, Grand Chief Matthew, xii; and Burnt Church protest, 183
Cope, Chief Jean Baptiste, 38
Cope, Peter, 45
Corbiere case, 63, 186
Cormier, Mireille, 133
Cornwallis, Governor Edward, 33
Court of Appeal, Nova Scotia, and *Marshall* case, 5
creation accounts, Aboriginal, 22
cultural changes: among First Nations, 67–8; among Maritime First Nations, 51–71
Cummins, John, member of parliament, 160
Cunningham, Don, 142

Davis Inlet, 60
DeBow, Richard, 189
Dedam, Alex, 173
Dedam, Anne, 141
Dedham, Douglas, 181
Dedham, Tim, 113
Delgamuukw case: Supreme Court decision on, 16, 92, 95, 90–1, 106, 188
Deloria, Vine: and western science, 23
demographic conditions: among contemporary First Nations, 53
Denny, Alex, 139, 167, 174
Denny, Paul: and *Syliboy* case, 89–90, 92
Dhaliwal, Herb, minister of fisheries and oceans, 9; and Aboriginal rights, 158; and agreements with First Nations, 179; and agreements with Maritime First Nations, 177–8; approach to solving *Marshall* confrontations, 147; and Atlantic First Nations chiefs, 144; and Burnt Church demands, 174; calls for resignation of, 145; and federal lobster agreements with First Nations, 158–9; handling of *Marshall* decision, 131–36; lobster negotiations, 164; March 2000 address on Maritime fishing and Aboriginal rights, 167; meeting with protesters, 143; negotiations over *Marshall* decision, 133–4, 212; response to non-Aboriginal protests, 141–2

Dickson, Chief Justice Brian, 86
discrimination: against First Nations, 75
disease: and First Nations, 29, 36
dislocations: Mi'kmaq and Maliseet communities, 47–9
Donham, Parker Barse, 142–3, 212
Douglas Treaties (British Columbia), 84, 159
Drybones case, 75–6
Duff, Wilson, 84
Dummer, Lieutentant-Governor William, 96
Dummer's Treaty, 38, 97, 202
Dummer's War, 32

Eagle Forest Products, 107, 113
Easter, Wayne, member of parliament, 13
economic conditions: in the Maritimes, 156; of Maritime First Nations, 55–9
Eel Ground, 67, 68; Aboriginal Fisheries Strategy agreement, 178
Eel Ground Community Development Centre, 176
Eel River Bar, 112, 117; fisheries agreement, 178
Eidsvik, Phil, 159
Embree, Judge John, 5
Escuminac Wharf Committee, 140
Eskasoni band, 47, 56, 89; fisheries agreement, 178; internal conflict in, 52

Fanon, Frantz, 74
federal government, Canada: fiduciary obligations to First Nations, 86; lack of preparations for the *Marshall* decision, 157–8; and lobster fishery, xv; and regulation of Aboriginal harvesting, 90
federal-provincial relations: and the *Marshall* decision, 157
First Nations: federal jurisdiction over, 45; government domination of, 36; harvesting, persistence of, 46; legal privileges of, 65–6; women, legal status of, 64–5
First Nations Environmental Network, 176
Fisheries and Oceans, Department of, vii, 9, 69, 128, 133, 137, 138, 140, 151,

157, 158; and Aboriginal food fishery, 176; arrest of Donald Marshall Jr, 3; arrest of Indian Brook fishing vessel, 180; enforcement of fisheries regulations, 162–3, 212–14; lobster negotiations, 164; Mi'kmaq fishing rights, 173–4; preparations for *Marshall* decision, 131; protests at Moncton offices of, 141; report of the Standing Committee on Fisheries and Oceans, 150–1; response to *Marshall* decision, 131–4; and west coast Aboriginal fishing rights, 159
Fisheries Resource Conservation Council, 130
Flanagan, Thomas, xii, 194
Fleming, Brian, 19–20
Fontaine, Grand Chief Phil, xii, 110
forestry: and Aboriginal rights, 155
Fort Beausejour, 38; capture of, 33
Fort Folly reserve, 120; fisheries agreement, 178
France: and First Nations, 32–3; role in the Maritimes, 31, 38
Francis, Brian, 101, 116
Francis, Edward, 140
Francis, Pat, 116
Fraser Paper, 107
Fredericton: Oxfam, 176
French-English conflicts in the Maritimes, 31–5
French-Indian War, 33–4
Frenette, Ray: New Brunswick premier, 100, 110, 111, 118
Fundy East Fishermen's Association, 149
Fundy Environmental Action Group, 176
fur trade, 29–30

Gehue, Cyril, 146
Gesgapegiag Mi'kmaq First Nation, 165; fisheries agreement, 177
Gespeg fisheries agreement, 177
Gitskan, British Columbia, 90–1, 92
Globe, Ballomy, 39
Graham, Alan, New Brunswick minister of natural resources, 100
Grand Cascapedia River, 165
Grand Council of the Mi'kmaq: early importance of, 26

Great London Exhibition, 1851, 37
Green, Brad, New Brunswick minister of Aboriginal affairs and attorney general, 125, 146, 156, 159, 160–1
Guerin case, and Aboriginal rights, 86–87, 92, 193
Gufstanson Lake controversy, vii

Halifax: development of, 33, 36; First Nations in, 62
Hamm, John, Nova Scotia premier, 135, 188
Harper, Elijah, 78
harvesting activities, First Nations, 48
Harvey, Lieutenant-Government John, 36
Hawk, Young, 108
historical responsibility, debate over relating to *Marshall* decision, 151–2
history, First Nations views of, xi
Hopper, Richard, 134
Horton fisheries agreement, 178
House of Commons: critique of federal lobster policy in, 147
housing conditions, of First Nations people, 60
Hubbard, Charles, member of parliament, 138
human rights and Aboriginal rights, 73
Hurley, Gary, 149
Hurley, Maisie, publisher of *Native Voice*, 84

Ile Royale (Cape Breton Island), 32
Ile St-Jean (Prince Edward Island), 32
immigrants, and reaction to Aboriginal rights, 152
Indian Act, 63, 75, 77, 201; restrictions on hiring of lawyers, 82
Indian Affairs, Department of, vii, xiii, 45, 63, 65, 74–6, 203
Indian Brook: food fishery at, 176; limited lobster fishery at, 146; Maritime First Nations and, 46–7; refusal to sign an agreement on lobster fishery, 180
Indian Island fisheries agreement, 178
indigenous protest movements, 48–9
inherent rights to resource and the *Marshall* decision, 181
Innu, 72

Inuit Committee on National Issues, 77
Irving, J.D. Corp., ix, 98, 100, 103–4, 107, 108, 109, 112, 116, 201; and First Nations hiring, 58; and First Nations logging agreements, 119
Irwin, Ron, minister of Indian affairsand northern development, 79

Jacques, Ronald, 120
Jamal, Mahmud, 103
James Bay Treaty, 72
Jerome, Bernard, 165
Jijug Enterprises Inc., 120
jobs, limited access for First Nations, 58
Johnson, Lloyd, 101
judicial activism, 102
Judicial Committee of the Privy Council, 82
Juniper Lumber, 98, 103, 107

Kahnawake First Nation: and Burnt Church, 182
Kennewick Man controversy, 23
Kikahan Committee of Tobique, 176
King Philip's War, 31
Kingsclear: fisheries agreement, 178; logging agreement, 121

La Forest, Gerald, 110
La Forest–Nicholas report on Aboriginal affairs in New Brunswick, 122
Lamer, A., Chief Justice of the Supreme Court of Canada, 172
Land and Forests Act (Nova Scotia), and Mi'kmaq rights, 83
land treaty, absence of in the Maritimes, 39–40
languages, survival of indigenous, 53–5
Lanteigne, André-Marc, Department of Fisheries spokesperson, 137, 179, 184
Lavallée, Betty Ann, 99, 159, 161, 170
lawlessness: government, 192
Lawrence, Governor Charles, 33
leadership: First Nations, and the logging controversy, 113; Mi'kmaq and Maliseet, 110
Lee, Philip, and the lobster crisis, 149
Lennox Island, Prince Edward Island, 13, 44, 66; and fisheries agreement, 177; food fishery at, 176
Lestigouche First Nation, 56

Levi, Chief Robert, 13, 98, 101–2, 117, 121, 125–6, 145, 148, 175, 190
Levi, Susan, 166
Listiguj First Nation, 120, 165
lobster: agreements with Maritime First Nations, 158–9, 177–8; agreements with Mi'kmaq, non-Aboriginal response to, 176; fishery, x, xv, 212 ff; media and protests over, 139; non-Aboriginal frustration with Aboriginal, 154–5; protests in summer 2000, 179; impact of *Marshall* decision on, 128, 130; fishing, Aboriginal, and public response, 128; attempted voluntary moratorium, 147; extent of illegal non-Aboriginal activity, 143; Mi'kmaq, after Supreme Court decision, 10; non-Aboriginal protests over, 139–41; non-Aboriginal response to Aboriginal, 152–3; licences, federal buyout of existing, 158; negotiations, non-Aboriginal support for Mi'kmaq position, 176–7; protest, residue of in the Maritimes, 163; protests and Royal Canadian Mounted Police, 140; protests, attempts at reconciliation, 143; seasons and fishing regulations, 129–30, 212–18
log exports: from New Brunswick to Maine and Quebec, 107–8, 112
Loggie, Wilmot, 136
logging: Aboriginal rights to, in Nova Scotia, 123; by First Nations after *Thomas Peter Paul* decision, 98; deals, New Brunswick government and First Nations, 110–12; industry, Aboriginal employment in, 123; Mi'kmaq right to commercial, 8; non-Aboriginal loggers working for First Nations, 117; rights, *Marshall* decision and potential Mi'kmaq, 19; Mi'kmaq case involving treaty claims, 173
Lord, Bernard: New Brunswick premier, 125, 16, 190
Lordon, Judge Denis, 117, 170; and Burnt Church protests, 182; and decision on *Bernard* case, 172
Louisbourg, 32, 33, 38
Loyalists: and the Maritimes, 34–5

Index

MacAleer, Wes, Prince Edward Island attorney general, 159
MacAskill, Ken, Nova Scotia minister of natural resources, 124
Macdonald, John A., 153
MacKenzie, James, federal mediator, 133, 148, 174
Mackenzie Valley Pipeline Inquiry, 77
MacLellan, Russell, Nova Scotia premier, 124
MacMillan Bloedel, 113
Madawaska Aboriginal Fisheries Strategy agreement, 178
Maillard, Pierre, 39
Mair, Rafe, and Aboriginal rights, 127, 193
Malécite de Viger fisheries agreement, 177
Maliseet: and the forestry industry, 122; habitation of traditional territories, 22–5; Loyalists and, 34; occupation of their lands, 35; origins and history of, 21–50; peace treaty, 38; Saint John River and, 27; society and economy, 23–8
Maloney, Chief Reg, 147, 180, 182
Maori (New Zealand), 74
Maritime Fishermen's Union, 14, 128, 130, 132, 133, 135, 136, 138, 142, 150, 154, 167, 174
Marshall Jr, Donald, vii, xvi, 185; case and legacy, 169; false imprisonment, 3; Mi'kmaq treaty rights case, 102–3; national significance of, 20; non-Aboriginal protests over Mi'kimaq fishing, 141; reaction to Supreme Court decision, 137–8; Supreme Court case, 3–20
Marshall Sr, Donald, 4
Marshall decision, Supreme Court: extent of, 13; meaning of, 186–206; public debate about, 10; reaction to, 127–68
Marshall, Joe B., 139
Martin, André, 140
Mascarene's Treaty, 96, 97, 202
Mawiw Tribal Council, 104, 111
McAskill, Don, 189
McCormick, Keith, Crown prosecutor, 98, 103, 105–6, 117
McCoy, Leslie, 97

McDonald, Butch, 101
McEachern, Judge Alan: and *Delgamuukw* case, 90
McEvoy, Professor John, 18, 98
McKenna, Frank, New Brunswick premier, 110, 153, 155
McLachlin, Justice Beverley, 16: appointment as Chief Justice of the Supreme Court of Canada, 172–3; dissenting opinion on *Marshall* decision, 12; and *Marshall* decision, 172
McMillan, Jane, 4
Meech Lake accord, 78
Membertou, Grand Chief, 7, 26, 38; and Christianity, 29
Membertou band, 3
Mercredi, Grand Chief Ovide, xii, 78, 79
Micmac Maliseet Council, 111
Micmac Warrior Society, 68
Micmac-Maliseet Coalition, 113, 118
Mi'kmaq: and Acadians, 32; appeal for land rights, 44; commercial fishing and harvesting, 42–3; cultural traditions, ix; distribution of, 26; genocide, 32; Grand Council, 139, 144, 167, 174; habitation of traditional territories, 22–5; logging, after *Thomas Peter Paul*, 107–26; occupation of their lands, 35; origins and history of, 21–50; petitions for government assistance, 36–7; rights as British subjects, 12; society and economy, 23–8; treaties, 1760–61, 5
Millbrook reserve, 5; fisheries agreement, 178
Miller, Virginia, 24, 28, 32
Miramichi Bay: confrontations over lobster fishing at, 139; federal response to Mi'kmaq fishing on, 148
moderate income: Mi'kmaq right to earn, 7, 11
Montagnais, 72
Moore, Charles, 135, 192
moose hunting: harvesting in Nova Scotia after *Marshall*, 189–90
Morrow, Denny, 149, 176
Musqueam band, 86, 88–9: controversy involving leases, 87

Nash, Jan, 99

Nation of Acadia Métis, 118
National Energy Board and Sable Island Natural Gas, 190
National Geographic, 73
National Indian Brotherhood. *See* Assembly of First Nations
national policy, federal government, 153
National Post, xii
Native Brotherhood of British Columbia, 49
Native Business Association, 118
Native Council of Canada, 77
Native Council of Nova Scotia, 159; and Aboriginal Fisheries Strategy agreement, 178
Native Council of Prince Edward Island: Aboriginal Fisheries Strategy agreement, 178
Native Loggers Business Association, 98, 114, 122
Native Women's Association of Canada, 49
Natural Resources, New Brunswick Department of, 109, 115, 189
Nault, Robert, minister of Indian affairs and northern development: response to *Marshall* decision, 146, 159–60
Neptune, Mitchell, 39
Nevitte, T., 190
New Brunswick: Aboriginal rights after Marshall, 157, 160–61; lessons from government's handling of *Thomas Peter Paul*, 197–8
New Brunswick Aboriginal Peoples Council, 98, 111, 118, 101, 159, 170; Aboriginal Fisheries Strategy agreement, 178
New Brunswick Conservation Council, 9
New Brunswick Court of Appeal: decision on *Thomas Peter Paul* appeal, 98–9
New Brunswick Native Loggers Business Association, 111
New Brunswick Salmon Council, 14
New Brunswick Wildlife Federation, 14, 189
New Zealand: lessons for the Maritimes, 203
Nicholas, Andrea Bear, 8

Nicholas, Graydon, 110
Nichols, Wayne, 122
Nisga'a, 76, 82: *Calder* case, 84–6
Nisga'a treaty, 85–6, 195, 204
non-Aboriginal loggers: hiring of by Mi'kmaq and Maliseet, 108
non-status Indians, 62–5; and *Marshall* decision, 159–60
Nova Scotia, and Aboriginal rights, 123, 157
Nova Scotia Assembly of Mi'kmaq Chiefs, 130
Nova Scotia Court of Appeal, 42

off-reserve First Nations, 62–5
off-reserve voting rights. *See* Corbiere case
Oka, vii, 72, 79, 182
O'Neill, Peter, 117
oral testimony: and First Nations cases, 92
Oromocto fisheries agreement, 158, 178

Pabineau reserve, 95; fisheries agreement, 178
Pasamaquoddy (First Nation from Maine), 38, 39, 139, 161; rights under the *Marshall* decision, 179
Patterson, Dr Stephen, 15, 43, 105; *Bernard* trial, 171; Standing Committee on Fisheries and Oceans, 150
Paul, Chief Benjamin, 190
Paul, Daniel, 26
Paul, Gaylen, 145
Paul, Chief Lawrence, 5, 14, 19, 133, 136, 139, 149, 151, 173, 188
Paul, Nicholas, 94, 96
Paul, Reg, 117
Paul, Chief Terrance, 7
Paul, Thomas Peter, xvi, 8, 92, 186; arrest of, 94; and Mi'kmaq logging, 94–126, 185, 193; personal legal difficulties of, 115. *See also Thomas Peter Paul* case
Paul, Tim, 94, 97, 110, 122
Penobscot, 40
People against Nuclear Energy, 176
Perley, Perry, 109
Pictou Landing fisheries agreement, 178
Pinchin, John, 152
Polches, Claude, 107

political leadership: growing confidence among First Nations, 67
politics, among local First Nations, 57
Pomquet Harbour, 3, 11
population: contemporary Aboriginal, 51; early estimates of, 25
Port Royal, 31, 32
Prince Edward Island Fishermen's Association, 142
prison: First Nations people and, 61
protests: Maritime First Nations and, 49

Raging Grannies of Fredericton, 176
reconciliation, Maritime approach to, xvii, 165–8
Red Bank fisheries agreement, 178
Redden, Harlen, 124
Reform Party. *See* Canadian Alliance
Regina v. *McCoy*, 97
regulation of fishery, by federal government, 11
Reid, Dr John,16, 43; *Bernard* trial, 171
Repap, 107, 116
residential school for Maritimes First Nations, xiii, 46, 54
resources: extension of *Marshall* decision to other, 159–61
Restigouche, 165
Restigouche Riparian Association, 165
Riley, John, 128
Roman Catholic Church, 29–30; and Mi'kmaq, 38
Rook, John, 103
Royal Canadian Mounted Police: Burnt Church protests, 144; increased manpower to quell protests, 143; lobster protests, 141–2; preparations for lobster protests, 162–3
Royal Commission on Aboriginal Peoples, 79
Royal Proclamation of 1763, 39, 86, 69, 80–1, 172

Sable Island natural gas: and *Marshall* decision, 188, 190
Sacred Mountain Society of Eskasoni, 176
St Anne Nackawic Pulp Company, 107
St Catherine's Milling and Lumber Company, 81
Saint John, 36; First Nations in, 62

St Mary's fisheries agreement, 178
Saint Thomas University, Native Studies Department, 8, 52
Scott, Duncan Campbell, 46
self-government: Aboriginal, 66–7; resource rights, 14
Shaugnessy Golf Club, 86
Shubenacadie, 47, 54; band council, 182; residential school, 46. *See also* Indian Brook
Sierra Club Canada, Eastern Canada Group, 176
Simon, Francis, 126
Simon case, and Mi'kmaq treaty rights, 87, 92, 94
Sioui case, and Aboriginal treaty rights, 87, 92
Smith, Melvin, and Aboriginal rights, 194
social conditions, among Maritime First Nations, 51–71
Sock, Leon, 104
Sparrow case, and Aboriginal harvesting rights, 88–9, 176, 193
St Mary's Bay, 130
St Mary's First Nation, 94
Standing Committee on Fisheries and Oceans: and *Marshall* decision, 150–1; report of and Aboriginal response to, 151
Stoffer, Peter, member of parliament, 132
Stone-Consolidated, 107
Stymiest, Judge, and Burnt Church fishing case, 105
subsistence rights, Supreme Court ruling on, 89
suicide, Aboriginal, 60
Supreme Court: Aboriginal response to clarification, 18–19; accusations of judicial activism, 16–17; appeal of *Thomas Peter Paul*, 99, 103–4; *Calder* decision, 76, 85–6; calls to suspend the ruling on *Marshall*, 135–6; clarification of the *Marshall* decision, 17–20; historical interpretation and the *Marshall* decision, 15–16; *Joshua Bernard* case, 171; *Marshall* decision, vii, xiv, 1, 6–20, 157; – , explained, 10–12; petitions to, 15; ruling on *Delgamuukw*, 91; unpredictability of, 158

Index

Swim, George, 152
Syliboy case, and Mi'kmaq treaty rights, 82–3, 92
Sylliboy, Ben, 144, 145; attitude towards Herb Dhaliwal, 148
Sylliboy, Robert, 144

Tantramar Environmental Alliance, 176
Terre-à-Terre (Down to Earth), 176
Thérieault, Bernard, New Brunswick minister of Aboriginal affairs, 110
Thériault, Camille, New Brunswick premier, 118, 121, 125
Thériault, Gilles, 133
Theriault, Harold, 136
Thomas, Warrior Chief Frank, 69
Thomas Peter Paul case, 51, 200; decision and response to *Marshall*, 137; First Nations protests, 100–2; judgment, 9; legacy of, 169; lessons from logging crisis, 120; New Brunswick's handling of, 164; public image of, 107; relationship with lobster protests, 155; sentencing of, 105–6; significance of the case, 106–7
Thompson, Glen, 145
Thunder East Corporation, 101
Tim Horton's, 127
Times & Transcript (Moncton), 15
Times Globe (Saint John), x
Tobique, 111, 119, 189; financial crisis in, 57; logging deal, 116–17
Tomah, Len, 161
Tompkins, Craig, 117
Toney, Chief Brian, 146; support for regular commercial lobster fishery, 149
traditional lands: Aboriginal rights to, 91
treaties: First Nations, 38–9; historical debates about, 42–4; Mi'kmaq and Maliseet, xiii, 11–12, 33–4; prospects for an accord arising out of court decisions about, 202–5; Treaties of 1760–61, 13, 15, 39, 40–2; Treaty 3, 81; Treaty of 1752, 33, 38; – , and contemporary Mi'kmaq harvesting rights, 87
Treaty Day Celebrations, Halifax, 139
treaty rights in Canada, 72–93
Treaty of Utrecht, 1713, 32

truckhouses, 38, 39, 42
Trudeau, Prime Minister Pierre: and *Calder* decision, 85
Truro, Nova Scotia, 144
Turnbull, Judge John, 104, 108–9, 113, 126, 193; criticism of judicial activism, 102; and *Thomas Peter Paul* case, 96–9, 125
Tyler, Douglas, New Brunswick minister of natural resources, 113, 119, 121, 123

Union of New Brunswick Indians, 11, 18, 49, 98, 110, 190
Union of Nova Scotia Indians, 4, 49, 124; and logging rights, 173
United Nations Human Rights Commission, 64, 180
Universal Declaration on Human Rights, 73
University College of Cape Breton, 52, 139
Upton, L.F.S., 26, 45
Urquhart, Harvey, 117

Van der Peet, *N.T.C. Smokehouse*, and *Gladstone* cases, and Aboriginal harvesting rights 90, 92
Vancouver Island First Nations, and the *Marshall* decision, 159
Volpe, Jeannot, New Brunswick minister of natural resources, 125, 160, 189
voting rights, First Nations, 75

Wabanaki Confederacy, 38. *See also* Abenaki
Wagmatcook fisheries agreement, 178
Ward, James, 177; and Burnt Church fishery, 175; and Fisheries seizures, 181
Warmer, David, 143
Warrior Societies, 116, 144; at Burnt Church, 181; Mi'kmaq and non-Aboriginal lobster protests, 141; *Thomas Peter Paul* protests, 101
Waycobah fisheries agreement, 178
Wayne, Elsie, member of parliament, 15, 135
Wendat (Huron), 87–8
West Nova Fishermen's Coalition: request to Supreme Court for a stay of *Marshall* decision, 17, 18

Wet'suwet'en, British Columbia, 90–1, 92
White and Bob case: and Aboriginal harvesting rights, 83, 92, 188
White Paper on Indian Affairs, 1969, 76
Wicken, Dr William, 10, 16, 33–4, 35, 43, 102, 171; and *Bernard* trial, 171
Wildsmith, Bruce, 4, 5–6, 102–3, 104; and *Bernard* case, 170–3; and Supreme Court clarification, 19

Woodstock: and Aboriginal Fisheries Strategy agreement, 178; logging deal, 116

Yarmouth, 137, 139, 140–1; illegal lobster fishing at, 143; lobster protest at, 142, 148; non-Aboriginal fishers protest at, 135
Yukon: lessons for the Maritimes, 203; territorial government and First Nations rights in, 157